D1732846

Overturned Chariot

A publication of the
School of Hawaiian
Asian & Pacific Studies
University of Hawai‘i

OVERTURNED CHARIOT

THE AUTOBIOGRAPHY OF
PHAN-BỘI-CHÂU

Translated by Vinh Sinh and Nicholas Wickenden

SHAPS LIBRARY OF TRANSLATIONS
University of Hawai'i Press
Honolulu

Library of Congress Cataloging-in-Publication Data

Phan, Bôi Châu, 1867–1940

Overturned chariot : the autobiography of Phan-Bôi-Châu /
translated with an introduction and notes by Vinh Sinh and Nicholas
Wickenden.

p. cm. — (SHAPS library of translations)

Translated from Chinese.

Includes bibliographical references and index.

ISBN 0–8248–1875–X (alk. paper)

1. Phan, Bôi Châu, 1867–1940. 2. Revolutionaries—Vietnam—
Biography. I. Title. II. Series.

DS556.83.P46A3 1997

959.7'03—dc21   97–19313
                                          CIP

University of Hawai'i Press books are printed on acid-free paper and meet
the guidelines for permanence and durability of the Council on Library
Resources.

Printed by The Maple-Vail Book Manufacturing Group

For Kyōko and Tan

— V.S.

In memory of Helen Froehlich,
most thoughtful of godmothers

— N.W.

Contents

The illustrations follow page 150

Translators' Preface

Though the process leading to the present edition and translation began when V.S. obtained copies of the literary Chinese manuscripts of Phan-Bội-Châu's autobiography in Vietnam in the late 1980s, the collaboration between us goes back before that time, when we worked together with Professor Matsuzawa Hiroaki (then of the University of Hokkaidō and now at the International Christian University, Tokyo) in preparing an English translation of *Shōrai no Nihon* (The Future Japan), published in 1886 by Tokutomi Sohō. There is a closer connection between the work of Tokutomi, the influential Japanese journalist and historian, and Phan, the champion of Vietnamese independence, than might at first appear, since the great Chinese reformer Liang Ch'i-ch'ao adopted many of the ideas advanced by Tokutomi (along with other Meiji writers), and in turn Phan, as he makes clear in this autobiography, looked to Liang as a mentor and guide. To Professor Matsuzawa, then, we wish to express our gratitude in the first place, for the continuing inspiration that this distinguished scholar has provided for our work.

This translation could not have been carried out without the assistance of many persons and institutions which we should like to acknowledge here. For their help in obtaining materials used in this work, we wish to express our warmest gratitude to the late Anh-Minh Ngô-Thành-Nhân, Chương Thâu, F. Durand-Evrard, the late Hoàng-Xuân-Hãn, Nguyễn-Thế-Anh, Nguyễn-Văn-Xuân, Phan-Huy-Lê, Shiraishi Masaya, Trần-Viết-Ngạc, and Trịnh-Văn-Thảo. The staff of the Interlibrary Loan department at the Library of the University of Alberta have been cooperative, efficient, and cheerful throughout the course of this project. For reading a draft of the work in whole or in part and offering valuable comments and suggestions we extend our sincere thanks to Ann Hall, Huỳnh-Sanh-Thông, Joseph F. Murray, and the two anonymous readers for the University of Hawai'i Press. Any shortcomings that may remain are of course the sole responsibility of the translators. Jerry Kowalyk's expertise and enthusiasm in providing computer-generated base maps has been of immense assistance. Ron Gardner kindly helped with difficulties in the computerized typesetting, and Alex Schwarzer genially supervised the production of the final copy. Zhao Yi-feng was most helpful as a research assistant.

In collecting materials for this work in East Asia and France, V.S. was aided by generous funding from the Social Sciences and Humanities Research Council of Canada.

V.S.
N.W.

Introduction

The name of Phan-Bội-Châu may not be readily recognized by many people outside Vietnam, but within his own country he is one of the most widely known and respected figures in recent history. Phan (1867–1940) was in fact the most prominent leader of the Vietnamese independence movement during the first quarter of the twentieth century, and a living link between the older generation that initiated, and the younger generation that carried to a conclusion, the struggle against French rule in Vietnam. The pioneers in this struggle were the scholars and local officials in the Mekong delta region. Beginning in the early 1860s, they launched a series of impetuous but sporadic uprisings to restore Vietnamese sovereignty, culminating in the nationwide *Cần-Vương* (Loyalist) movement of 1885–1895. By the 1930s the adherents of the Vietnamese independence movement had become more aware of its place in the broader context of anticolonialism, yet at the same time their ranks were beginning to be split by differences over ideology. That between these two periods Vietnamese resistance to foreign domination did not lose its cohesion and vigor was thanks mainly to Phan and his associates. For this reason, during the more than twenty years following 1954 when Vietnam was divided between North and South, his memory was honored and numerous studies of his life and writings were published in both parts of the country. He had gained a stature in the modern history of Vietnam comparable to that of Sun Yat-sen in modern China; and it is interesting to observe, as Phan recounts in this autobiography, that he had made the personal acquaintance of Sun, and maintained close contacts with many of Sun's associates during the years when he was active in Japan and China.

II

The origins of France's connection with Vietnam can be traced back to the late eighteenth century, when Nguyễn Ánh (1762–1820), struggling against rivals for power, solicited military assistance from the French. In order to obtain such assistance, he entrusted his eldest son, Prince Cảnh, to the missionary Pigneau de Béhaine to be taken to Paris as a kind of hostage. In return, the French were looking above all for privileges for their traders and missionaries. Overcoming his opponents, Nguyễn Ánh proclaimed himself emperor in 1802, assuming the title Gia-Long and becoming the first of the Nguyễn dynasty.

At the time of Gia-Long's death in 1820, his youngest son ascended the throne, instead of the son of the late Crown Prince Cảnh as tradition would have dictated. The new emperor adopted Minh-Mạng as his era name and reigned until 1841, being succeeded by his son. The line of Prince Cảnh did not die out, however; Marquis Cường-Để (1882–1951), who was eventually brought forward by Phan-Bội-Châu and his associates as their nominal royal leader, was one of his direct descendants. Unfortunately, in the meantime Minh-Mạng and his successors by their anti-Christian policies provided the French with some justification for armed intervention in Vietnam, which eventually led to their taking control of the country as their first colony in East Asia.

By the time of Phan's birth in 1867, the French had been making incursions into Vietnam for approximately ten years. Under France's unrelenting military pressure, Emperor Tự-Đức (reigned 1848–1883) had been forced to cede the three southern provinces in Cochin China in 1862. Extending their interests to the north, the French then proceeded to demand the right to trade along the Red River, which would also give them access to southwestern China. By another treaty in 1874, following a French attack on Hanoi and other cities in the Red River delta in the previous year, the Vietnamese court at Huế was compelled not only to agree to open the Red River to the French for trade but also to cede sovereignty over all of Cochin China to France.

Anti-French resistance had already sprung up in the Mekong delta in the 1860s; now the scholar-gentry *(văn-thân)* and the peasantry rose up in many parts of the country. But as all their attempts at resistance were ill equipped, sporadic, and lacking coordination, they were quickly put down and could not prevent the French establishing a protectorate over the remainder of Vietnam in 1883. As far as the French were concerned, the very name of Vietnam ceased to exist, and the country was divided into three zones—Tongking, Annam, and Cochin China—under different forms of administration. The sense of the "loss of the country" *(vong-quốc),* poignantly expressed again and again in Phan's writings, took its rise from these events.

In protest against the French conquest of her tributary state, China dispatched troops to Tongking in 1883. The ensuing Sino-French conflict lasted for two years and ended with China's humiliating defeat. It should be noted that even before China's full-scale intervention, remnants of the forces engaged in the Taip'ing Rebellion, most notably the Black Flags, had been fighting alongside the Vietnamese in the Tongking area. The leader of these Black Flags was the notorious Liu Yung-fu (known in Vietnamese as Lưu Vĩnh-Phúc), whose name will recur time and again in this autobiography.

On 4 July 1885, under the guidance of the passionate but erratic regent Tôn-Thất-Thuyết, the young Emperor Hàm-Nghi (1870–1947; reigned 1884–1885) was placed at the head of an insurrection against the French at the imperial capital. This attempt at a coup was promptly suppressed. Thuyết then conducted the Emperor to a mountain refuge in the Province of Quảng-bình. From there the Cần-Vương proclamation was issued in the Emperor's name, calling for an all-out struggle against the French. In response, uprisings took place throughout the country.

An outstanding figure among the leaders of the resistance at this time was Hoàng-Hoa-Thám (1858–1913), commonly known as Đề Thám, a former outlaw and a gifted strategist, who eagerly responded to the Cần-Vương proclamation and in 1886 created a guerrilla base at Yên-thế in northern Vietnam (in what is now Hà-bắc Province). Đề Thám managed to hold out against the colonial authorities for more than a quarter of a century, until 1913. His dogged resistance earned him the nickname of "the Tiger of Yên-thế." When Phan began his activities as a resistance organizer, one of his first moves, in 1903, was to attempt to confer with Đề Thám, but they were unable to meet at that time, as the latter was ill. Later, however, in 1906, when Phan returned to Yên-thế, Đề Thám entertained him lavishly and provided a base for his comrades.

The most important leader in the Cần-Vương movement, however, was unquestionably Phan-Đình-Phùng (1844–1896), a member of the scholar-gentry who had once been the chief censor at the Nguyễn court and who was widely respected for his courage and integrity. Phan-Đình-Phùng organized a guerrilla army in Nghệ-Tĩnh and Quảng-bình that kept the colonial forces at bay until 1896, when he died of dysentery. Phan seems to have cherished hopes of joining Phan-Đình-Phùng; probably it was only a concern lest overt political activity on his part might endanger his father that stopped him from doing so. It is quite clear that Phan-Đình-Phùng was a source of inspiration to him, standing out as a model of a patriotic intellectual in a time of national crisis.

III

The Province of Nghệ-an is a hard and barren land, well known as the birthplace of a host of resistance leaders against foreign intervention throughout Vietnamese history. It was here, in the village of Sa-nam in Nam-đàn District, that Phan, called at first Phan-Văn-San, was born in 1867 into a family poor but proud of its scholarly traditions. Sa-nam was the native village of Phan's mother; when he was three his family moved to Đan-nhiễm, his father's native village, also in Nam-đàn District and not far from Sen village, where Nguyễn-Ái-Quốc (later to be identified with Hồ-Chí-Minh) was born. Phan was in fact an acquaintance of Nguyễn-Ái-Quốc's father, and the young Nguyễn-Ái-Quốc and Phan apparently met from time to time; they would communicate with each other again when Nguyễn-Ái-Quốc had become a figure of national significance.

Until Phan was five years old, as his father Phan-Văn-Phổ was teaching away from home, Phan was brought up mainly by his mother, Nguyễn-Thị-Nhàn, who recited to him passages from the *Classic of Poetry (Kinh thi;* in Chinese, *Shih ching),* so that basic Confucian values were instilled in him from his earliest years. At the age of five, Phan was allowed to attend his father's classes, where it took him, as he says, a mere three days to memorize all of the *Three-Character Classic (Tam-tự-kinh;* in Chinese, *San-tzu-ching),* a primer of Chinese classical studies. Amazed by his son's unusual learning ability, Phan's father then decided to teach him further Confucian texts such as the *Analects (Luận-ngữ;* in Chinese, *Lun yü).* Without paper, Phan diligently practiced writing on banana leaves. He tells us that at the age of six, he managed to create his own little imitation of the *Analects* to ridicule his classmates, for which he was chastised by his father. At thirteen, Phan was sent to study under a local scholar who took the trouble to borrow on his behalf books from the wealthier houses in the neighborhood that helped him to extend his knowledge considerably. The Confucian outlook that Phan acquired in his earliest years would remain with him until the end of his life.

Meanwhile, in 1874, as a child of seven, Phan responded to the fierce Bình-Tây (Put Down the French) movement of the scholar-gentry in his home district by playing "Bình-Tây" at school, "using bamboo tubes for guns and lychee pits for bullets." Needless to say, little Phan was in no position as yet to have a full understanding of the issues at stake, but inheriting as he did the ardent patriotic sentiments and concern for the fate of the country characteristic of the scholar-gentry of Nghệ-Tĩnh, he instinctively wished to take sides with the resistance. He later described his childhood emotions as follows:

> I was endowed with a fiery spirit. From the days when I was
> a small child, I read the books that our ancestors had handed
> down to us, and every time I read the stories of those in the past

> who were ready to die for the righteous cause, tears would come
> running from my eyes, soaking the books.[1]

Phan's ardent patriotism, like his Confucian values, was something he absorbed from the milieu of his early childhood that remained central to his character and activities ever after.

In 1883, aged sixteen, in response to the risings against the French occupation of Tongking, Phan drafted an appeal calling for "putting down the French and retrieving the North" *(Bình-Tây thu-Bắc),* which he posted along the local roads, but to his disappointment there was no response. He realized for the first time that it was necessary for him to make a name for himself, because people would not pay attention to anyone whose social status had not yet been guaranteed by success in the mandarinate examinations. Again, in 1885, when the scholar-gentry in Nghệ-Tĩnh rose up in response to the imperial Cần-Vương proclamation, Phan organized about sixty of his classmates who were also preparing for the examinations into the "Army of Loyalist Examination Candidates" *(Sĩ-tử Cần-Vương Đội).* But while this "Army" was still considering ways to raise funds and manufacture weapons, Phan's ambitious plan was forestalled by a sudden French attack. The lesson he drew from this fiasco, as he declares in this autobiography, was that in order for an undertaking to succeed, plans must be weighed carefully, as hasty and heedless actions were bound to fail. However, Phan's readers will observe that his failures of this nature were by no means at an end, but would recur throughout his active career.

In the next fifteen years Phan concentrated on preparing for examinations, while supporting himself and his family by teaching and writing. Discreetly, he studied works by the classic Chinese and Vietnamese military writers such as Sun Tzu, Chu-ko Liang, and Trần-Hưng-Đạo to prepare himself for later participation in the national struggle.[2] The reason why Phan assumed a low profile during this

---

1. *Ngục-trung-thư* (NTT), 11–12 (with some revisions to the translation).

2. The first two men were known in Vietnamese as Tôn Tử and Gia-Cát Lượng, respectively.

period was concern for his family responsibilities. He was the only son of his parents; his father was now an old and ill widower (his mother having died in 1884), and Phan, with his strong sense of filial piety, naturally accepted the financial burden of supporting him and avoided activities that might compromise him politically.

Although Phan had come to be recognized as the foremost among the literary talents of the Nam-đàn District (*Nam-đàn tứ-hồ,* literally "Four Tigers of Nam-đàn") since his early youth, contrary to all expectation, it took him six tries before his name was finally posted at the head of the list of passing candidates *(giải-nguyên)* at the regional examinations in Nghệ-an in 1900. Why was it that such an obviously talented candidate took so long to obtain a *cử-nhân* degree? There is an anecdote that may shed light on this question. After continual failures in his examination attempts, we are told, Phan went to take lessons from an accomplished instructor in a nearby district who had coached most of the candidates who had successfully passed the higher levels of the mandarinate examinations in the region. Given some examinations for practice during his first few days at this instructor's private school, Phan failed each time. When he asked why, the instructor told him that although he was an outstanding student, his style of writing did not meet the requirements for the regional examination—it was too advanced, suitable only for the higher-level metropolitan or court examinations. What this suggests is that Phan, though highly capable, was too strong willed and independent minded to conform to the narrow, stereotyped expectations of most examiners.

Phan's academic fortunes seemed to have come to an abrupt end in 1897, when he was declared to be excluded for life from taking the examinations on account of carrying notes into the examination site. In his autobiography, Phan simply mentions this incident without defending himself. The commonly accepted explanation is that one of his friends, meaning to be helpful, had without Phan's knowledge placed in his bag some materials which were found by the porter at the gate of the examination site. The authorities seem to have become convinced of Phan's honesty; he received a pardon three years later, and when he took the regional examination in 1900, he placed first, as mentioned above. (It was at that point that he changed his name to Phan-Bội-Châu.) Though in 1903 he was not successful in his sole attempt at the highest level of the examinations—the metropolitan examination in Huế—he had by then acquired the academic status he felt he needed.

Why was it that Phan, despite the nonconformist streak in his character, devoted so much effort to the conventional goal of passing the examinations? One might suggest two main reasons. To begin with, while his father was alive he wished to please him. In addition, he realized that academic status was a necessity if he were to be taken seriously as an anticolonial activist. Phan emphasizes, however, time and again that he did not wish to use his literary talents to forge an official career in the way so many of his contemporaries did. It is clear that he despised the careerists.

In later years, Phan regretfully looked back at the deficiencies of the system of education in which he had been brought up. In his own words:

> Alas! The broom in our house was worn out, yet we still thought it was valuable. When one has treasured something for a long time, one becomes completely accustomed to it. I myself was so bound by the conventions of those days that I wasted my days and months for half a lifetime in the examination-taking business. That must indeed be judged a very large stain upon my life![3]

Modeled after the Chinese, the Vietnamese examination system *(khoa-cử)* required its candidates to be well versed in Chinese classics *(kinh-sách)* and strictly to follow set formats in their examination essays. It did not provide the learners with knowledge about the modern world, nor did it encourage them to think independently or creatively. The written languages in which Phan's training left him well versed were literary Chinese and Vietnamese demotic characters *(chữ*

---

3. NTT, 11 (translation revised).

Nôm). He had difficulties even with the modern Vietnamese romanized script *(quốc-ngữ)* which became popular in Vietnam while he was living abroad; far less did he acquire proficiency in modern Western languages. Owing to his lack of grounding in the relevant languages, although he was fascinated by Japan's modernization since the Meiji Restoration and wished to create a new Vietnam in the image of Meiji Japan, his knowledge about Japan—still more, about the West—was bound to remain superficial. Despite the shortcomings of his traditional education, though, Phan never questioned the values inspired by his Confucian heritage, which shaped his outlook to the end of his life. His attitude in the last analysis was perhaps best reflected in a brief note to this autobiography:

> Chinese studies are not necessarily to be blamed for the stale writings on the mandarinate examination in the old days. Western studies are not necessarily to be blamed for the slavishness and inferior writings of nowadays. Dismal circumstances have buried alive countless promising youth; how deplorable it is!

In other words, not the literary substance but the ossified method of his education was what he deplored. Nevertheless, for knowledge of the modern world he would have to turn elsewhere.

The principal sources of Phan's information about the modern world were Chinese reformist writings, generally known as *Hsin-shu* or "New Books" (in Vietnamese, *Tân-thư*), by writers such as Liang Ch'i-ch'ao (1873–1929). These Chinese writers themselves, as it happened, derived their information mainly from Japanese books about the West, so that at the time of their first introduction to Vietnam, Western ideas had been filtered successively through the two media of Japanese and Chinese.[4] It must have been around 1897, when he had the opportunity of traveling to Huế where these reformist materials

---

4. For a discussion of the circuitous transmission of Western ideas from Japan to Vietnam by way of China at the end of the nineteenth and the beginning of the twentieth century, see Vĩnh Sính, "Chinese Characters as the Medium for Transmitting the Vocabulary of Modernization from Japan to Vietnam in the Early Twentieth Century," *Asian Pacific Quarterly*, October 1993: 1–16.

were available, that Phan first encountered the *Hsin-shu*. The great intellectual impact that the *Hsin-shu* had on him during his sojourn in Huế is attested by Phan himself:

> Mai-Sơn Nguyễn-Thượng-Hiền . . . lent me books such as *Chung-tung chan-chi* (History of the War in the Middle East) and *Fa-P'u chan-chi* (History of the Franco-Prussian War) [by Liang Ch'i-ch'ao], and *Ying-huan chih-lüeh* (A Brief Description of the Maritime World) [by Hsü Chih-yu]. Through reading these books, I began to have a rough idea of the rivalries in the world, and I was profoundly struck by the tragic prospect of the ruin of nations and the extinction of races.

It is worth adding that to Phan-Bội-Châu, as well as to a number of his contemporaries such as Phan-Châu-Trinh (1872–1926), the "New Books" were the principal source of inspiration not only when they were in Vietnam but even after they had gone abroad to continue their political activities. Phan-Bội-Châu recounts that after his arrival in Japan in 1905, he was so preoccupied with the work of coordinating the Đông-Du (Go East) movement that he did not have time for serious study of the Japanese language. For this reason, he continued to rely for his knowledge of Japan and of the world beyond on the writings that were being published in Chinese by both the Liang Ch'i-ch'ao and the Sun Yat-sen groups in Japan. For instance, Phan learned everything he knew about the career of the Italian revolutionary Giuseppe Mazzini (1805–1872), whose name is mentioned quite frequently in his writings, through reading a biography by Liang Ch'i-ch'ao that Liang lent to Phan when the two first met each other in Yokohama. As a result, Phan, like many of his comrades, was limited in his understanding both of those he regarded as Vietnam's primary enemies, the French, and of those he regarded as her potential models and allies, such as the Japanese and the Germans.[5] Still, in spite of such limitations, he could never revert to a purely traditional outlook.

---

5. It may be observed that Nguyễn-Ái-Quốc was among the first anticolonial Vietnamese to be in a position to acquire a firsthand understanding of conditions in Western countries.

IV

Phan's father's death in 1900 released him from family obligations to embark on his chosen career as a leader in the struggle for Vietnam's independence. His subsequent life can be divided into four stages, in each of which he significantly modified his policies and plans in response to changing circumstances and the evolution of his own ideas.

The first stage, 1900–1905: During these years, Phan either resided in Huế or traveled throughout the country to establish contact with sympathizers and remnants of the Cần-Vương movement. To begin with, what Phan saw as his task was to pick up the torch of anticolonial armed resistance from such earlier scholar-gentry as Phan-Đình-Phùng. Phan's early efforts to stimulate armed uprisings proved futile; but through the medium of the Chinese " New Books," he, like some others, was becoming aware both of the Hundred-Day Reform movement of 1898 in China and of Japan's remarkable success in modernization since the Meiji Restoration in 1868. In 1904 Phan was a leading figure in the group that created the Việt-Nam Duy-Tân Hội (Vietnam Modernization Association), the first anticolonial organization in Vietnam to show an awareness of the problem of modernization. Moreover, as Liang Ch'i-ch'ao—whose writings greatly influenced the members of the Modernization Association—had gone into exile in Japan and was continuing to write on the necessity of drawing lessons from the Japanese experience, his avid Vietnamese readers were impelled to broaden their horizons and look beyond the Middle Kingdom, their traditional source of inspiration and assistance, to the newly emerged East Asian power of Japan.

The second stage, 1905–1909: In 1905, the Vietnam Modernization Association dispatched Phan to Japan with the idea of seeking Japanese military assistance. Visiting Liang Ch'i-ch'ao in person in Yokohama, Phan told him of the Association's plans, only to have Liang flatly dismiss them. " Once Japanese troops had entered within your country's borders," Liang warned, " it would surely be impossible to find an excuse to drive them out." As Liang trenchantly admonished

Phan: "Your country should not be concerned about not having a day of independence, but should be concerned about not having an independence-minded people." Liang stressed that the Vietnamese must ultimately rely on the strength of their own country, rather than foreign assistance, to bring them success in their drive for independence. "The actual strength that your country has within itself," he added, "is the intelligence of its people, the vitality of its people, and the talents of its people." Though in the long run Phan proved unable to follow, or perhaps even fully to appreciate, Liang's remarkably sagacious advice, he nonetheless began at this point to realize how necessary it was to educate Vietnamese youth to take part in the anticolonial struggle. Unexpectedly, therefore, his visit to Japan became the starting point of an unprecedented movement to send Vietnamese youth to that country for study, which would later come to be known as the Đông-Du (Go East) movement. At its peak in 1907, the Đông-Du movement brought some two hundred Vietnamese youths to Japan, notwithstanding the obstacles placed in the way of Vietnamese travel abroad by the colonial authorities.

In that same year, however, France and Japan concluded a treaty by which they pledged to respect each other's spheres of interest in East Asia. In the course of 1908 and 1909, the Japanese authorities ordered the Vietnamese students' organization to disband and expelled Marquis Cường-Đễ and Phan from the country. The Đông-Du movement thus came to an abrupt end. Nonetheless, despite its short duration, this movement exerted a unique and significant influence on modern Vietnamese history. Among its immediate consequences were the founding of the Đông-Kinh Nghĩa-Thục (Đông-Kinh Private School) in Hanoi (1907),[6] which aimed to provide an independent and modern education

---

6. The Đông-Kinh Private School was modeled after the Keiō Gijuku, the school founded in Tokyo in 1868 by Fukuzawa Yukichi (1835–1901), the famous Japanese educator, whom Phan held in great esteem. *Đông-Kinh* is not only the old name of Hanoi but also the Vietnamese equivalent of the name of Tokyo. *Nghĩa-thục* is the Vietnamese equivalent of Gijuku, a (private) "community school," somewhat reminiscent of an English "public" school. The name thus reveals the admiration felt

for its pupils, and the emergence of a peasant movement demanding a lowering of taxes in central Vietnam (1908). In the longer term, though Phan's vision of a new and independent Vietnam in the image of Meiji Japan was very much his own, it captured the imagination of many of his fellow countrymen and conditioned a series of political movements in subsequent years. Even now (1998), some ninety years later, as Vietnam contemplates various models of "renovation" *(đổi mới)*, a reappraisal of the lessons to be derived from the Đông-Du movement is once again being called for.

It should be pointed out that Phan was always something of a Pan-Asianist in his outlook, in the sense of believing that the people of the "same culture and same race" *(đồng-văn đồng-chủng)* should stand together against Western encroachments. Although he never clearly defined the group of nations he had in mind, it seems certain that it included China, Japan, Korea, and Vietnam, in all of which Chinese script and Confucian tradition formed the basis of formal culture.

China, in his view, occupied a special place among these nations. From the outset of his journey overseas, he made a point of establishing close relations with the Chinese students and activists living abroad. Using classical Chinese characters, he could communicate with them more easily than with the Japanese, and he was not deterred by the fact that they represented a wide spectrum of political orientations and were not always on cordial terms with each other. It was particularly important to him to make contacts with Chinese from the provinces bordering Vietnam—Kwangsi, Kwangtung, and Yunnan—in anticipation of future collaboration. As Phan began to perceive Japan as an imperialist power not unwilling to cooperate with the Western powers at the expense of its Asian neighbors, he seems to have looked more and more to China, along with other Asian countries that were suffering from the "same sickness" *(đồng-bệnh)* as his own country, to provide support for Vietnam. For this reason he joined a group

---

by Phan and his comrades for Fukuzawa's educational institution, dedicated to the teaching of modern subjects, which was the inspiration for theirs.

of Japanese and other East Asian activists in founding, in 1907, the Society for East Asian Alliance *(Đông-Á Đồng-minh Hội)*. He claims also to have played an active role in establishing the Alliance of Yunnan, Kwangsi, Kwangtung, and Vietnam *(Điền-Quế-Việt-Việt Liên-minh Hội)*.[7] In this way he laid down the foundations he believed were necessary to enable the Vietnamese independence movement to draw on support from China.

Phan could hardly have helped but feel a growing sense of disappointment with Japan, which during these years was consolidating its position as one among the imperialist powers and must therefore have appeared in his eyes to be aligning itself with "brute force" *(cường-quyền)*. At the same time, he never entirely ceased to admire Japan and to hope that the Japanese would one day come round to support the Vietnamese cause, and he continued to hold the Pan-Asianist belief that an alliance of China and Japan against the Western powers was the natural way to bring about the independence of Vietnam as well as other Asian countries.

The third stage, 1909–1925: Expelled from Japan, Phan at first made Hong Kong his base of operations. It was here that he heard the news that Hoàng-Hoa-Thám had launched an uprising in Yên-thế. Anxious to equip his comrades to take action in concert with Hoàng, Phan used a sum of money just sent to him from home to purchase arms, then journeyed to Singapore and Thailand in an endeavor to find a route to smuggle the arms into Vietnam. Not only did his plans come to naught; inside Vietnam, the movement suffered serious reverses, and one of his key comrades lost his life. At his wits' end, Phan donated most of the arms to the Chinese revolutionary party of Sun Yat-sen. Meanwhile, he and a few of his comrades had moved to Kwangtung, where they lay low for about half a year, selling Phan's writings to support themselves and availing themselves of the generous hospitality of a Chinese benefactress.

---

7. Of the two *Việts* here, the first stands for Kwangtung and the second (written with a different character) for Vietnam.

In the autumn of 1910, following the example of an ancient Chinese hero who had gone to farm in a remote place while waiting for an opportunity to overthrow the ruler of his country, Phan left Kwang-tung with more than fifty comrades to go farming in Siam (now Thailand). Phan's sojourn in Siam was shorter than he expected. No sooner had he established himself there than news reached him of the success of the Republican Revolution of 1911 that brought down the Manchu government in China. Sensing an opportunity to turn the situation of his movement around, Phan gave up his farming venture and hastened back to China to attempt to forge an Asian alliance—with China and Japan in the forefront—against the European powers. The possibility of such an alliance had indeed preoccupied him for many years. Only in retrospect, in his autumnal years, would Phan admit that his endeavors at this time were "highly impractical." At the time he must have been filled with buoyant optimism, as Sun Yat-sen was elected provisional president of China and many others among the Chinese whom he had known since his days in Japan came to occupy high positions in the new government.

The stunning early successes of the Chinese revolutionary movement seem to be what impelled Phan to bring about a major shift in the orientation of his own Vietnamese movement. In the meeting among the comrades that Phan convened after his arrival in Kwangtung, not only was the old Vietnam Modernization Association replaced by a new Vietnam Restoration League *(Việt-Nam Quang-phục Hội)* on the model of its Chinese counterpart, but the political objective of the movement was changed from the reestablishment of Vietnam as an independent monarchy to the creation of a democratic republic, like the new China. Phan had strong hopes that his friends among the officials of the Chinese government would provide the new League with the financial and military support needed to overthrow the colonial regime in Vietnam.

Contrary to Phan's expectations, however, the inchoate Chinese government faced disorder and instability that challenged its very existence, so that it could offer no more than token aid in response to his requests. Phan was told by Ch'en Chi-mei, one of his old Chinese acquaintances, that his Restoration League had better start with education, "as a people without education would not be able to succeed at insurrection." Phan had not entirely welcomed advice to that effect when Liang had proffered it in 1905, and Ch'en's well meant offer of training for young Vietnamese in China was no longer enough for him. He now gave first priority to fomenting a campaign of armed insurrection, in the belief that this was the only course of action that offered any prospect of producing an immediate effect. In the event, violent incidents would cost the lives of many of the young men he had trained, without bringing about the hoped-for result.

From 1912 until 1925 Phan's base of operations remained China, allowing for a number of side trips to Japan and Korea. Less than two years after his return to China, in January 1914, he was arrested and imprisoned in Kwangtung by Lung Chi-kuang, a warlord and a supporter of Yüan Shih-k'ai who at that point was ruling China as a dictator. Phan was suspected of having formed a liaison with an anti-Yüan faction. He remained a captive for rather more than three years (in retrospect, he himself refers to "four years"), at times expecting that he would be summarily executed, and for a while in danger, as he later discovered, of being handed over to the French authorities in Indochina as a "bargaining counter." It was only in the spring of 1917, after Lung had suffered serious setbacks, that Phan managed, by means he does not disclose, to make his way to freedom. Phan's earlier autobiography, *Nguc-trung-thu* (A Booklet Written in Prison), was written during his early days in the Kwangtung prison, under threat of imminent death.[8]

In the years down to 1925, Phan was extending his foreign contacts beyond China and Japan. Following the ancient maxim "The enemy

---

8. This autobiography (cited as NTT) is available in English as "Phan Boi Chau's *Prison Notes*" in *Reflections from Captivity*, translated by Christopher Jenkins, Trần Khánh Tuyết, and Huỳnh Sanh Thông, edited by David G. Marr (Athens, OH: Ohio University Press, 1973), 9–66.

of my enemy is my friend," he made a number of attempts to solicit support from Germany, in view of Germany's worsening relations with France. His first contacts with German diplomats went back as far as 1906, when he visited the German consulate in Hong Kong. In 1915, when Germany seemed to have made considerable gains in the course of the First World War, one of Phan's associates was sent to Siam to establish contact with the German and Austrian representatives in Bangkok. Ironically, shortly afterward the diplomatic situation changed unexpectedly: Siam declared war on Germany and aligned itself with France, and the Siamese government presently acceded to the French request to extradite Phan's comrade back to Hanoi to face execution.

The revolutionary fervor in China following the student demonstrations at Peking University that broke out on 4 May 1919, known as the May Fourth Movement, opened up the possibility of contact with the Russians, with whom Sun Yat-sen was then seeking close relations. Wishing to pursue this possibility, Phan traveled to Peking to meet Ts'ai Yüan-p'ei, the chancellor of Peking University, widely respected as "the Father of the Chinese Renaissance," and Ts'ai introduced Phan to some Russians who were in Peking at the time. In a brief meeting with the Russians, Phan sounded out the prospect of sending Vietnamese students to the Soviet Union; this prospect, however, never materialized. Ultimately, the Germans and the Russians proved still less useful to the cause of Vietnamese independence than the Japanese or the Chinese.

There was even a brief period in 1919 when Phan was prepared to canvass the possibility of collaboration, up to a point, with the French. Early in that year, Lê Dư and Phan-Bá-Ngọc—eldest son of possibly the most prominent leader of the Cần-Vương movement, Phan-Đình-Phùng, and long a close associate of Phan-Bội-Châu—presented him with a persuasive argument for collaborating with the then governor-general, Albert Sarraut, a Socialist whose policy of *liberté dans la modernisation* they had come to regard as offering a viable prospect for progress within Vietnam. For a short time Phan must have been convinced, as he wrote what he describes as a "lengthy essay," *Pháp-Việt đề-huề chính-kiến-thư* (A Political Opinion Concerning Franco-Vietnamese Collaboration), in which his arguments seem to reflect those put to him by Phan-Bá-Ngọc. Phan-Bội-Châu went so far as to have an interview with a French official who came to Hangchow to meet him; the conditions presented to him proved unacceptable, however, and the negotiations went no further. Four years later, again in Hangchow, Phan-Bá-Ngọc was assassinated by a young militant who had obtained his gun from the Marquis Cường-Để, who was then residing in Tokyo.

Phan-Bá-Ngọc's reputation has ever since been that of a traitor; Phan-Bội-Châu in this autobiography certainly represents him as such, though in the very last years of his life he would return, without crediting Phan-Bá-Ngọc's influence, to an attitude toward the French very like Phan-Bá-Ngọc's. On closer analysis, the motives behind Phan-Bá-Ngọc's seeming change of front may well have been far from simple. A man of unusual political astuteness (as Phan-Bội-Châu himself admits), Phan-Bá-Ngọc could have seen the implications of Japanese intervention in China at a time when the other world powers were preoccupied with the war in Europe, and inferred that the balance among the imperialist powers in the Far East was already tilting against the French. With "the expansion of Japanese influence reaching its peak," collaboration with the French could have appeared to him to be the only way to forestall "a lot of trouble for the French and a great catastrophe for the Vietnamese."[9] If such was Phan-Bá-Ngọc's position, it is quite possible to see why Cường-Để would not have tolerated it, unremitting hostility to the French being the most consistent political principle of his career. (In a Japanese report sent to the French authorities, however, it is stated that he arranged to have Phan-

---

9. The quoted phrases are from "Pháp-Việt đề-huề chính-kiến-thư," in Nguyễn-Quang-Tô, *Sào-Nam Phan-Bội-Châu [1867–1940]: Con người và thi văn* (Sào-Nam Phan-Bội-Châu (1867–1940): The Man and His Writings) (Saigon: Bộ Văn-hóa Giáo-dục và Thanh-niên, 1974), 191.

Bá-Ngọc assassinated simply as a personal enemy.)[10] As for Phan-Bội-Châu, his acceptance at this point of the idea of collaboration was undoubtedly merely tactical, based on Phan-Bá-Ngọc's arguments. When thereafter, for a time, he repudiated Phan-Bá-Ngọc's position, he seems to have been significantly influenced both by Cường-Để and his supporters and by the many other militant comrades who, like he himself, were inclined by temperament to a policy of armed insurrection.

After the May Fourth Movement, Sun Yat-sen aligned himself with the Soviet revolutionary regime. In January 1924 he reorganized the Kuomintang (Nationalist Party), which adopted new party principles and general regulations and issued a new manifesto in an endeavor to revitalize itself. Observing these changes, Phan drew the conclusion that "the current trend was gradually turning toward a worldwide revolution." He promptly wound up the Vietnam Restoration League and replaced it with the Vietnamese Nationalist Party *(Việt-Nam Quốc-dân-đảng)*, of which, as Phan himself tells us, "the organizational structure was for the most part modeled on that of the Chinese Kuomintang, with some omissions and additions."

It was in December of the same year that Nguyễn-Ái-Quốc arrived in Canton and talked with some of the Vietnamese revolutionaries there. In the report that he wrote to the presidium of the Comintern he described an individual who cannot have been anyone else but Phan-Bội-Châu.

> I have met here a number of the Vietnamese nationalist revolutionaries. In their group is a man who left his country twenty years ago. In the subsequent period he organized several uprisings against France. These uprisings led merely to the death of a few French officers and soldiers and the capture of some guns, and the reason for his failure was that he did not receive any support or help.

---

10. Tokyo, Japanese Diplomatic Archive, *Futsukoku naisei kankei zassan—Zokuryō kankei: Indoshina kankei Annan ōzoku hompō bōmei kankei* A6701-1-1-1, Taishō jūgonen jūgatsu [October 1925].

The sole objective of this man is to avenge his country for
the massacres committed by the French. He does not understand
politics and above all he does not understand how to organize
the masses. In our communications I have explained to him the
necessity for organization and the futility of ill prepared actions.
He has agreed with me. The work that we have started is as follows: (i) I have drawn up a plan of organization, a copy of which
is attached herewith; (ii) having agreed to this plan, he has given
me a list of fourteen Vietnamese who have been working with
him up to now.[11]

Phan intended to return to Canton to discuss the revision of the Vietnamese Nationalist Party's constitution and program of activities with
his comrades. The full impact on Phan of the advice Nguyễn gave him
is hard to gauge, since Phan was arrested before he had an opportunity
to go back to Canton. Later, Phan would reminisce that after Nguyễn-
Ái-Quốc had communicated with him he realized that his own work
had been futile, but that the task of achieving the independence of Vietnam was now safe in the hands of this " very reliable " individual.[12]

It would be going too far to suppose that Phan's amicable contact with the Russians, his reconstruction of the Vietnamese Nationalist Party along the lines of the then Russian-inspired Kuomintang, or
the very respectful reception that he gave to the advice of Nguyễn-Ái-

---

11. Nguyễn-Ái-Quốc to the Presidium of the Communist Party, 18 December 1924,
translated from Hồ-Chí-Minh, *Toàn tập* (Collected Works) (Hanoi: Sự Thật, 1980),
I, 314; also quoted in Phạm Xanh, *Nguyễn-Ái-Quốc với việc truyền bá chủ nghĩa
Mác-Lê Nin ở Việt Nam (1921–1930)* (Nguyễn-Ái-Quốc and the Dissemination of
Marxism–Leninism in Vietnam [1921–1930]) (Hanoi: Thông tin lý luận, 1990), 109.
That Phan did not actually meet Nguyễn-Ái-Quốc in person at this time is clear from
their surviving correspondence, particularly Phan to Lý Thụy (an alias Nguyễn-Ái-
Quốc was then using), n.d. (possibly 15 February 1925, in the opinion of the editor),
in Aix-en-Provence, Archives nationales, Fonds SPCE, Phan-Bội-Châu, Annexe N° 6
à Note Noel N° 144. It was from the fourteen Vietnamese whose names were given
by Phan to Nguyễn-Ái-Quốc that the latter chose the core members of his League of
Vietnamese Revolutionary Youth *(Việt-Nam Thanh-niên Cách-mạng Đồng-chí Hội)*.
12. Đào Duy Anh, *Nhớ nghĩ chiều hôm* (Twilight Reminiscences) (Saigon: Trẻ,
1989), 57.

Quốc imply that he had developed a serious interest in revolutionary socialism as such. These things must be seen in the light of Phan's willingness to be adaptable in his policies, without ever losing sight of his one overriding objective: the independence of his country.

The fourth stage, 1925–1940: In June 1925, as he arrived in Shanghai on what he intended to be a brief trip on behalf of the movement, Phan was arrested by French agents, transported back to Hanoi, and confined in the Hỏa-lò prison. To avoid public disturbances, the colonial authorities at first did not release Phan's real name, but their subterfuge was soon discovered. At the criminal trial that followed, all the charges went back to 1913, the year in which he had been sentenced to death in absentia. The most serious of the charges were incitement to murder and supplying an offensive weapon used to commit murder in two incidents, which had resulted in the death of a Vietnamese governor (12 April 1913) and two French majors (28 April 1913).[13] Speaking in his own defense, Phan said that he opposed the French authorities only by political means and would not advocate murder. He told the court that if he were guilty of anything, it was of the following:

(i)   Your government desires Vietnam to be a French colony, but I desire it to be independent.

(ii) Up to now Vietnam has been an autocracy, but I desire it to become a democracy.

(iii) The authorities ban our people from going abroad to study, but I escaped to go abroad and encouraged students to go overseas for study.

(iv) I write books to rally the Vietnamese to rise up and demand that the authorities carry out political reforms to fulfill their God-given role of enlightening the public.[14]

---

13. Tôn-Quang-Phiệt, *Phan-Bội-Châu và một giai đoạn lịch sử chống Pháp của nhân dân Việt-Nam* (Phan-Bội-Châu and a Stage in the History of the Anti-French Resistance of the Vietnamese People) (Hanoi: Văn Hóa, 1958), 217–218.
14. Ibid., 218.

One of the two French lawyers who volunteered to defend Phan said: "Phan-Bội-Châu criticized the emperor and the French colonial government because he earnestly wished his country to be free from hardship and poverty . . . . Phan-Bội-Châu is the purest of the pure."[15] In the end, the criminal court sentenced Phan to penal servitude for life.

The announcement of this sentence aroused a great clamor from the liberal sector of the public. Even when the court was still in session, one individual volunteered to serve the sentence in Phan's stead; after being dragged out of the court by the police, this man wrote a petition to the court making the same request. A number of newspaper and magazine editors, student organizations, and private individuals sent telegrams to Alexandre Varenne, the new governor-general of Indochina (and a sometime Socialist deputy), to demand Phan's release. Faced with an increasingly vociferous public, Varenne requested an amnesty for Phan from Paris, and he was let out of prison on 24 December 1925.

In an attempt to keep Phan under control, it was arranged that he should stay in Huế at the house of a former member of the Đông-Du movement who by this time had become an active collaborator with the colonial regime, Nguyễn-Bá-Trạc. The house was under surveillance by bodyguards, so that visits by Phan's admirers were somewhat inhibited. In the face of rising public protest against this "house arrest," the *résident-supérieur* of Trung-Kỳ and the Nguyễn court agreed to allow Phan's supporters in Huế to arrange for him to live in a house on top of the slope above the Bến-ngự (Imperial Quay), purchased with a fund donated by his fellow countrymen from Nam-Kỳ. This thatched house was divided into three sections and had a garden of medium size. It was at this modest house that Phan received his admirers and well-wishers of all shades of opinion and visitors from all parts of the country.[16]

---

15. Ibid., 219.

16. The house still stands; Phan's grave is in the garden, marked by a recently erected bust of Phan.

The year Phan was taken back to Vietnam also saw the repatriation from France of another great Vietnamese patriot and contemporary of Phan's: Phan-Châu-Trinh. The two Phans were acquaintances, but they followed sharply divergent political paths. In contrast to Phan-Bội-Châu, Phan-Châu-Trinh unequivocally maintained throughout his career that "reliance on foreign help is foolish and violence is self-destructive" *(vọng ngoại tắc ngu, bạo động tắc tử).* What he advocated was a moderate policy of working within the French colonial system in order to make progress *(ỷ Pháp cầu tiến bộ).* When Phan-Châu-Trinh died suddenly in March of the following year (1926), some fourteen thousand people attended his funeral in Saigon, and the entire country went into mourning. The memorial service in Huế was presided over by Phan-Bội-Châu, whose moving eulogy for Phan-Châu-Trinh reveals a sincere appreciation of the latter's determinedly non-violent anti-colonial struggle, deepened perhaps by his introspection at this time on the tragic failures that had resulted from his own more impetuous methods. The funeral of Phan-Châu-Trinh and the campaign shortly before that to demand Phan-Bội-Châu's release may be regarded as the first widespread, public, and powerful expressions of nationalism that modern Vietnam had ever witnessed.

Phan passed his last fifteen years in Huế, living a quiet life that contrasted with the ferment of anticolonial passion welling up within Vietnamese society. His expenses were mostly defrayed by his acquaintances, and were at all times quite modest. His strongest supporter and most sympathetic and understanding friend was undoubtedly Huỳnh-Thúc-Kháng (1876–1947). A *literatus* like Phan and the holder of a *tiến-sĩ* (doctoral) degree, Huỳnh had known Phan before the latter went to Japan and became his constant companion from the time Phan settled in Huế until his death. Huỳnh was the editor-in-chief of *Tiếng dân* (The People's Voice), a newspaper published in Huế from 1927 until 1943; to this newspaper Phan occasionally contributed, for a time taking charge of its column of advice to aspiring poets. Huỳnh, unlike Phan, followed parliamentary methods in his resistance to the colonial regime; in fact, for a short time before founding his newspaper, Huỳnh had been President of the Trung-Kỳ Assembly. When Hồ-Chí-Minh established his provisional government following the August Revolution of 1945, Huỳnh was appointed minister of Home Affairs, and in 1946 was its acting president when Hồ was away in Paris for negotiations with France. In the years between 1929 and 1936, during which political repression was intense, it was Huỳnh and the staff of his newspaper who looked after Phan's daily necessities. Together with Phan-Châu-Trinh, Huỳnh was perhaps the person who had the most penetrating insight into both the positive and negative aspects of Phan-Bội-Châu's career.

Phan wrote this autobiography during 1928–1929, at the suggestion, as he tells us, of the people around him. His purpose was to leave a record of his activities for his fellow countrymen of later generations to draw upon, and holding that, as he stated at the outset, "My history is entirely a history of failure," he expected them to learn mainly from his mistakes. According to those who knew the conditions under which Phan drafted his autobiography, he wrote it (in literary Chinese) only at night. For paper, he obtained used notebooks of the type traditional in East Asia, with folded double-ply leaves. These he would disassemble and use the blank inside surfaces of the leaves to write on. In the morning he would fold the leaves up again and reassemble them in their covers so as to look once more like ordinary used notebooks. He took this precaution to preserve the manuscript from confiscation in case his house were to be searched by the colonial authorities.

In addition to this autobiography, Phan in his later years wrote two major works: *Khổng-học-đăng* (The Light of Confucianism) and *Chu dịch* (The Book of Change).[17] Both are of considerable length; Phan seems to have devoted a great deal of time and care to distilling in them the conclusions of his lifelong study and observation of Chinese culture. A much shorter book that he wrote under the title *Xã-hội chủ-*

---

17. Published respectively by Anh-Minh (Huế, 1957) and Khai-Trí (Saigon, 1957). Both are included in the ten-volume set of Phan's collected works edited by Chương Thâu (Huế: Thuận Hóa, 1990).

nghĩa (Socialism)[18] was a rather superficial treatment of its subject based on some outdated secondary sources in Chinese.

In the last period of his life, Phan occasionally gave evidence of a more conciliatory outlook than formerly on the question of dealing with the French colonial regime. In 1929 and again in 1931, during the time of the Nghệ-Tĩnh Soviet movement, he volunteered to act as a mediator between the colonial authorities and the local "communist elements," though his offer was not taken up by the French. In the late 1930s, as Japan's military forces drew closer to the border of Indochina, Phan called for "Franco-Vietnamese collaboration," a policy that, as he said, he had enunciated some twenty years previously.[19] When he wrote this autobiography he still seems to have been somewhat embarrassed at having defended such a policy, placing most of the responsibility for his doing so, as explained above, at the door of his longtime associate Phan-Bá-Ngọc. The subsequent signs of increasing moderation in Phan-Bội-Châu's attitude toward the French regime in Indochina have until now gone virtually unnoticed.

During his years at Huế, Phan seems to have found his main relaxation in taking trips in a boat on the Hương (Perfume) River. It was on his boat that he received his friends, and from it he talked to the young admirers who came, also by boat, to see him and listen to him. The most widely held image of Phan, still cherished by many among the older generation in present day Vietnam, is that of an old, bearded man standing with his cane on his boat at the Imperial Quay. He is affectionately remembered as *Ông già Bến-ngự* (the Old Man of the Imperial Quay).

In both his writings and his conversations during these years, Phan seems to have expressed a great deal of optimism about the future generation. The following conversation in the boat on the Perfume River with a visitor from his hometown, recorded by the

---

18. Published in 1946 (Vinh: Sinh Minh).

19. Documents showing Phan's views in the last years of his life are contained in Fonds SPCE, Phan-Bội-Châu, 1928–1940.

late Đào-Duy-Anh, a well known Vietnamese scholar, gives us some insight into Phan's expectations for the future. When his visitor expressed despair over the prospects for Vietnamese independence on the ground that Phan had been "the people's hope for many years past, but had finally found himself tied up here," Phan replied: "You should not think so. That my revolutionary career finally ended in failure is because I have passion but no ability. But there is no doubt that our nation will achieve independence eventually. Now there are people more able than our generation to see to the completion of the work left unfinished by us. Have you ever heard of Nguyễn-Ái-Quốc?"

The visitor responded, "There are newspapers reporting that Nguyễn-Ái-Quốc was arrested and died in Hong Kong two or three years ago."[20] Phan replied, "No, I am quite sure that he is still alive, and if he is alive, our country will achieve independence. They were able to arrest me without much trouble, but how could they arrest him? And even if they did arrest him, they would certainly have to release him eventually, because of his ability, and on top of that he has a wide circle of friends and supporters all over the world."

"Is it not true," the visitor asked, "that [the prophecy current in Nghệ-Tĩnh] *Bò đái thất thanh, Nam-đàn sinh thánh* (When the Bò Đái Stream stops trickling, a saint will be born in Nam-đàn) refers to yourself?[21] If someone like you had to fail, what hope is there for other people?" Phan rejoined: "As far as examinations go, it is true that I was once quite famous. Our people, out of the habit of respecting the *literati,* tend to attribute fame to them for all kinds of things. But if a saint were to be born in Nam-đàn, that person could be no one else but Nguyễn-Ái-Quốc."[22]

20. Nguyễn-Ái-Quốc was in fact arrested by the British authorities in Hong Kong in June 1932, but was defended by a British lawyer and acquitted early in 1933.
21. The Bò Đái Stream is on Mount Thiên-nhận, on the other side of the Lam River from Nam-đàn District. The Bò Đái Stream actually dried up some one hundred years ago, but the prophecy continued to be repeated, as it expressed the longing of the local people for independence.
22. Đào Duy Anh, *Nhớ nghĩ chiều hôm,* 56.

Phan died on 29 October 1940, about a month after the troops of imperial Japan moved into Tongking, and little more than three months before Hồ-Chí-Minh made his dramatic appearance on the Vietnamese scene in February 1941.

V

As a typical Confucian *literatus,* Phan deliberately refrained from discussing his private life in his autobiography, recounting only his public career. A few facts about his private life may nevertheless be appropriately given here.

Phan was married to Thái-Thị-Huyên, also from Nam-đàn, when he was twenty-two years old. The marriage had long been arranged between the parents on both sides, who were acquaintances. As Phan was the only son and his wife did not bear him children, she "married for him" a second wife to fulfill Phan's father's desire for an heir to carry on the family; such a practice was not uncommon in traditional Confucian families. He had with this second wife one son and one daughter; after his second marriage his first wife also bore him a son. The two women, we are told, were on good terms with each other, "like sisters of the same family."[23]

When Phan successfully passed the regional examinations in 1900, the year during which his father died, it would normally have been expected that he would become an official, and his wife might naturally have looked forward to sharing in his prestige. In fact, as already mentioned, Phan refused to follow the ordinary career path of his contemporaries. Before leaving Vietnam to embark on his eventful life abroad, to avoid any possible complications for his wife Phan gave her a letter of divorce already signed by a witness and by himself. She made no complaint but simply agreed to all that he did.

The only time that Phan again met his wife was after he had received the pardon that released him from Hỏa-lò prison, when the

23. Lê-Tràng-Kiều, "Bà Phan Bội Châu" (Mrs. Phan-Bội-Châu), *Tân Việt-Nam*, 5 July 1945, 15.

train carrying him from Hanoi to Huế stopped en route at Vinh station in Nghệ-an. In a brief meeting with Phan at the railway station, his wife said to him: "We have been living apart for more than twenty years. Now that I have been able to see you one more time, I am very happy. From now on, my only wish is that you will hold to your initial aspiration. Do whatever you like, and do not worry about your wife and children."[24] She appears to have been determined above all not to cause him extra anxiety. When Phan was living in Huế, once in a while his sons, their wives, and his grandchildren came to visit him, but never his wife. Even when she died, she told the children not to let Phan know the date of her death. The sacrifice of one's private life for the sake of the people was an ideal expected of those living up to the highest standards of a Confucian society.

The following remarks that Phan later made in a conversation with his children give some insight into his feelings toward his wife:

> From the time I was thirty-six until I left our country, your mother secretly knew everything about all of my activities for the cause of the country, but never did she say a single word. The exception was one day when I happened to be sitting by myself, when your mother, leaning against a nearby pillar, said to me: "You are setting out to catch a tiger [the colonialists]; the tiger has not been caught yet, but so many people have already heard what you are up to. Why is that?" When your mother said that, I pretended as if I did not hear. I was really silly. Now that I am telling you this, I should say that during the ten years before I left our country, though very impoverished, I had many friends and my resolve never faltered; a great part of that was owing to your mother.[25]

From the impressions formed by numerous people who came into contact with Phan, it appears that he was by nature a sociable, open-hearted man who took great pleasure in talking to people from different walks of life. In fact, in his later years, seeing visitors occupied a great

---

24. Ibid., 16.
25. Quoted in Nguyễn-Quang-Tô, *Sào-Nam Phan-Bội-Châu*, 48–49.

part of his schedule. Once there was a female correspondent of the *Hà-nội báo* (Hanoi News) who wished to write an article on "Đời tình ái của nhà chí sĩ Phan-Sào-Nam" (The Love Life of a Man of High Purpose, Phan-Bội-Châu). Phan seems to have been quite open to her rather personal inquiries.

From their conversation, the correspondent gathered that Ấu-Triệu was the woman Phan respected most among his female comrades during his active career. She asked: "From what you have said, I suppose Ấu-Triệu was a close comrade of yours in the past?" Phan replied, "Yes, you are right. She helped me in many ways. She was a person of honesty and integrity. I have great respect for her."[26]

The correspondent then said: "I am amazed by the fact that men of your generation could respect a woman without loving her. But now [1936], it seems to me that it is not unusual to see men who have married their female comrades, because respect is the starting point of love." Phan responded: "You are quite right, but there was no such thing between the female comrades and myself, partly because we were influenced by Confucian ethics, partly because our belief in our cause was extremely powerful. As that was so, our private feelings could be held in check. But nowadays young people fall in love very easily, because circumstances are much less difficult."

She followed this up: "Now, you say that because of the influence of Confucian ethics and the pursuit of a great undertaking, private feelings were held in check. Are you implying that there was a kind of love, superficial or profound, that once flashed through your mind?" Phan said, "Yes. To be honest, there was such a flash, but of a person one highly respects, one would not dare to think in that way, even though just in a flash." The correspondent pursued this theme: "Yet, if it were possible to open the heart, one would see the word 'love,' though just

---

26. Ấu-Triệu (d. 1910), whose real name was Nguyễn-Thị-Đàng or, according to other sources, Lê-Thị-Đàn, was a native of Thừa-thiên. She worked actively to support the Đông-Du movement and the movement demanding the lowering of taxes in Trung-Kỳ (1908). She was arrested and subjected to severe torture; in order not to be forced to reveal secrets, she committed suicide in prison.

in a flash. 'Would not dare' is only a shell covering the surface." At his wits' end, Phan burst out laughing.

Resuming her questioning, the correspondent went on: "Apart from Ấu-Triệu, whom you respected, was there anyone else you were attracted to?" "I should confess," admitted Phan, "that at one time I was attracted to Bạch-Yến. I was simply attracted, without telling her that I liked her, but it looked to me as if she knew it, too. In spite of that, I did not talk to anyone about it. Fortunately, I went abroad, therefore I was able to avoid this attraction. During more than twenty years of activities with female comrades, I was only attracted to Bạch-Yến."[27] According to Nguyễn-Quang-Tô, a scholar who came from the same home town as Phan, Bạch-Yến must be a misspelling of Bạch-Liên, also known as Thanh, who was Nguyễn-Ái-Quốc's elder sister and a supporter of the Đông-Du movement.[28]

VI

At the outset of this autobiography, Phan asserts: "My history is entirely a history of failure," and it is true that in his career he never achieved the results for which he strove. His own assessment of the causes of his failure focused on what he saw as the deficiencies in his own character—"excessive self-confidence," "excessive openness in dealing with people," and so on. From a historical perspective, however, it is possible to see that there were much broader factors tending to limit his achievement.

Though always dedicated to the overthrow of the colonial regime in Vietnam, Phan was never truly a social revolutionary. His idea of revolution, derived from the classical Chinese tradition in which he had been immersed from childhood, was simply a replacement of personnel at the top rather than a fundamental alteration of social structures, and it was a change that could be brought about by the

---

27. *Hà nội báo*, no. 6 (December 1936), quoted in Nguyễn-Quang-Tô, *Sào-Nam Phan-Bội-Châu*, 126–127.
28. Ibid., 386.

dramatic and decisive actions of a few heroic leaders, not one requiring a populist movement for its accomplishment. When it appeared that his attempts to emulate the old Chinese and other Oriental heroes would not suffice to bring about the kind of revolution he sought, he lamented that he had not been born, like those heroes, at a more favorable place or time. For the same reason, he tended to overestimate the role of the *literati*—to which he and most of his comrades belonged—in the independence movement. He once went so far as to assert: "Alas! It is only the *literati* who can read books and make sense of them, only the *literati* who can think of great ideas, only the *literati* who can bear the burden of persevering all the way."[29]

Given these deeply ingrained characteristics of Phan's social and political attitudes, it is not surprising that—notwithstanding his leading role in the first movement to send Vietnamese youth overseas to study —he never wholly committed himself to the principle that widespread education is a necessary concomitant to a successful change of regime. Perhaps he never fully recognized the significance of Liang Ch'i-ch'ao's earnest counsel that "the actual strength that your country has within itself is the intelligence of its people, the vitality of its people, and the talents of its people," even though this spurred him to initiate the Đông-Du movement. He seems to have had no systematically worked out concept of the kind of education that should be given to Vietnamese youth; certainly he articulated no practical educational program. He tells us himself that he was inspired by Mazzini's motto "Education and insurrection go hand in hand," but he used this motto simply to justify his persistence in plans for immediate militant action *(bạo-động)*, to which he confessed he was instinctively attracted. The result was not only that a high proportion of the Vietnamese youth brought to Japan and China through the agency of his movement were sent to military colleges, but also that a number of those whose education had cost so much effort died while trying to carry out some

---

29. Phan-Bội-Châu, *Hòa-lệ cống-ngôn* (An Exhortation Bathed in Tears), as quoted in Hoài Thanh, *Phan-Bội-Châu* (Hanoi: Văn Hóa, 1978), 180.

spectacular act of violence of the kind Phan continued to believe was necessary to provide the spark for a general uprising.

A related impediment to Phan's success as a resistance leader was his failure to acquire an understanding of the French and their regime. The circumstances of his life (unlike those of some of his younger fellow countrymen, including Nguyễn-Ái-Quốc) were such that he never learned the French language or encountered any individual Frenchman in a situation in which his remarkable gift for human relations could have come into play. He seems not to have recognized that attacks directed against individuals or small groups among the French would do little to alter the policy of the French state. The best tactic he could think of, apart from such attacks, was to call rather indiscriminately for the assistance of other foreign countries that were, or seemed to be, at odds with France; these included Germany and Russia, but above all China and Japan. The one rapid and effective way to secure Vietnam's independence, he believed, was through an alliance of Asian countries, with China and Japan at the forefront. In his instinctive Pan-Asianism and his confidence in the goodwill of France's opponents in Europe, there was much that was naive and highly subjective; he was assuming that France was the only country that could entertain colonial designs vis-à-vis Vietnam.

It follows that Phan himself could never have fully recognized the actual significance of his work. He was right, of course, to feel the greatest sense of accomplishment when he recalled his role in organizing the Đông-Du movement to bring the youth of his country to study in Japan. But he could not have realized that, short-lived though this was, it was the first step toward giving Vietnam full access to modern ideas. Similarly, when he reorientated the Vietnamese resistance movement from monarchism to democracy, he was bringing it into line with what seemed to him the spectacularly successful Chinese nationalist movement, rather than affirming the principle of social revolution; but in retrospect this appears as the first effective step toward the abandonment of the traditional form of polity in Vietnam. At an earlier stage in his career, when he was in Japan, Phan had begun to popularize the practice of referring to his country as "Việt-Nam" (Vietnam, the South of the Viet people) rather than "Annam" (the Pacified South), a name that obviously owed its origin to the Chinese world view and was retained by the French.[30] He rightly perceived the significance of the fact that youths from all the Three Regions of the country were coming together voluntarily for the first time, as students in Japan, to participate in a single unified movement. The force of Vietnamese unity had been mainly conspicuous hitherto in reaction to foreign intervention. At the same time, Phan was among the first of his countrymen in the modern age to encounter the practical problems of striking a balance within a Vietnamese national movement between the unity and the diversity of the Vietnamese people. He expressed some diffidence about his ability to come to terms with these problems, but his ideal of Vietnamese nationhood was a legacy that would live on. Finally, Phan's voluminous writings, in particular his passionate poetry, were perfectly attuned to appeal to the feelings and desires of his countrymen then and since, arousing their patriotic sentiments and national pride in times of crisis. Many participants in the Vietnamese resistance movement of later years would cite a few lines of Phan's poetry that had awakened their enthusiasm in their youth. Phan was far from unconscious of his literary gifts, but their effect was greater than he could know.

VII

The present translation of Phan-Bội-Châu's autobiography is based on the original text in literary Chinese, *Phan-Bội-Châu niên-biểu*, with *chữ Nôm* (Vietnamese demotic script) mixed in at a few places. Two manuscripts of this original text have been used, one owned by Huỳnh-Thúc-Kháng (cited as HTK), and one commissioned by Hoàng-Xuân-Hãn (cited as HXH). The readings of the two manuscripts are virtually identical except for some minor points—for example, in HXH the

---

30. The name "Việt-Nam" was first coined in the time of Emperor Gia-Long.

character *thời* that indicates "time" has been changed to *thần,* which can also mean "time" but is not in popular use.

Two basic *quốc-ngữ* translations exist, both of which have also been consulted throughout. One was dictated orally by Phan-Bội-Châu himself. This version was edited by Huỳnh-Thúc-Kháng and published by Anh-Minh (cited as AM).[31] The other was translated by Phạm-Trọng-Điềm and Tôn-Quang-Phiệt (cited by the latter's initials as TQP).[32] Both of these *quốc-ngữ* versions have their merits and shortcomings. The merit of AM lies in the fact that it contains some extra information not found in the original text, added by Phan-Bội-Châu himself as he dictated the translation. (This information has been included in the footnotes to the present translation.) Concerning the AM version, Huỳnh-Thúc-Kháng aptly wrote: "If the spirit in the literary Chinese text is ten, then that in the *quốc-ngữ* translation is five, because Phan was not skilled in *quốc-ngữ,* and as there was no time to make corrections it is not smooth. Nonetheless, the important ideas are not incorrect."[33] The greatest shortcoming of AM is that the publisher sometimes let his politics influence the printed version. Anh-Minh, a staunch supporter of the Ngô-Đình-Diệm government in South Vietnam, added headings that do not exist in the original, such as "Contact with the Russians and [Phan's] discovery of their cunning." He also deliberately left out the passage in which Phan recollects his favorable impressions of the Russians.[34] As for the TQP translation, it generally

---

31. *Tự-phán* (Huế: Anh-Minh, 1956).

32. The first edition (1955) of this translation was entitled *Tự-phán* (Self-Assessment). In the second edition the title was corrected to *Phan-Bội-Châu niên-biểu* (The Autobiography of Phan-Bội-Châu) (Hanoi: Văn Sử Địa, 1957); this latter is the edition cited here.

33. In the "Preface" to *Tự-phán,* x.

34. There is still a typescript of the text on which AM is based, without these editorial alterations. The *quốc-ngữ* version included in volume II of *Phan-Bội-Châu toàn tập* (Phan-Bội-Châu's Collected Works) edited by Chương Thâu (Huế: Thuận Hóa, 1990) makes use of this typescript, with some minor revisions. The version included in *Phan-Bội-Châu niên-biểu,* edited by Nguyễn-Khắc-Ngữ (Saigon: Nhóm Nghiên-cứu Sử-Địa, 1971), is also based on this translation, with some corrections and notes.

presents a faithful version of the original text, but in places it is not free from minor errors.

The French translation by Georges Boudarel[35] is highly readable, though based as it is on TQP, it reproduces some of its errors. Boudarel's thorough annotations are particularly helpful. He has drawn at certain points on information in the records of the French *Sûreté*, which is of great interest but naturally cannot always be accepted without critical scrutiny.

There are some factual discrepancies concerning dates and events between this autobiography and Phan's earlier autobiography (cited as NTT).[36] These are pointed out in the notes to the present translation. In spite of such flaws, the autobiography here presented for the first time in English remains an essential source for anyone seeking to understand not only Phan-Bội-Châu's career and character, but also the longer sequence of often moving and tragic events in which he played his part. In the assessment of the significance of this work that he wrote in 1946, Huỳnh-Thúc-Kháng declared: "As Phan writes his autobiography, it becomes also a panorama depicting the changing phases of Vietnam's history over the last sixty or seventy years."[37] The following pages thus offer to the modern reader unique insights into both the man and his milieu, with all their lights and shadows.

Proper Names

In this volume, Vietnamese and other East Asian names are given in their customary order, with the family name first and the personal name last. Where a Vietnamese is referred to, the form of the name used is

35. "Phan-Bội-Châu: Mémoires," *France-Asie/Asia* 194–195, 22, no. 3/4 (1968): 4–210.

36. For a discussion in English of the problems these raise, see Nguyễn Khắc Kham, "Discrepancies between *Ngục Trung Thư* and *Phan Bội Châu Niên Biểu*" in Vĩnh Sính, ed., *Phan Bội Châu and the Đông-Du Movement* (New Haven, CT: Yale Center for International and Area Studies, 1988), 22–51.

37. In AM, "Preface," X.

that by which the person would have called himself or herself as an adult, thus retaining the person's local pronunciation (e.g., *Vũ* or *Võ*, *Hoàng* or *Huỳnh,* etc.).

Aliases may be mentioned either in square brackets or in the notes. During Phan's time, it was not unusual for a person to be known by more than one name. The reasons for changing one's name could be many, but generally speaking there were three: (i) unhappiness with the name given at birth; (ii) a desire to obtain better fortune under another name (thus Phan himself changed his name from Phan-Văn-San to Phan-Bội-Châu when he took the regional mandarinate examination for the sixth time, probably hoping for better luck); (iii) political reasons (thus Phan adopted several aliases and pseudonyms during his active years in Japan and China; Nguyễn-Ái-Quốc is believed to have had dozens of pseudonyms).

In contrast to present-day Vietnam where the use of personal names has become very popular, even when referring to persons with formal titles (e.g., "President Thiệu" for the former president Nguyễn-Văn-Thiệu of South Vietnam), in the Vietnam of Phan's time it was customary for *literati* like Phan to use family names, full names, or pseudonyms (or pseudonyms with family or full names) in addressing each other formally. For this reason, no one would use his personal name (Châu) to refer to Phan, and the same tradition was still observed by those a generation or more younger, such as Nguyễn-Ái-Quốc or Hồ-Chí-Minh (thus one might refer to Mr. Nguyễn-Ái-Quốc or Mr. Nguyễn or to President Hồ, but never to Mr. Quốc or President Minh).

For Vietnamese monarchs, the title "Emperor" is adopted here, because on formal occasions within their own territories they referred to themselves by the equivalent title *(Hoàng-đế)*. In respect of their tributary relationship to the Chinese emperor, of course, they were regarded simply as client kings.

The Vietnamese names for the Three Regions under French rule, *Bắc-Kỳ, Trung-Kỳ,* and *Nam-Kỳ,* equivalent to Tongking, Annam, and

Cochin China, are always used by Phan in the original text and have been retained in this translation.

Finally, hyphens have been used in proper names wherever they are appropriate. Chinese names and other words have been transliterated according to the Wade-Giles system, Japanese names according to the Hepburn system.

Reckoning of Dates

Phan always gives dates using the Vietnamese (and Chinese) lunar calendar. In this calendar, each year is designated by two terms: The first refers to one of the " Ten Heavenly Stems " and the second to one of the " Twelve Earthly Branches," or the twelve animals of the zodiac. There are twelve lunar months in a year (intercalary months occur occasionally). Each month is divided into three " decades " *(tuần),* i.e., periods of ten days. (These are not to be confused with the *tuần* in modern Vietnamese, which refer to seven-day weeks.) Phan would therefore refer to the first decade *(thượng-tuần),* second or middle decade *(trung-tuần),* or third decade *(hạ-tuần)* of any given month. We have naturally followed his practice in this translation, adding wherever necessary the approximate equivalent in the Gregorian calendar.

Abbreviations

AM   *Tự-phán*, translated orally into *quốc-ngữ* by Phan-Bội-Châu (Huế: Anh-Minh, 1956).

CT   *Phan-Bội-Châu niên-biểu*, in *Phan-Bội-Châu toàn tập* (Phan-Bội-Châu's Collected Works), edited by Chương Thâu, vol. II (Huế: Thuận Hóa, 1990). [Based on the same text as that used by AM, but without AM's additions and deletions, and with minor editorial revisions.]

GB   "Phan-Bội-Châu: Mémoires," translated by Georges Boudarel, *France-Asie/Asia* 194–195, 22, no. 3/4 (1968): 4–210. [Based on TQP.]

HTK   *Phan-Bội-Châu niên-biểu*, manuscript in literary Chinese owned by Huỳnh-Thúc-Kháng (photocopy).

HXH   *Phan-Bội-Châu niên-biểu*, manuscript in literary Chinese from the collection of Hoàng-Xuân-Hãn (photocopy).

NTT   "Phan Boi Chau's *Prison Notes*," in *Reflections from Captivity*, translated by Christopher Jenkins, Trần Khánh Tuyết, and Huỳnh Sanh Thông, edited by David G. Marr (Athens, OH: Ohio University Press, 1973), 9–66.

TQP   *Phan-Bội-Châu niên-biểu*, translated by Phạm-Trọng-Điềm and Tôn-Quang-Phiệt, second edition (Hanoi: Văn Sử Địa, 1957).

THE AUTOBIOGRAPHY OF

PHAN-BỘI-CHÂU

★

Preface

I WAS CAPTURED while abroad, brought home, and confined in prison.[1] Fortunately, owing to the generous solicitude of my compatriots, I have been able to carry on through my remaining years of life. It has been possible for me to meet and renew my ties with family members, friends, and comrades, from the sight of whom I had been utterly cut off for decades past.

Those who like me, those who detest me, those who blame me, those who place hope in me, those who know me, and those who do not know me—all wish to learn the full story of Phan-Bội-Châu. Alas! My history is a history of countless failures without one single success. For some thirty years, while I roamed hither and yon, calamity struck those involved with me throughout the land—association with me brought imprisonment, and ill effects spread among my compatriots. In the depths of each night I have beaten my breast and gazed up at heaven and wiped away my tears. I have been stumbling and falling for twenty years and more. I feel ashamed not to have lived up to the duties of my station in this world. I look up to the nameless martyrs like one without food or drink.

Yet since ancient times, in epochs of transition when the old meets the new, how many have there been who achieved complete success in the task of sweeping away the rubbish to let the stream run pure? The fact that it took several revolutions for France to establish her republic is a clear illustration of this. We should at least study the path of an overturned chariot in order to derive instruction from failure, and presently consider how to change our course so as to arrive at success.

---

1. Hỏa-lò prison in Hanoi.

We should seek for a way of life in the midst of ten thousand deaths; we should find an effective cure after our wings have been nine times wounded.

Plans of action should be kept secret so that there is no concern about disruption. Hearts and minds should be united to cleanse blood with blood.[2] On the day that marks success, shall not the history of Phan-Bội-Châu be to the later generation like that of the chariot that went before them? The solicitude of my family members and friends has pressed me hard: "Write your history quickly, while you are still alive." I therefore humbly oblige, draft this volume, and entitle it *The Autobiography of Phan-Bội-Châu.*

---

2. CT adds an extra sentence: "One cannot reconstruct society without using blood to cleanse blood."

Self-Assessment

MY HISTORY IS entirely a history of failure, and the maladies that have caused this failure are indeed obvious. All the same, I do not venture to say that there is nothing of which I can be proud. Before I enter into the main narrative, I should like to set out in broad outline the following points:

— My self-confidence is excessive. I tend to think that there is nothing impossible to carry out in this world. This is on account of my fault in not weighing my ability or measuring my virtue.

— My openness in dealing with people is excessive. I tend to think that there is not a single person in this world whom it is not possible to trust. This is on account of my fault in not being wary and calculating.

— In dealing with affairs and people, I pay attention only to big things. Where small things are concerned, for the most part I deliberately make snap judgments. For this reason, on many occasions, because of small things a big plan has failed. This is on account of my fault in being slapdash and imprudent.

The above three items are the most serious maladies. For the rest, I shall rue them in my heart, but it is not possible to list them here.

— I am venturesome and daring. Even against ten thousand people, I do not back down. Particularly in my youth, my audacity was enormous.

— In my association with others, once I have encountered a fine thought, it is impossible for me to forget it for the rest my life. Frank advice and severe admonition I gladly receive.

— In any undertaking in my life, I always look forward to reaching the goal, and achieving victory at the last moment; even though means and strategies may change, I am not distressed.

The above three items I should consider those of my strengths that are worthy of note. Those who sympathize with me and those who blame me will recognize all this.

What follows will be divided chronologically into three periods.

— The first period is my obscure years, unworthy of being narrated; but as these were the formative years of my life, I dare not omit them.
— The second period is the time of my youth, the years before I went abroad, which included various activities: lying low while readying myself for the future, forming secret plans, and making contacts with outstanding individuals.
— The third period comprises the history of my activities after I went abroad.

THE FIRST PERIOD

IN THE TWELFTH MONTH of the Year of the Hare, the twentieth year of the reign of Tự-Đức of the Nguyễn dynasty [26 December 1867], I was born to my father, Phan-Văn-Phổ, and my mother, Nguyễn-Thị-Nhàn, in my mother's native village of Sa-nam, Đông-liệt District, in the region between Mount Hùng[1] and the Lam River.

My family for generations had been one of scholars, always living in genteel poverty. When my grandfather died, my family became even poorer. Fortunately, my father, being a proficient scholar whose ink bottle served as his rice paddy and his brush as his hoe,[2] was able to support the family. When my father was thirty years old, my mother became his wife. When my father was thirty-six, I was born; that was five years after the loss of Cochin China. My first cry as a babe sounded like an ominous warning: "You are already one whose country has been lost."[3]

When I was three years old, my father took me to my grandfather's village. He built a house to the south of Mount Mồ, in which my

---

1. Mount Hùng is commonly called Mount Đụn [or Độn]. When Mai-Hắc-Đế fought against the T'ang forces and was defeated, this is where he went to die. There is a royal shrine on the mountain; therefore people of later generations changed its name to Mount Hùng. [Author's note.] — Mai-Hắc-Đế, the self-proclaimed "Black Emperor" of what was then known as Annam, led his unsuccessful uprising against China in A.D. 722. [Translators' note.]

2. *Nghiên điền bút canh:* a reference to teaching.

3. In Sino-Vietnamese, *Vong-quốc:* the term was popularly used by both Vietnamese and Chinese at the turn of the century to describe a country that had lost its independence and been subjected to colonial rule.

family is living now, in the village of Đan-nhiễm, township of Xuân-liệu. My father often went far away to teach at private schools. Until I was six years old, the responsibility for my upbringing and education fell solely to my mother. My mother's character was benevolent and charitable. Although my family was poor, when relatives, friends, or neighbors encountered pressing difficulties, we did our best to help them. We would share our last coin or our last grain of rice. Bringing me up throughout my childhood, she never used a single word that was improper; I lived with my mother for sixteen years, yet I absolutely never heard her cursing anyone. To those who were rude she only returned a smile. During her childhood she had been in her elder brothers' company as they read books, and she was able to remember what the books said to her dying day. When I was four or five years old, without being able to recognize characters, I could recite by heart several chapters in the *Book of Poetry*, having heard them from my mother's lips.

When I was six, my father took me to his private school and taught me Chinese characters. In three days I learned all of the *Book of Three Characters* and was able to repeat it without missing a single word. My father, taken by surprise, began to teach me the *Analects,* having me read and copy the characters, then instructing me to write out from memory what I had read in the book. In every lesson more than ten pages were read. Being poor, we were not able to acquire enough paper, so I used banana leaves instead. Once they were memorized, I burned them.

When I was seven, I learned the Classics and their commentaries; I was able roughly to comprehend their meaning. Once, imitating the *Analects*, I composed *Phan Tiên-sinh Luận-ngữ* (The Analects of Master Phan), which had several passages making fun of my classmates. My father, finding out about this, punished me smartly with his switch. After that I would not venture to compose a book in jest again.

When I was eight, I was able to compose brief pieces in the then popular style. I entered for the trial examinations[4] of the village, the district, and the prefecture, in which I always came first.

When I was nine, in the Year of the Dog, the twenty-ninth year of the reign of Tự-Đức [1874], the scholar-gentry in the Nghệ-Tĩnh region[5] rose in revolt under the name of *Bình Tây* (Put Down the French), appealing to the other districts and prefectures to join them. The leaders were Trần Tấn, a licentiate *(tú-tài)*[6] of Thanh-chương; Đỗ Mai, a licentiate of Diễn-châu; and Lê Khanh, a licentiate of Hà-tĩnh. On hearing this, I assembled the children at my school; using bamboo tubes for guns and lychee pits for bullets, we ourselves played at *Bình Tây*. For this I was severely punished. I did not give up, however, since delight in action and love of novelty are in my very nature.

When I was thirteen, I was able to compose neoclassical poetry and prose. Most of this even the senior teachers in the village could not comprehend. My father wished me to be trained under excellent teachers, but there was no great private school in the neighboring villages, and being poor, I was unable to go far away to study. I therefore continued to follow lessons with my father and with Master Nguyễn in Xuân-liệu village. This master, named Kiều, was deeply versed in Chinese studies.[7] He had obtained his *cử-nhân* degree[8] and received an appointment at the Bureau of Compilation, but had

---

4. In Sino-Vietnamese, *tiểu-khảo,* literally "little examinations;" those who passed these tests did not receive a degree, but might be awarded some piece of land that could be used as a means of support for further study.

5. The area including the two provinces of Nghệ-an and Hà-tĩnh.

6. In Chinese, *hsiu-ts'ai*, literally "flowering talent;" the lowest degree, which entitled its holder to participate in the provincial mandarinate examinations.

7. In Sino-Vietnamese, *hán-học,* the body of knowledge that formed the basis of official learning in traditional Vietnam, until the Chinese-style mandarinate examinations were abolished in 1919.

8. In Chinese, *chü-jen*, literally "recommended man;" this degree was officially granted to one who had passed a regional examination and was entitled to proceed to the metropolitan examination.

abandoned officialdom and retired to teach at home. Having taken me on, he became immensely fond of me; sometimes on my behalf he borrowed books from the libraries of the great houses for me to read. Owing to the reading of this literature, my knowledge was greatly extended. It is regrettable that at that time I was burying my head in the stale literature on the mandarinate examination, so that I could not benefit much.[9]

When I was seventeen, in the Year of the Sheep, the thirty-sixth year of the reign of Tự-Đức [1883], Bắc-Kỳ[10] was totally lost. North of Ninh-bình,[11] though, patriots rose in arms like swarms of bees. I, too, was caught up in the excitement, and wished to respond to the call of the patriot band in Bắc-Kỳ, but I had no power to do so. Thus in the depths of the night, by the light of my lamp, I drafted an appeal: *Bình-Tây thu-Bắc* ("Put down the French and Regain the North"). I surreptitiously affixed it to the big trees along the Mandarin Road, hoping it would attract attention. However, as my station was humble and my words were insignificant, it was an empty writing, without effect. Within a few days the appeal was torn down and destroyed. For the first time I realized that it was indispensable to make a name for myself. Henceforward I bent every effort to cultivating my writing for the mandarinate examination. My literary reputation became more and more widespread; I passed first in several regional examinations.

When I was eighteen, in the Year of the Monkey, the first year of the reign of Kiến-Phúc [1884], my mother departed from this life in the Fifth Month. It was not permissible for me to enter for examination during the period of mourning for my mother. Not only that, the circumstances of our family were extremely straitened; my two

---

9. Chinese studies are not necessarily to be blamed for the stale literature on the mandarinate examination in the old days. Western studies are not necessarily to be blamed for the slavish and inferior literature of nowadays. Dismal circumstances have buried alive countless promising youth; how deplorable it is! [Author's note.]

10. The Vietnamese name for the area known to the French as Tongking.

11. A town at the southern edge of Bắc-Kỳ.

younger sisters had no one to look after them; my father, as a widower, added the cooking to his duties. To obtain a bare living, I began to use my brush as a means of support from this time on.

When I was nineteen, in the Year of the Cock, the first year of the reign of Hàm-Nghi, in the Fifth Month [May 1885], the capital city Thuận-hóa (Huế) was lost. In the Seventh Month, French soldiers seized the citadel of Nghệ-an. The scholar-gentry in Nghệ-Tĩnh one and all responded to the Imperial Proclamation calling for a Cần-Vương (Loyalist) uprising by rounding up a rabble of militiamen who opposed the bullets with their bodies. They were filled with zeal for the great cause, but this is what should be called stupid loyalty.[12]

It was from this time that I too began to practice this childish and ludicrous patriotic game. By now, the officials and the scholar-gentry had mustered all the local able-bodied men, formed them into bands, sharpened sticks to make pikes, and dispatched them over hill and dale. Though only a student, I could not hold myself back; unable to contain my indignation, I bestirred myself to mobilize my class-mates. Trần-Văn-Lương[13] was the first to support me; more than sixty people rallied to the cause. We intended to organize an Army of the Examination Candidates, but there was no one who could assume the responsibility of leader. Though the one who started the business, I was the youngest among the group, with only slender ability and slight reputation; it was not suitable for me to assume such a charge. There being no alternative, Trần and I went to see the *cử-nhân* Đinh-Xuân-Sung and tried to persuade him to become our leader. Đinh, being full of righteous indignation, accepted. A list of names was then drawn up and a military badge decided on, but both funds and weapons were unavailable. We thereupon set about drawing up a list of donors and manufacturing weapons.

---

12. *Ngu-trung;* this expression and the following sentence evidently reflect Phan's judgment in his later years, in view of his earlier inclination to militant resistance.

13. A *cử-nhân* who chose not to become an official. [Author's note.]

However, within less than the space of ten days[14] French soldiers suddenly burst on the scene, burning and ravaging, shooting and killing. Smoke and flames obscured the sky. Shattered and disheartened, everyone accused Trần and me of putting on a poor show. My father also reproached me severely. I had to go and ask Đinh to give back the list of names and disband the Army of the Examination Candidates. Luckily matters were still wrapped in secrecy and all traces were quickly destroyed; no one was found out. This activity was really a most childish game. Through it, however, I acquired one good lesson: I came to realize that to become a hero it is necessary to prepare discreetly, and to carry out a great undertaking it is necessary to weigh all possible plans. Those who move too quickly and take action heedlessly are, like a violent tiger trying to cross a river, bound to fail.

FOR MORE THAN TEN years afterward, I devoted myself single-mindedly to self-improvement. Moreover, I tried to study further the literature in vogue at the time, in the hope of making my name more widely known and of establishing my reputation in the world, which might serve as a springboard for future activities. In addition, I discreetly sought out books on the art of war by the ancient strategists, such as *Tôn-Tử thập-tam-thiên* (Thirteen Chapters of Sun Tzu), *Vũ-hầu tâm-thư* (The Essential Chu-ko Liang), *Hổ-trướng xu-cơ* (Inner Secrets of Military Command), *Binh-gia bí-quyết* (Keys for Military Strategists), etc.[15] In the depths of the night, I copied

---

14. *Tuần*, a "decade," the traditional Vietnamese ten-day "week," of which there were three in a month. A description of the old Vietnamese system for reckoning time will be found in the Introduction, p. 37.

15. The first two books are by the two best-known Chinese strategists. *Hổ-trướng xu-cơ* is a work of Đào-Duy-Từ (1572–1634), a scholar and military strategist under the Nguyễn lords, best known for building the famous strategic wall in Quảng-bình Province known as the *Lũy Thầy* to prevent invasions by the Trịnh from the north. *Binh-gia bí-quyết*, more commonly known as *Binh-gia yếu-lược* (Essentials for Military Strategists), is by Trần-Hưng-Đạo (?–1300), the foremost military hero in Vietnamese history, who twice defeated the Mongol invaders in the thirteenth century.

them out privately in my room in order to learn them by heart, with the expectation of using them as models for action in times to come.

When I was twenty, in the Year of the Dog, the first year of the reign of Đồng-Khánh [1886], that was the time when my lifelong aspiration for revolution really began to take shape. My animosity and hatred toward the enemy, when occasion arose, poured forth unreservedly. Holding what Mr. Mai and Mr. Tấn had done in high respect, I composed a book entitled *Song-tuất-lục* (Records of Two Years of the Dog). Its earlier part was a detailed account of the uprising in Nghệ-Tĩnh in the Year of the Dog [1874]; the latter part briefly reviewed the Cần-Vương movement in the next Year of the Dog [1886]. To both parts were appended short commentaries that highly praised Mr. Mai and Mr. Tấn; both, being rebel leaders, had been executed, so that no one would dare to utter their names in public, and I was the first to record their story. My colleagues and pupils compelled me to burn the manuscript. Nonetheless, through this I acquired a good lesson. Alas! While one's reputation is not sound and one's wings are not fully fledged, yet one has the wish to fulfill a dream overnight —simply to express it is already difficult, let alone to realize it in practice!

From twenty-one to thirty-one years of age, there was a period of ten years during which I lay low and stayed in the background, for two reasons. The first was the straitness of my family's circumstances. My family, from my great-grandfather onward through four generations, always had only one son; my father, though not the first child, was the sole heir, and I too had no brothers. My father was old, ill, and a poor widower who relied on me as his mainstay. Having an innate sense of filial piety, I was always averse to anything that might compromise my father, and tried my best to avoid it. For this reason I confined myself to teaching and professional writing. The money that I earned was fairly ample; by means of it I could constantly support my father without any lack. When there was still something extra in the wallet, the money would be spent at once on the needs of visitors. The fugitive outlawed patriots and the remnants of the Cần-Vương movement all liked to maintain secret contact with me. My failure in later days was really engendered at this time. Yet it was also in the course of these ten years that I met those through whom I made the friends I have most cherished in my life. How laborious and difficult it must be for the Creator to shape the success and failure of an individual!

The second reason was the vicissitudes of my academic fortune [in the mandarinate examinations]. Since my childhood I had been reading books and gaining a notion of the great cause,[16] and from the outset I did not wish to be just a common villager. I often used to recite the lines:

> *Each night I always tell myself out loud*
> > *To leave a name to future generations;*
> *But what worse way to stand out from the crowd*
> > *Than fame for passing the examinations!* [17]

In spite of everything, I had to conceal my resentment and keep up my resolve, attempting the provincial examination six times before my name was posted up at the head of the list of the passing candidates. At that time I wrote the following lines to "congratulate" myself:

> *Eight or nine of ten things go against my wishes;*
> *The wind outside the bamboo screen brings sadness.*

---

16. *Đại-nghĩa.* Though Phan never spells out what this term implied, we can gather that it meant first and foremost the expulsion of the French from Vietnam; any other goals, including domestic reform, could only be considered after that. Phan's militancy, and indeed his rigidity, are encapsulated in this notion.

17. Lines from Sui-Yuan's poem in Chinese. Mr. Nguyễn-Ái-Quốc, when he was ten years old, heard me reciting these lines on a convivial occasion, and he is still able to recall them now. [Author's note.] — Sui-Yuan was a Chinese poet of the early Ch'ing dynasty. The original text reads simply "literary fame," but the allusion seems to be to success in passing the literary examinations for the mandarinate. More than twenty years must have passed between the original meeting of Phan-Bội-Châu and Nguyễn-Ái-Quốc in Vietnam and their correspondence when both were in China late in 1924. [Translators' note.]

> *A passing flutist midst three hundred persons;*
> *Alone, a Nan-Kuo shamed before the courtiers.*[18]

Such was my contempt for worldly fame!

IN THE COURSE OF my life I have had two bosom friends whom I especially cherished, one being Đặng-Thái-Thân of Hải-côn, also known as Ngư-Hải,[19] the other being Nguyễn Hàm of Quảng-nam, also known as Tiểu-La.[20] It was the happy chance of our common interest in literature that brought me together with Mr. Đặng; it was the remnants of the Cần-Vương movement that brought me together with Mr. Nguyễn. The occasions were different but the end results were the same. The way in which our temperaments coincided was truly wonderful!

At the time, because of my impoverished situation, I was teaching at home. My pupils numbered several hundred. Whenever I explained a text to my pupils, I would repeat over and over again the deeds of the men of high purpose *(chí-sĩ)* in the past. In particular, I was very fond

---

18. My old friend Mr. Thai-Sơn took great pleasure in this poem. [Author's note.]
— The story goes that Nan-Kuo, although only pretending to play the flute, found employment in the orchestra of three hundred flutists maintained by King Hsüen-Wang of Ch'i. When the king was succeeded by his son, the flute players were auditioned individually and Nan-Kuo had to run away rather than face exposure. [Translators' note.]

19. Đặng-Thái-Thân (1874–1910), a native of Nghệ-an, was a disciple and close comrade of Phan. Along with Phan and others, he was a founding member of the Vietnam Modernization Association. After Phan went to Japan, he was in charge of the affairs of the Association north of Huế, and acted as liaison with Phan. Phan gives a narrative of the circumstances of his death in 1910.

20. Nguyễn Hàm, also known as Nguyễn Thành (1863–1911), a native of Quảng-nam, was the son of a high mandarin. He participated in the Cần-Vương movement in his home province; when this was crushed by the French in 1887, he was arrested and imprisoned for some time. After his release, he farmed in his home town. Phan met him for the first time in 1903; he was the strategist of the Vietnam Modernization Association. Arrested once again, he died in prison on Poulo Condore in 1911.

of recounting the stories of Hoàng-Phan-Thái and Phan-Đình-Phùng, wishing to make a strong impression. The only person who fully understood my thoughts was Mr. Đặng. The writings in which I expressed my disgust at the times and my indignation at society, as well as my association with the fugitive patriots and the remnants of the Cần-Vương movement, I kept secret and allowed no one to know; only Mr. Đặng was sure to be apprised of all these things. He and I were literary friends for twelve years and revolutionary friends for eleven years. Though he died owing to his failure, he took his own life to preserve his integrity unsullied by the enemy's hand. I feel ashamed indeed when I think of our friendship!

Earlier on, in the Year of the Cock, the first year of the reign of Hàm-Nghi [1885], the capital had fallen and the king had had to take his departure. The Cần-Vương movement had burst forth as clouds rise up and water boils over. In La-sơn in Nghệ-Tĩnh, Phan-Đình-Phùng was the leader for eleven years; in Thanh-hà in Nam-Ngãi,[21] Nguyễn-Hiệu was the head for four years, before the movement died out. At the time, I was immature and my wings were not fully fledged. My family had no other son; I dared not lift up my head, but I secretly kept in touch with those in charge of the remnants of Mr. Phan's movement. I was closely acquainted with the adjutant *(tán-tương)* Nguyễn Quýnh of Hương-sơn, the agent *(đốc-biện)* Hà-Văn-Mỹ of Nghi-xuân, the deputy commandant *(phó-lãnh)* Ngô Quảng, and the quartermaster *(quản-cơ)* Lê Hạ, as well as the battalion commanders *(đội)* Quyên and Quế.[22] Of all these, Nguyễn Quýnh was the closest to me. Because he was an important member of Mr. Phan's movement and continually traveled back and forth with the associates of Mr. Nguyễn's movement in Thanh-hà, he knew Tiểu-La very well. Whenever he talked about the movement in Nam-Ngãi, he praised Tiểu-La in the highest terms.

---

21. The region comprising Quảng-nam and Quảng-ngãi.

22. These individuals could have received their titles from the resistance leader Phan-Đình-Phùng around 1885, when he followed Emperor Hàm-Nghi to their base in Tân-sở.

It was not until three years before I went overseas that I met Tiểu-La for the first time and conferred with him in person; but in spiritual terms, my association with him had already been going on for more than ten years. When I met him at last, he gave his heart to me at once, and did everything in his power to support me. It was the members of the Cần-Vương movement who first introduced me to him.

WHEN I WAS THIRTY-ONE, in the Year of the Cock, the eighth year of the reign of Thành-Thái [1897], I was excluded for life from taking examinations on account of bringing notes to the examination site.[23] For a time I wandered around Bắc-Kỳ. Eventually I found my way to the capital, Thuận-hóa [Huế], where I taught at the house of Mr. Võ in An-hòa, who is Võ-Bá-Hạp's father. During my spare time from teaching, it was through the medium of literature that I was brought into contact with some notable personalities. Khiếu-Năng-Tĩnh, principal of the Imperial Academy,[24] treated me with high regard. My enduring friendship with Thai-Sơn Đặng-Nguyên-Cẩn began at that time.[25] Mai-Sơn Nguyễn-Thượng-Hiền[26] read my

---

23. According to Tôn-Quang-Phiệt, Phan's friend Trần-Văn-Lương, meaning to be helpful, had, without Phan's knowledge, placed some books in his bag, which were found by the porter at the gate of the examination site. Phan received a pardon three years later, when he took the examination and came first, as he later relates.

24. Khiếu-Năng-Tĩnh (1835–?) was a well known literary figure, an erudite scholar, and a prominent educator in nineteenth-century Vietnam.

25. Đặng-Nguyên-Cẩn (1867–1923) was a native of Nghệ-an. He passed the metropolitan examination in 1895 and was appointed educational director in Nghệ-an, then in Bình-thuận. Arrested for his association with the Đông-Du movement, he spent thirteen years in prison, being released in 1921.

26. Nguyễn-Thượng-Hiền (1868–1925), a native of Hà-đông and a son-in-law of the Regent Tôn-Thất-Thuyết. He obtained the *cử-nhân* degree at the early age of seventeen and was at the top of the list of those who passed the metropolitan examination in 1885, but before the results could be officially announced, Huế fell to the French. In 1892 he sat for the metropolitan examination a second time and then passed the court examination—the interview in the presence of the emperor—with distinction, but not wishing to become a mandarin, he accepted only after repeated invitations the post

prose-poem[27] *Bái thạch vi huynh* (Bowing to the Rocks as to an Elder Brother), which contained the lines:

> *In my destined endeavor to fill up the sea,*
> *For your aid I forgot not to ask;*
> *Now, mending the sky with a minuscule patch,*
> *I once more look to you in my task.*

He appreciated those lines immensely. It was he who showed me the writings of Kỳ-Am Nguyễn-Lộ-Trạch.[28] After I had read *Thiên-hạ đại-thế-luận* (The Great Trends in the World), new ideas began to spring up in me. He also lent me books such as *Chung-tung chan-chi* (History of the War in the Middle East) and *Fa-P'u chan-chi* (History of the Franco-Prussian War) [by Liang Ch'i-ch'ao], and *Ying-huan chih-lüeh* (A Brief Description of the Maritime World) [by Hsü Chih-yu]. Through reading these books, I began to have a rough idea of the rivalries in the world, and I was profoundly struck by the tragic prospect of the ruin of nations and the extinction of races. He also related to me the story of the gallant deeds of Tăng-Bạt-Hổ, whose name I treasured in my heart. The idea of breaking down the bars and escaping from my cage was beginning to germinate. Owing to the constraint of circumstances, however, I could not give vent to my frustration and had to wait for an opportune time. It would be more than another two years yet before I could realize my hidden aspirations.

---

of education director in Ninh-bình. In 1907 he retired to join Phan in Japan. He went to Siam around 1915 to establish contact with the German and Austrian ministers in Bangkok in order to pursue anti-French activities. After the subsequent setbacks to the movement, he went to China and retired to a Buddhist temple in Hangchow.

27. *Phú,* a form developed in China during the Han period, rich in imagery and hyperbole.

28. A native of Kế-môn, Thừa-thiên Province, a renowned scholar who had a profound understanding of the great trends in the world but refused to enter for the examinations. [Author's note.]

THE SECOND PERIOD

WHEN I WAS THIRTY-FOUR, in the Year of the Ox, the twelfth year of the reign of Thành-Thái [1900], I placed first in the regional examination [in Nghệ-an].[1] Now I had a mask behind which to hide myself from people's eyes. My father died in the Ninth Month of the same year, after a lifetime of seventy years. The heavy charge of my family suddenly fell away, and my shoulders were lightened; thus I began to set about realizing my revolutionary plans.

As a start, with Ngư-Hải [Đặng-Thái-Thân] and other comrades I secretly worked out a plan that could be divided into three stages:

— The first was to establish contact with the remnants of the Cần-Vương movement and the outlawed patriots to call for a military uprising. The goal was to assail the enemy vengefully, with the primary means being violence.

— The second was to throw our support behind a leader sought from among the royal lineage; to make contact secretly with influential persons in hopes of gaining their support; and to bring together the patriots from the South to the North to get things co-ordinated.

— The third was—since the above two stages would certainly require outside assistance—to send someone abroad to ask for help.

---

1. The principal examiner for the mandarinate examination in Nghệ-an in 1900 was Khiếu-Năng-Tĩnh, whom Phan had met in Huế in 1897. Khiếu, who had taken a liking to Phan, was apparently responsible for helping him to obtain a pardon canceling the decision of 1897 by which he would have been excluded from the examination.

Our goal was exclusively to restore Vietnam and to establish an independent government. Apart from this, there was as yet no other idea.

THE TWO-YEAR PERIOD of the Ox and the Tiger [1901–1902] was the time to carry out the first stage. I took grateful leave of the houses in which I had been a tutor and began to teach back at my own home. Ostensibly I was assembling pupils to expound literature, but covertly I was gathering people to discuss the affairs of the movement. Tán Quýnh, Phó Ngô, and the former disciples of Bạch-Xỉ like Kiểm and Cọng, along with the secret friends of Hắc-Long like Đồ Cả and others, all came to frequent my house. Sometimes I went up to the borderlands of Thanh-hóa, Nghệ-an, and Hà-tĩnh to enlist the support of famous outlaws, so that the tribal leaders *(đầu-mục)* like Cầm and Mao[2] all had heart-to-heart conversations with me and became my allies.

In the summer of the Year of the Ox, I, together with Phan-Bá-Ngọc, the son of Phan-Đình-Phùng of La-sơn; our like-minded friend Vương-Thúc-Quý; and the scattered members of the Cần-Vương movement in the Nghi-xuân district, like Trần Hải and others, altogether amounting to several dozen men, planned to use the occasion of the French commemoration of Bastille Day[3] to capture some French weaponry by means of hand-to-hand fighting, with a view to taking over the citadel of Nghệ-an. On that day everyone gathered below the city, but, oddly enough, our collaborator inside failed to keep his promise, and the whole thing had to be called off. After the event, word of the plan leaked out to an agent of the French *Sûreté,* Nguyễn Điềm,[4] who secretly reported it to the office of the *résident.* Fortunately, at the

2. Cầm-Bá-Thước and Hà-Văn-Mao, leaders of the Cần-Vương movement in the highlands of Thanh-hóa, who had participated in the uprising against the French headed by Đinh-Công-Tráng in 1886.

3. In the original text, *Cộng-hòa kỷ-niệm,* literally "commemoration of the Republic."

4. It is interesting to note that this man passed fifth in the same regional examination in Nghệ-an in which Phan passed first.

time the governor of Nghệ-an was Đào Tấn, who thought that what I had done was right, and did his best to protect me; that was why the entire affair did not end in disaster. After that, I was more careful about recruiting inside collaborators.

In the autumn of the Year of the Tiger [1902], I sent some men to have an audience with General Hoàng-Hoa-Thám in his post at Phồn-xương in the district of Yên-thế, Bắc-Kỳ; they were Tán Quýnh and one of my pupils. As these visitors were strange to Hoàng, he did not trust them; therefore they came back without having accomplished anything significant.

In the Eleventh Month in the winter of the same year [December 1902], I resolved to go to see Hoàng myself. Taking the occasion of the exposition inaugurating the bridge over the Red River in Bắc-Kỳ, I asked Governor Đào Tấn to provide me with a travel permit to see it. I then traveled around Bắc-Kỳ to visit the surviving members of the Cần-Vương movement. The former agent *(đốc-biện)* in Nam-Định Province, Khổng-Định-Trạch, was at the time a prominent figure in the underground movement in Bắc-Kỳ. Whenever I went to the North I always stayed at his house.

When I arrived at Phồn-xương, I left my companion, Kiếm-Phong Nguyễn Kỳ, outside the post and went inside by myself. This time the right-hand men of Hoàng-Hoa-Thám—Cả Đinh, Cả Huỳnh, and Hoàng's eldest son, Cả Trọng—brought their followers and retainers to welcome me courteously. I remained at the post for more than ten days. Since Hoàng was ill at the time, he deputized Cả Trọng to attend to me instead, and promised to see me on a later occasion, intimating that if Trung-Kỳ called for an uprising he (Hoàng) would be willing to support it. Previously, a good many people from Nghệ-an and Hà-tĩnh had gone to the North and talked about Hoàng when they returned, but no one had made any close inside investigation. As I entered the post and looked around, I realized for the first time that Hoàng's command, encompassing several districts in the hill country, was like an island of independence, even after the loss of our country.

Hoàng was a man of modest origins. He started out as a boy looking after water buffalo. Throwing himself into the Cần-Vương movement as a fighter, owing to his achievements he was promoted to provincial commander *(đề-đốc),* having frequently routed the French soldiers. The French resorted to a hundred means to solicit him, but he never allowed himself to be subverted. The French were then constructing the railway from Hanoi to Kwangsi, and the part between Lạng-sơn and Bắc-giang was often attacked and destroyed by Hoàng's troops so that the track could not be laid. Vexed by this, the French had to enter into an agreement with Hoàng according to which one district and four townships in the hill country were ceded to him; every eight years this treaty would come up for renewal. During the campaign in the two years of the Cock and the Dog [1897–1898], Hoàng's name resounded throughout Asia and Europe, which made the hearts of millions of people in our country beat as one. Is not Hoàng like Washington and Garibaldi?

IN THE SPRING OF the Year of the Hare [1903], it was time to carry out the second stage. Under the pretext of going to the capital to attend the Imperial Academy, I traveled throughout Quảng-bình, Quảng-trị, Quảng-nam, Quảng-ngãi, and down to parts of Nam-Kỳ to look for more comrades. On the one hand, I secretly established contact with members of the royal family to try to find someone like Liu Pei or Lê Trang-Tông;[5] on the other hand, I looked for a collaborator or two among the incumbent officials, thinking that among them there might be someone like Chang Liang or Ti Jen-chieh.[6] Alas! The conditions

---

5. Liu Pei (162–223), in Sino-Vietnamese Lưu Bị or Lưu Tiên-Chúa, attempted to restore the Han dynasty in the period of the Three Kingdoms. Lê Trang-Tông (reigned 1533–1548) was brought back from exile in Laos in order to displace the Mạc dynasty and restore the Lê as rulers of what was then called Đại-Việt.

6. Chang Liang (d. 187 B.C.) was descended from a family who had long been ministers of the Han state; after it was conquered by the Ch'in he spent his entire patrimony in attempting to assassinate the First Emperor. In this he failed; however, after Liu Pang founded the Former Han dynasty (unconnected with the Han state)

of the country that is our enemy today are very different from those of the one that was our enemy in the past, and our servile officialdom at the present time is quite unlike that of the old days. I was really exceedingly naive and silly to have had such plans.

Scarcely more than ten days after I entered the Imperial Academy in the capital, Nguyễn Quýnh and I went to the district of Thăng-bình in Quảng-nam to visit Tiểu-La. The very first time that he saw me, he showed the pleasure of someone meeting the friend of a lifetime, conversing heart-to-heart the whole night long. He introduced me to a person called Tôn-Thất-Toại; from this it appeared that he had thought of the Liu Pei plan ahead of me. After having met Toại, I was a bit disappointed and wished to find someone superior. If there were no such person, then we should content ourselves with Toại. Toại had been involved in an attempt to restore independence and had been pursued; he had escaped to Quảng-nam, and Tiểu-La had been hiding him for five or six years. On meeting this man, however, it appeared to me that his caliber and knowledge were commonplace. This is the reason why I was not happy.

Tiểu-La said to me: "Now that we are to embark upon our enterprise, the first thing is to win the hearts of the people. At present, those who long for the past wish only to honor the sovereign and expel the enemy; they do not think beyond that. Consider: Ch'u Huai-wang and Lê Trang-Tông were no more than a kind of tool in the hands of bold-spirited men at the time when they were beginning their enterprises.[7] Moreover, now that we are planning a great enterprise, a good deal of money will certainly be needed. Nam-Kỳ is the store-house of money and provisions in our country. Nam-Kỳ is the land that the Nguyễn dynasty opened up; it feels under great obligation

---

in 202 B.C., he was honored as one of the Three Heroes. Ti Jen-chieh, in Sino-Vietnamese Địch Nhân-Kiệt or Địch Lương-Công, was a minister under Empress Wu-Hou (655–690) of the T'ang dynasty, noted for taking various measures against corruption and social evils.

7. Ch'u Huai-wang, in Sino-Vietnamese Sở Hoài-Vương, became king of the State of Ch'u in the Warring States period.

to the Nguyễn dynasty. The financial resources with which Gia-Long restored the country all came from there. Now, were we to bring forward a descendant of Gia-Long, then the endeavor to appeal to the people in Nam-Kỳ should be easy. Since I was a member of the former movement in Quảng-nam and Quảng-ngãi and have some empty fame, if I made any move I could be found out easily. You are now attending the Imperial Academy in the capital. Try to look for someone among the royal family, especially someone descended from the line of the crown prince who was the eldest son of Gia-Long. If we could find one, then that would be the first move in the chessgame."

With this I concurred. Upon returning to the Imperial Academy in the capital, I bore it in mind whenever I met any member of the royal family. I kept my ears and eyes open to everything about a younger son of [Emperor] Hiệp-Hòa and the eldest son of [Emperor] Đồng-Khánh, but neither one measured up to my expectations. Eventually I came to know that the crown prince of the Eastern Palace, Anh-Duệ,[8] still had a grandson called Marquis Cường-Để.[9] With my friend Nguyễn

---

8. This was the personal title of Prince Cảnh, the eldest son of Emperor Gia-Long, who went to France in 1787 with Pigneau de Béhaine as a hostage to secure French military assistance. Minh-Mạng, his younger brother, was enthroned in 1820, and the succession to the throne remained in his line down to Bảo-Đại. Cường-Để was a descendant of Prince Cảnh. The "Eastern Palace" *(Đông-cung)* is the traditional designation for the residence of the heir to the throne, or by extension the crown prince himself. The usage is a Vietnamese adaptation of the Chinese system.

9. Cường-Để, also known as Nguyễn-Phúc Hồng Dân (1882–1951), was a descendant in the fourth generation of Emperor Gia-Long. His title *(Kỳ-Ngoại-Hầu)* literally meant "outside-of-the-capital marquis." Brought into the movement to resist the French by Phan and others, as related here, he was made titular head of the Vietnam Modernization Association on its foundation. Early in 1906 he went to Japan and studied first at the Shimbu Gakkō and then at Waseda University. After his forced departure from Japan in 1909, he went successively to Hong Kong, Siam, and China, returning to Nam-Kỳ via Singapore in 1913 to make contacts and raise funds. Returning to Hong Kong, he was able to escape to Europe after being arrested. He came back to Japan in 1915; according to his own account, Inukai Tsuyoshi promised him that if France were defeated in Europe, Japan would help Vietnam to gain independence. Inukai further advised the Marquis not to accept any assistance from the Germans and

Thiếp of Quỳnh-lưu,[10] under the pretext that we were practitioners of geomancy and astrology, I visited the Marquis's residence by the An-cựu River. To begin with we used fortune-telling to draw him out; having found that this man harbored great aspirations, we then let him know what we really had in mind. He responded favorably, and gave his assent. We thereupon entered into a solemn bond. I hastened back to inform Tiểu-La, and we promised to meet the Marquis in February of that year at the house of the former provincial administration commissioner *(Bố-chính)*, Phan[-Quý-Thích]. The two [Tiểu-La and the Marquis] got on extremely well. Afterward, the Marquis introduced me to Metropolitan Governor *(Phủ-doãn)* Trần of Thừa-thiên Province and the governor *(tổng-đốc)* of Nghệ-an.[11] They all secretly gave their approval.

As to the secret plan of making contact with the incumbent officials, however, there still had not been any lead to follow up. I therefore wrote *Lưu-cầu huyết-lệ tân-thư* (A New Booklet on the Ryūkyūs Written in Blood and Tears) and personally gave it to Hồ Lệ of Duy-xuyên, then minister of Military Affairs; it was through him that this booklet was circulated to high officials in the ministries, the bureaus,

also not to go too far away from Japan in case the right time arrived for Japan to come to his aid. From that time until he was assassinated in 1932, Inukai subsidized the Marquis, giving him an allowance of 100 yen a month, several years later raised to 150 yen. After the Japanese coup in Vietnam in March 1945, the Marquis expected to replace Emperor Bảo-Đại, but his hopes were never fulfilled, as Bảo-Đại was retained on the throne by the Japanese. The Marquis died a disappointed man in Tokyo on 5 April 1951. His memoirs were published by his son Tráng Liệt under the title *Cuộc đời cách mạng Cường-Để* (The Revolutionary Career of Cường-Để) (Saigon: Nhà in Tôn-Thất-Lễ, 1957).

10. Nguyễn Thiếp is the name given in both the original Chinese texts. The Vietnamese translations give the name as Hồ Thiếp.

11. *Phủ-doãn* is the title given specifically to the governor of the prefecture or province in which the dynastic capital is located, as distinct from governors of other comparable administrative units who hold the less prestigious title of *tổng-đốc*. Huế is situated in Thừa-thiên.

and the cabinet. The grand academician of the Eastern Hall *(Đông-các Đại-học-sĩ)*, Nguyễn Thắng, and the minister of Personnel *(Lại-bộ)*, Nguyễn Thuật, both invited me to their chambers and talked with me briefly, advising me to be careful in my language so as to avoid getting into trouble. I went back to see Hồ Lệ and conversed with him for a long while. He sighed deeply and said to me: "When it was still possible to do something, there was no one who thought of it; now that there is no freedom of any kind, how can one say anything?" Hồ was, among those then holding office, one of the strongest characters. As this was all that could be got from him, what, then, was one to expect from others? The original plan thus became hopeless. However, aiming for a deer, I got a buck; intending to catch a fish, I got a pearl; indeed, things went above and beyond my expectation.

After Hồ Lệ received my booklet, he immediately asked his adherents to copy it. In addition, he showed it to the scholar-gentry from his native region. Thus it came to be actively circulated among the educated people in Quảng-nam and Quảng-ngãi, so that men of high purpose like Tây-Hồ Phan-Châu-Trinh, Thái-Xuyên Trần-Quý-Cáp, and Thạnh-Bình Huỳnh-Thúc-Kháng became my staunch friends for life, and even persons of high purpose like Ngũ-Lang and Ấu-Triệu all came to know of me at that time thanks to the intermediacy of this *New Booklet on the Ryūkyūs*.

The booklet was divided into five parts. The first part gave a painful account of the humiliation brought about by the loss of the country and the sapping of its liberties, and foretold ultimate catastrophe in the future. The main parts discussed in detail measures to cope with the emergency and plan for survival: (i) opening the people's minds; (ii) stirring up the people's morale; (iii) fostering the people of talent. The last part appealed to the incumbent officials, encouraging them to undertake imperishable deeds.

WHEN THE BOOKLET had been circulated, Tiểu-La Nguyễn Thành said to me: "Now you can go to the South." He then purchased a travel permit for me, provided me with expenses for the journey, and asked one of his pupils, called Tư Doãn, to accompany me. Previously I had heard the name of Trần Thị, of Thất-sơn in Châu-đốc Province, who had been a heroic figure among the outlaws and had sought refuge in the guise of a Buddhist monk; I wished to see this man and make an inquiry whether or not any vestiges of the groups led by Trương Định and Hồ Huân still remained.[12] Moreover, I wished to let the patriotic people in Nam-Kỳ know in advance about the Marquis, in preparation for an appeal later.

Early in the Twelfth Month of the Year of the Hare [January 1904], I arrived in Saigon. I looked around for a few days, then traveled through the Six Provinces to enlist support for the movement.

Late in the month I arrived in Thất-sơn and visited Trần Thị in his mountain temple.[13] This man's speech was firm and spirited; his age was above fifty, yet his appearance was still full of vigor. Previously he had been several times suspected by the French and put into prison; after regaining his freedom he had entered the temple. He was a person who missed the Sung and longed for the Chou.[14] I told him the story of the Marquis and he was immensely pleased, promising me that the following spring he would go to the capital to have an audience with the Marquis. On receiving me, he said one thing to me that I could never forget. That was: "As a rule, when you wish

---

12. Trương Định (1820–1864) was a native of Quảng-ngãi Province. As to Hồ Huân, Phan is probably referring to Nguyễn-Hữu-Huân (1816–1875). Both were early leaders of the anti-French resistance in Nam-Kỳ.

13. Trần Thị literally means simply "a man whose family name is Trần." According to Nguyễn Hầu, his original name was Trần Nhựt Thi (?–?). This rather mysterious figure was an early leader of the movement to oppose the French and restore the independence of Vietnam. His Buddhist name was Hòa-thượng Phi-Lai.

14. I.e., he was a loyalist. After the Chou dynasty collapsed, there were many who were nostalgic for its grandeur; likewise, when the Mongols overthrew the Sung dynasty and replaced it with that of the Yüan, many still treasured their memories of the Sung and vowed to restore them.

to plan something in secret, to discuss it in broad daylight and the open air is appropriate; to do so late at night and in a secret room is inappropriate, because late at night and in a secret room your ears and eyes cannot forestall trouble from afar, merely giving spies an opportunity."

From Thất-sơn I went to Sa-đéc to meet a person called Ký-Liêm, who introduced me to Councilor *(Hội-đồng)* Nguyễn-Thành-Hiến.[15] This man later went abroad with me and worked with me for more than seven years. He lived in Hong Kong, but owing to his involvement in an assassination plot, he was taken into custody by the French and escorted back, and he died in Hanoi prison. Alas! This gentleman was truly one of the outstanding figures of Nam-Kỳ!

Late in the First Month of the new year [February/March 1904], from central Nam-Kỳ I went back by land through Phú-yên, Bình-định, to look around for men of high purpose. I heard that in Bình-định there was a person called Blind Thúi (Mù Thúi), who was originally a heroic figure of Hải-dương Province. Owing to his involvement in the Kỳ-Đồng Incident,[16] he received a life sentence and was sent into exile in Hà-tiên. While he was being transported, passing by Quy-nhơn, he used a knife to put out his eyes. The authorities stopped transporting him and he ended up living there. He refused to let others know his

15. Also known as Nguyễn-Thần-Hiến (1856–1914). A native of Hà-tiên, his father was prefect of Vĩnh-long and later governor of Hà-tiên in the reign of Emperor Tự-Đức. Very well educated, when he was about twenty years old it was said that he had as much knowledge as those who had passed the highest examinations. He was a key supporter of the Đông-Du movement in Nam-Kỳ, to which he donated a large part of his family fortune. He traveled between Hong Kong, Shanghai, and Japan during 1910–1913 to acquire arms in preparation for an uprising in Vietnam. He was arrested by *Sûreté* agents in Hong Kong on 16 March 1913 and transported back to Hanoi. He died in Hỏa-lò prison on 26 November 1914.

16. Kỳ-Đồng (?–?), whose real name was Nguyễn-Văn-Cẩm, a native of Thái-bình Province, launched an uprising against the colonial authorities in 1888 and was arrested. In an attempt to gain his allegiance, the French sent him to study in France, but after his return Kỳ-Đồng again joined the resistance movement and was eventually sent into exile overseas.

name, asking them to call him Thúi.[17] It was to give vent to his anger
at his failure that he used this self-mocking name. When I came to
visit the place where he lived, he had died three days earlier. I was
profoundly grief-stricken and wrote the following verses to mourn him:

> *Hearing your fame came I; grand as the ocean,*
> *Your name imprints my heart as ne'er before.*
>
> *Sadness I felt, and now feel deeper sadness;*
> *Of gallant souls like you, are there yet more?*

I heard that the interpreter [Nguyễn-Đức-]Hậu, was also living in exile on the borders of Bình-định Province, and I wished
to go to visit him. But as I arrived in Phù-cát District, I saw a
number of French soldiers and Vietnamese militiamen on their way
through the district, carrying him captive. We only looked at each
other from a distance; we were not able to exchange a single word.
Later, when I went abroad to Hong Kong, I heard an extraordinary
story about him. In the reign of Tự-Đức, while accompanying a
Western merchant ship to Hong Kong, he heard that Chinese bandits
had kidnapped more than ninety Vietnamese women, to sell them to
Hong Kong merchants. Being a ready writer of English, he lodged
a complaint with the British officials in Hong Kong, whereupon the
British authorities made arrangements to escort the women back to
our country. Our court in recognition awarded him the ninth rank
of officialdom, but he did not accept. Afterward, he was involved in
secretly plotting an insurrection and received a severe sentence. Alas!
This being the lot of a man of such capacity, how could our country
fail to be lost![18]

---

17. Literally, "Stinky."

18. The interpreter Hậu personally negotiated with the British officials in Hong Kong.
All the repatriated kidnapped women said as much. [Author's note.]

I WENT BACK TO Quảng-nam to stay over at Tiểu-La's home for just one night, then returned to the capital. A long absence of an intern of the Academy, I was afraid, would arouse people's suspicions. In the Third Month of the same year, I failed the second stage of the metropolitan examination *(hội-thí)*. On the same day, I secretly left for Quảng-nam and met Trần Thị of Thất-sơn at Tiểu-La's home. I immediately took Trần Thị to the capital to have an audience with the Marquis. Afterward, Trần Thị and I went back to Quảng-nam to meet with Trình Hiền of Ô-da[19] and several tens of men to discuss our plan of action. Trần Thị agreed to go to Nam-Kỳ to raise funds. I went to Bắc-Kỳ once more, with the promise that in early April we would invite the Marquis to come here [to Tiểu-La's home] to hold a secret convention.

I bade farewell to Tiểu-La and traveled through various regions north of Quảng-bình to make secret contacts with the Catholics. It was at this time that a mutual understanding was initiated with senior Catholics like Mr. Thông of Mộ-vịnh, Mr. Truyền of Mỹ-dụ, Mr. Thông of Quỳnh-lưu, and Mr. Ngọc of Quảng-bình. The overhanging clouds and murky fogs that separated Catholics and non-Catholics were swept away in an instant. That in itself was truly an inspiring feat. In this matter Ngô Quảng was most instrumental. After he had lost his position, Ngô Quảng had entered his name on the register of the Catholics. Now, with him taking me along, it was like riding in a light vehicle along a familiar road. Everything went as we wished. The great support rendered to the patriotic cause by the Catholic people after I went overseas was thus not coincidental.

---

19. Trình Hiền, also known as Đỗ-Đăng-Tuyển or Đỗ-Tuyển (1856–1911); his pseudonym was Sơn-Tẩu, and he was commonly called Ô-Da (sometimes spelled Ô-Gia) from his birthplace, Ô-da. An active comrade of Phan's, even though he himself was a Confucian scholar he argued for the introduction of practical studies into Vietnamese education. Arrested in 1910, he drank poison on the way to prison but survived, then jumped into the river but was saved by his guards. In 1911 he was sent to Lao-bảo Prison, but on the way he went on a hunger strike and died.

THE APPOINTED TIME, early in the Fourth Month [May 1904], arrived. I attended the meeting. The Marquis also came. The number of those participating was more than twenty. Tiểu-La's residence was often frequented by visitors, therefore the household help and the neighbors took this as a matter of course. Besides, Tiểu-La was a past master in the art of deception, so that no disclosure would be made by informers. The meeting was opened in the morning and concluded at noontime. Only the members knew the name of the Association.[20] There were no records; the agenda and schedule were all conveyed by word of mouth. The Marquis was designated as president of the Association and was addressed as "Chief" *(Ông Chủ),* and disclosure of the term "Association" *(Hội)* was prohibited. Nguyễn Hàm, Phan-Bội-Châu, Trình Hiền, Lê Võ, Đặng-Tử-Kính, Đặng-Thái-Thân, and the others were all members, addressing each other as "Brother" *(Anh em).* On the same day, agreement was reached on three important items:

(i) to extend the influence of the association within the shortest possible period of time, to expand the membership, and to collect substantial membership fees;

(ii) to continue to be active after the insurrection, requiring the preparation of various materials within the shortest possible period of time;

(iii) to formulate a plan and method for going abroad to seek help.

The first two items were to be the joint responsibility of the above-mentioned members. The last item was exclusively entrusted to the secret deliberations of Nguyễn Hàm and Phan-Bội-Châu. As long as the emissaries had not left the country yet, other members were not to be informed about this in order to avoid leaks. For this reason, before my going overseas very few members would know about it.

---

20. I.e., the Việt-Nam Duy-Tân Hội (Vietnam Modernization Association), which was actually created at this meeting.

The same day, as the meeting was about to conclude, my young attendant, named Xuân,[21] arrived in haste from the capital. As soon as he came in and saw me, he whispered into my ear some unexpected news. Tiểu-La noticed this and took me out into the garden. I told him what it was: "Three days ago the *résident-supérieur* in Huế, M. Auvergne, right out of the blue, sent a telegram requesting the principal of the Imperial Academy, Khiếu-Năng-Tĩnh, and the director of the Historical Institute, Cao, to advise me to come and see him because he had something to ask me. Both the officials of the institutions, when they received the message, were quite perplexed and taken aback. I'm afraid that our plan has leaked out." Tiểu-La laughed and said: "There's nothing to be afraid of! He has only heard tell of something and wants to find out whether it is true. If the plan had really leaked out, you would certainly have been arrested already; what need would there be to send a telegram? Now you had better go back to the capital at once and see the *résident-supérieur* immediately. After that you may return to the Imperial Academy. By then his suspicions will have been cleared up."

I acted on Tiểu-La's good advice and went to the office of the *résident-supérieur*. He dismissed everyone else in the room, and showed me a secret report from his informers. Not a word in the report was based on anything but hearsay, without any supporting evidence. To each of his questions I responded with an appropriate answer. He did not cause me any trouble. As he questioned me, he looked hard at my face several times; my face did not change color. Finally, with perfect composure, I bade him farewell and left. I told people that the *résident-supérieur* had asked me why, in spite of my literary fame, I had failed the metropolitan examination, and everybody believed that. I kept what had happened to myself, but after that I acted even more guardedly and secretively.

---

21. Son of the former provincial military commander *(đề-đốc),* whom I had been bringing up ever since he was thirteen years old. [Author's note.]

ALL THE WHILE, our comrades were exerting themselves to the utmost in the activities of the movement. On the whole, some headway was being made with each of the previously mentioned plans. Tiểu-La and I dedicated all our efforts to sending someone overseas, which required the following:

— funds;
— someone with diplomatic skill;
— a guide.

Tiểu-La said: "As far as funds are concerned, Sơn-Tẩu and I can take care of them. Someone with diplomatic skill is certainly hard to find at the moment. Since there is no one else, you will have to go yourself. About the guide, I have been thinking carefully for a long time.

"I suppose, given the present circumstances of the world powers, no country except one of the 'same culture and same race'[22] would agree to help us. China has already abandoned our Vietnam to France; moreover, at present she is in a deteriorating condition and lacks the wherewithal even to save herself. Japan is the only country of the yellow race[23] that has modernized; since she defeated Russia her ambitions have expanded. If you went there and persuaded her as to the pros and cons, she would surely be moved to help us. Even if Japan did not send troops, her help in funds would certainly make it easy to purchase weaponry. For this reason, as far as the plan of 'crying at the Ch'in court to ask for help'[24] is concerned, there could be no more appropriate place to go than Japan.

---

22. *Đồng-văn đồng-chủng;* an expression revealing the basic assumption behind the call for common action among the four East Asian countries (China, Japan, Korea, and Vietnam) following the mid-nineteenth-century expansion of the Western powers.

23. In Sino-Vietnamese, *Hoàng-chủng.*

24. Shen Pao-tzu, a man of the State of Ch'u, went to ask for help from the State of Ch'in when his country was surrounded by Wu forces. Before the Ch'in came to any decision, he had cried at the court for seven days continuously. Moved by this, the Ch'in sent troops to relieve the Ch'u.

"Now, Tăng-Bạt-Hổ, following the collapse of the Cần-Vương movement, escaped to Kwangtung and Kwangsi; then, carrying [Vietnamese] imperial credentials, he went on to Port Arthur to make friendly contact with a representative of Russia. As this did not work out, Tăng turned back and went to Formosa (Taiwan) to enlist the support of Liu Yung-fu.[25] But when Formosa was annexed by Japan and Liu took flight, Tăng went on to Siam to make his way back to Vietnam. At present he is in hiding in Hanoi. His devotion to our country is more ardent than ever. I have already sent him a letter to invite him to come south, and he should be arriving any day. If he were the one entrusted with being your guide, you would have no concern about losing your bearings."[26]

AT THAT POINT I resolved to plan to go to Japan. Before I departed, there were some things that needed to be dealt with. For one thing, I should make arrangements and entrust things to my friends.[27] As outside assistance was only for the purpose of enhancing the reputation of our forces at home, our domestic organization must accordingly be in perfect order. Things would be impossible without planning in advance.

---

25. In Sino-Vietnamese, Lưu Vĩnh-Phúc (?–1917). Exiled from China, he came to northern Vietnam in 1863 and became a leader of the "Black Flags" (*Cờ đen*) who assisted the Vietnamese in their efforts to resist the French. Before returning to his base in Kwangtung, in 1895 he went to Formosa to combat the Japanese.

26. Tăng-Bạt-Hổ (1858–1906) was a native of Bình-định. He joined the Black Flags of Liu Yung-fu, and during 1885–1887 participated in the Cần-Vương movement. Leaving the country after its collapse, he worked as a sailor on merchant ships, traveling to China, Siam, Russia, and Japan. Phan supplies an account of his subsequent career and contributions to the cause of Vietnamese independence, down to his premature death in Huế in 1906.

27. AM gives a longer version of this passage, not found in the original text, which reads: "Before I departed, there were two things that needed to be dealt with: (i) bidding farewell to my friends. Since the path ahead of me was hidden in the distance and the day of my return was uncertain, I should shake hands with my friends for a last time; (ii) making arrangements and entrusting things to my friends."

In the Seventh Month of that year [August/September 1904], on the pretext of extending congratulations to those who had passed the metropolitan examinations, from Tiểu-La's home I visited Huỳnh-Thúc-Kháng's home in Thạnh-bình. There I happened to meet Tây-Hồ Phan-Châu-Trinh and Thái-Xuyên Trần-Quý-Cáp,[28] who were both at the house. We talked all night long; it was highly agreeable. When I mentioned that I was about to go upon a long journey, they looked at each other and laughed, and wished me every success. Alas! That occasion turned out to be the last one on which Thái-Xuyên and I met each other. One of us went to the guillotine and shed his blood, dyeing with its hue the mountains and rivers; one of us spent his life vainly traversing lakes and oceans; but both with spirits immutable, like gold and rock. As long as my mission has not been fulfilled, what can I say to you, dear Thái-Xuyên, in the other world?

Meanwhile, Tăng-Bạt-Hổ arrived from Bắc-Kỳ; the first day he turned up at Tiểu-La's house, I met him there. He was in his early forties, black-haired, thick-set, and with an air that inspired confidence. At first glance one could tell that he had seen much of the world and undergone many trying experiences. His conversation about the overseas situation was exceedingly well informed; in particular, with regard to the prominent figures in China at that time he showed himself extraordinarily knowledgeable, as if he were talking about the few precious objects in his house. I was as happy to meet him as if he had been sent from Heaven. When the conversation came round to the matter of going East [to Japan], spontaneously and resolutely he volunteered to undertake the task of being my guide, and said to me: "The two of us staying abroad will certainly need someone to go back and forth from time to time to convey news, so as to maintain a link between home and abroad. This is by no means a light duty; the person who undertakes it should be someone with experience, who can

28. Thái-Xuyên Trần-Quý-Cáp (1870–1908) was a native of Quảng-nam Province who held a *tiến-sĩ* degree. An active supporter of resistance against the French and of the Đông-Du movement, he was executed in the aftermath of violent demonstrations in his home province.

endure hardship and who possesses courage and knowledge." On the spot, I proposed Đặng-Tử-Kính; Tiểu-La also agreed. Đặng-Tử-Kính was approaching his forties; he had devoted himself to the former Cần-Vương movement for several years and was also a most active member of the new movement. He was the uncle of Ngư-Hải [Đặng-Thái-Thân].[29]

The plan of action had thus been decided. As there were still a few things I had not dealt with yet, I had to stay on for some months more before I could begin to carry the plan out. In the Eighth Month [September/October 1904], I again went to Bắc-Kỳ to see Mai-Sơn [Nguyễn-Thượng-Hiền] and the Agent (đốc-biện) Khổng[-Định-Trạch], as well as other comrades. In the Ninth Month [October/November], I returned to Nghệ-Tĩnh to meet the members of the movement there. In the Tenth Month [November/December], I went down to Quảng-bình to seek a pledge of support from the important figures of the church like Mr. Thông, Mr. Truyền, et al. They all met one evening at a church in Ba-đồn. Most of the people who took part in this meeting were remaining members of the group of Hiền and Hậu, whose resentment against the French was very profound. In addition, there were those who had been persuaded to come by Học-Thiện and Tú-Định. All of them were ready and willing to support me.

In the Eleventh Month [December 1904/January 1905], I took leave of the Imperial Academy, asking permission to go home in the Twelfth Month. I made use of the opportunity to say goodbye to my acquaintances at the Academy, with the promise that we should meet again at the Academy in the following year to wait for the metropolitan examination. I had been an intern at the Imperial Academy for two years altogether, but my like-minded friends there were limited to one or two. That was the most one could expect from the academic circle in the capital!

---

29. Đặng-Tử-Kính (d. 1928), a native of Nghệ-an, was a close comrade of Phan's, who went to Japan in 1905 and to Siam in 1909. He took charge of finances for the entire movement. He died while in Siam.

Early in the Twelfth Month [January 1905], together with Ngư-Hải [Đặng-Thái-Thân] and Đặng-Tử-Kính, I visited Tiểu-La's home to meet with secret comrades like Trình Hiền of Ô-da, Tôn-Thất-Toại, Châu-Thư-Đồng,[30] and others, to discuss how to lay out the division of duties. Going abroad to seek aid would be the responsibility of Tăng-Bạt-Hổ, Đặng-Tử-Kính, and myself. Carrying on the tasks of the movement inside the country would be entirely entrusted to Tiểu-La and Ngư-Hải. Our deliberations were now concluded.

I then bade farewell to Tiểu-La. The journey of ten thousand leagues began at that point. From then on, Đặng-Tử-Kính alone would be going back and forth from time to time to Tiểu-La's home, but for Tăng-Bạt-Hổ and myself, this would be the last day with Tiểu-La. Alas! The rarity of the comrades of a lifetime, the immensity of the ocean and the sky; the cock's cry in the midst of the storm, the spirit's endless futile round of dreams—how sorrowful it is!

The next day I returned to the capital, visited the Marquis at his home, and reported to him the plan of going East. In addition, I also let him know in advance of our intention to have him go abroad with us. The Marquis agreed.

IN THE MIDDLE of the Twelfth Month [January 1905], I returned home. During the previous several years, when I was secretly traveling between North and South, I had passed by Nghệ-an five or six times altogether, but I had not stopped at my home. People in my native town only thought that I was attending the Imperial Academy and devoting myself to my studies. Now that my long journey was about to begin, I returned home one more time for a few weeks to restore the shrine and

---

30. Châu-Thư-Đồng (1845–1908) was a native of Quảng-nam and a close friend of Tiểu-La Nguyễn Thành. He worked as a liaison for the Đông-Du movement in Hội-an. In 1908, when the movement to demand the lowering of taxes took place in his home district, he was arrested by the colonial authorities. To protect others, he assumed all responsibility for the movement in his town; he was sentenced to life imprisonment in Lao-bảo, where he went on a hunger strike and died.

the tombs of my family; this was also a way of giving the impression that I had no other plans.

I had agreed with Tăng-Bạt-Hổ that he should come to my home on the thirtieth day of the Twelfth Month [3 February]. Lê Võ and Đội Quyên also joined us, each providing us with some funds for our journey. Trần-Đông-Phong of Đại-đồng gave fifteen bars[31] of silver. This generous act of dedication to the cause was especially commendable as this was the first time he and I had met face to face. Altogether, the travel funds amounted to three thousand piasters. Apart from the sums given by our comrades, all had been procured by Tiểu-La. Actually, Châu-Thư-Đồng gave three hundred piasters on his own; all the rest was gathered together through the campaign—that is to say, through Tiểu-La's work.

On the first day of the First Month of the Year of the Snake [4 February], I sent Tăng-Bạt-Hổ in advance to the North to wait for me at Khổng-Định-Trạch's home, as I was concerned that if there were a stranger around at the time of my departure, it would arouse people's suspicions. On the fourth day, as the celebration of the New Year had been completed, I wrote letters inviting several dozen comrades to my house for a farewell dinner. In addition, I bade farewell to the people in my village, saying that I was going back to the Imperial Academy in the capital in hopes of becoming a mandarin.

On the day of my departure, Lê Võ went with me as far as the city of Nghệ-an; only Đặng-Tử-Kính and Trần Bỉnh of Hà-tĩnh accompanied me to Nam-định. Trần was an outstanding personage among the Catholics. He could read Western books, and on his own had manufactured Western-style guns and bullets with incredible skill. At the outset, when I was planning an armed insurrection, I had established contact with him. After I had gone abroad, he took to the hills to manufacture guns. In the end he was stricken by grave illness and died.

Thus I began my journey. I stopped by the house of the *cử-nhân* Trần-Văn-Lương to stay overnight. Trần lived in genteel poverty, but he was an old schoolmate of mine; hearing vaguely of my journey, he

---

31. *Nén*, weighing approximately 5.5 kilos.

had scraped together everything he had in the house to give me ten piasters. He said to me: "We have been good friends for ten years. Now we shall be separated by ten thousand miles. I am now using one piaster to pay my debt for each year of our friendship. Apart from that, I don't know what else to do." I laughed heartily and accepted.

On arriving at the city of Nghệ-an, I paid a call on Thai-Sơn [Đặng-Nguyên-Cẩn], who at the time was education commissioner (*đốc-học*) in Nghệ-an. He said to me: "Go on your way. Inside the country the most urgent thing is to enlighten the people's intelligence and to educate those with talent. People like Tập-Xuyên [Ngô-Đức-Kế] and I will take care of that." I introduced Ngư-Hải to him. We stayed and talked all night long.

The next day we took a train to Nam-định. When I entered Agent Khổng-Định-Trạch's home, Tăng-Bạt-Hổ was there already. Again we had to delay for several days to wait for our funds to arrive. This was because at the time we left home we did not dare to carry a large amount of money. We therefore asked a certain person of Quảng-nam and a certain person of Hà-tĩnh to carry the money separately. On the fifteenth day of the same month [18 February], these two gentlemen arrived. Trần Bỉnh bade farewell to turn southwards. Tăng-Bạt-Hổ, Đặng-Tử-Kính, and I took our journey to Hải-phòng by way of Hanoi. In each of these two places, Tăng-Bạt-Hổ had secret friends, so that everything went as one would wish.

On the twentieth day of the same month [23 February 1905], we boarded a Western merchant ship from Hải-phòng to Móng-cái. From here on, this is entirely the history of my life abroad.

THE THIRD PERIOD

IN THE YEAR OF the Snake [1905], I was thirty-eight. On the twentieth day of the First Month of this year [23 February], as we were leaving Hải-phòng, Tăng-Bạt-Hổ told me: "There are two ways to enter China by water from here. One is to cross over to Chushan, entering China across the border of Fangcheng County; this route is quite arduous, but it would be easy to preserve secrecy. The other is to go to Móng-cái and cross the bridge, entering China across the border of Tunghsing County; this route is quite straightforward, but it would be difficult to maintain our disguise. This time, it would be prudent for us to cross over to Chushan."

At nine in the evening our boat docked at Ngọc-sơn; the three of us left the boat and landed. As we had adopted the guise of itinerant merchants, none of the Frenchmen on the boat had asked us any questions. After walking for about half a day, we arrived at a fishing village. Tăng-Bạt-Hổ handed me a cross and told me to wear it around my neck. As this whole village is solidly Catholic, to be seen with a cross makes one not unacceptable. We then entered a fisherman's house, the owner being an old acquaintance of Tăng's. When we ate and drank with the owner, we raised our hands to our foreheads to make the sign of the cross and said a prayer, and the owner was very pleased. At twelve o'clock on the same day the owner rented a fishing boat on our behalf to cross the river. After a couple of hours the boat drew alongside the shore—we were already entering the territory of Fangcheng County in China!

On the twenty-second day of the First Month [25 February], we stayed over on a houseboat in the town of Chushan, the proprietor of which, named Hsi Lung, was another old acquaintance of Tăng-Bạt-Hổ's. When we had set down our luggage, I felt like a swan that had escaped from its cage, instinctively going wild with excitement, for in this place there were no ears and eyes of the French!

FROM CHUSHAN TO Canton there are two ways. One is by land, crossing a river into Tunghsing, proceeding by way of Chinchow as far as Lienchow, and taking a steamship from Peihai to Hong Kong. The other is by water, taking a sailing boat past Chinchow as far as Lienchow, then changing to a steamship for Hong Kong. If one meets with a favorable wind, then it is possible to make the whole trip by sailing boat. At that time, the proprietor was about to go to Hong Kong on business; we thus boarded the same sailing boat to go up to Peihai. It took six days. At Peihai we boarded a steamship to Hong Kong.

Unexpectedly, I acquired a good friend called Lý Tuệ, who was chief cook on the ship. As he went back and forth looking over the passengers, he suspected the three of us of being escapees. He liked talking to me, but I dared not yet reveal to him the truth of the matter; all I could do was simply to make an appointment to meet him at a hotel when we reached Hong Kong. In the first decade of the Second Month, the ship arrived at Hong Kong; he promised to meet me at the Taian Hotel. I went there and stayed for one night. Tăng-Bạt-Hổ left me to go by himself to Shaokuan, to visit the former ministers Tôn-Thất-Thuyết and Trần[-Xuân-]Soạn.

Next day, Lý Tuệ came to see me. His good understanding of the just cause and his profound detestation of what the French were doing, which transpired in our conversation, led me to tell him the real intention of our journey. He was deeply moved, and volunteered to do the best he could for our new movement. From that day on, whether money was being dispatched undercover or students were being sent out surreptitiously, he was in charge of everything secret on the ship. There was not a single mishap with either money or letters, yet he absolutely never mentioned anything about remuneration. His sense of loyalty grew stauncher all the time. His younger brother Lý Tư, as well, was not inferior to him in this respect. I have now heard that the two of them were sent into exile. Alas! Many there are in our country garbed in green sleeves and yellow sashes,[1] yet dedication and righteous indignation must be sought for among the kitchen help. This should be put on record for everyone to know!

DURING MY FEW days' stay in Hong Kong I toured round the city. Observing the colonial policies of the British, I was greatly astonished. Not to mention that the streets were well laid out and clean and that commerce was flourishing, the fact that foreigners could enter the port freely was truly beyond what I could have imagined. In spite of our alien costume, nobody bothered to ask about our travel permit or our nationality—this for me was something I had never experienced in my life.

There were several dozen Chinese schools and newspapers, one of the latter being the *Shang-pao* (Commercial Gazette), which belonged to the monarchist faction, another being the *Ch'ung-kuo Jih-pao* (Journal of China), which was an organ of the revolutionary faction. I went to the *Commercial Gazette* to ask to see its editor, Hsu Chin, who would not receive me. I then went to the *Journal of China*. Its editor, Feng Chih-you, welcomed me at once. I conversed by brush with him for some considerable time. He expressed his sympathy for our plan. Feng said to me: "Hold on for ten years. Our party will be successful in expelling the Manchus; then we can assist your country. Now is not yet the time. Nevertheless, in view of the relationship of the Middle Kingdom to its tributary states [such as Vietnam], to ask for aid from the Chinese inside the Ch'ing government would not necessarily be unhelpful. Since the present governor of Kwangtung is

---

1. An allusion to the court mandarins.

hsuen, who is an official of the Manchus but a Chinese—in fact a native of Kwangsi, which stands in a relationship of interdependence, like lips and teeth, with Vietnam—if you went and talked to him, you might well gain a helping hand."

Since I had only just left our country, I was a complete novice in foreign affairs. Having heard this, I took Feng's advice at face value. I composed a letter, and asked Tăng-Bạt-Hổ to go to Canton and request an acquaintance of his named Chou, one of Shen's secretaries, to convey it to Governor Shen.[2] Chou promised that when he obtained a reply from Shen he would dispatch someone to Hong Kong to invite me. In this letter, the first diplomatic piece that I ever produced, wildly excessive hopes can be observed. I stayed in Hong Kong for a long time waiting for Shen's reply, but in the end there was not a single word. I eventually came to realize that despotic governments are not human, be they the Manchu or our own government—just badgers from the same hole! I then left for Shanghai.

WHILE STILL AT HOME, I had read *Mu-tzu ch'eng-p'ien* (The 1898 Reform), *Ch'ung-kuo hun* (The Chinese Spirit), and two or three batches of the *Hsin-min Sung-pao* (Journal of the New Citizen); these were all works by Liang Ch'i-ch'ao.[3] I had come to admire this man greatly. Now, on the ship to Shanghai, I met Chou Chun, a Chinese

---

2. This letter was published with an introduction by Chương Thâu in *Nghiên cứu lịch sử*, no. 90 (September 1966).

3. Liang Ch'i-ch'ao (1873–1929), after participating as a young mandarin in the abortive reform movements in China in 1895 and 1898, was forced to escape to Japan. There he published a journal advocating reform of the Chinese Empire, and a number of important studies of Western thinkers. He also traveled to (among other places) Hawai'i, Australia, the United States, and Canada. In 1911 he accepted the legitimacy of the republican regime and returned to China, where for a time he participated in the government, attempting to bring about fiscal reform; having failed in this, he withdrew from politics in 1917 and spent his last years in academic life. He is considered the leading Chinese intellectual of the early years of the twentieth century; for some remarks on his influence on Phan-Bội-Châu, see the Introduction.

who had been studying in the United States and was returning home; he gave me Liang's address in the Yanagi-kan, Yamashita-chō, in Yokohama. I was indeed overjoyed, and thought that on arriving in Japan I should certainly go to meet Liang first thing.

In the first decade of the Third Month [April 1905], the ship arrived at Shanghai. My desire to go on to Japan was very pressing, but at that time the Russo-Japanese War had not yet ended. Japanese merchant ships had been requisitioned by the government; consequently there were no Japanese ships in Shanghai. Other steamships going to Japan were also held up and did not leave because of the hostilities. We had no choice but to stay on in Shanghai for more than a month.

In the middle decade of the Fourth Month, the Russo-Japanese War came to an end;[4] Japanese merchant ships began to arrive at Shanghai. We asked Chao [Kuang-fu] from Hunan, a Chinese who was studying in Japan, to be our guide to go with us to Yokohama. The most awkward thing was that I did not understand Japanese and was not well versed in spoken Chinese; brush-conversation and talking by gesture were very troublesome. What a great shame for a diplomat!

In the last decade of the Fourth Month [late May/early June 1905], our ship arrived in Kōbe. Our luggage was quite heavy; as yet we were not familiar with the Japanese language and customs. Fortunately, Chao was good enough to guide us to an inn where we could stay overnight. We then took an early train bound for Yokohama. En route, everything necessary on the train was taken care of by Chao. We were chance acquaintants, but got on just like brothers. He never minded the trouble he took and did not expect any compensation; this is really a fine quality of the people of a great nation. Then again, my Chinese composition may have helped too.

When I first met Chao, I found out that he was a member of the revolutionary party; therefore I dared not tell him that I was going to meet Liang. This was because the revolutionary and the monarchist

4. What Phan is referring to is the Japanese victory in the Battle of Tsushima, 27 May 1905.

parties were just like ice and hot coals; I had already heard as much when I was in Hong Kong. When the train arrived in Yokohama, Chao bade farewell to me, saying: "I am going on to Tokyo now. This is Yokohama. I have asked the Japanese railway guard to take care of anything you need." I was taken aback, but reluctantly acquiesced.

I then got off the train and went to the gate of the station. My luggage was nowhere in sight. I stood there helplessly for a long time, until a Japanese wearing a white cap and a sword came up to me. I took a small notebook out of my pocket. He wrote the question: "Why don't you leave?" I answered: "I cannot find my luggage." He wrote: "I have paid for a reservation at the inn for you. Your luggage will be sent there." He then called three rickshaws, saw us onto them, and spoke a few words to the rickshaw men. In a short while we arrived at the Tanaka Inn. We hardly had time to sit down before our luggage turned up. This was all because according to the regulations of the Japanese railways, passengers and luggage, people and animals are not transported in the same carriage, even in the fourth class. In order to maintain hygiene and to protect the passengers, each carriage must have a notice indicating the maximum number of passengers and the limit on the luggage the passengers are allowed. The train conductor will take good care about this and keep watch over it. On a train, no one would take lost objects. Tăng-Bạt-Hổ and I once left something behind on a train, but several days later we found it in the same spot. All this made me sigh to myself: "The standards of conduct of the people of a stalwart nation, even in this simple thing, looked at from the viewpoint of our nation, are as distant as the sky from the abyss!"

A FEW DAYS LATER I drafted a letter of self-introduction to Liang Ch'i-ch'ao. The letter contained sentences like this: "Since the day of my birth, we have been destined to know each other; after ten years of reading your writings, I feel as if you are my old acquaintance," and so on. Liang accepted the letter; greatly moved, he invited me to come in. Our conversation was mostly translated by Tăng-Bạt-Hổ;[5] for more complicated matters we used brush-conversation. Liang wished to have a fuller discussion, so he promised to meet me again the following day.

Our brush-conversation lasted three or four hours. In summary, the most essential ideas were the following:

(i) "Your country should not be concerned about not having a day of independence, but should be concerned about not having an independence-minded people."

(ii) "In your plan for restoring independence there are three important factors: (a) the actual strength that your country has within itself; (b) the support of Kwangtung and Kwangsi; (c) the moral support of Japan. Should your country have no actual strength, then the other two factors will not bring felicity to your nation." He also added: "The actual strength that your country has within itself is the intelligence of its people, the vitality of its people, and the talents of its people. The support of Kwangtung and Kwangsi would be in the form of soldiers and supplies. The moral support of Japan would be in the form of diplomacy, as the first strong Asian nation to recognize your country's independence."

(iii) As I touched upon the matter of seeking Japanese aid, he said to me: "I am afraid that this plan is not good. Once Japanese troops had entered within your country's borders, it would surely be impossible to find an excuse to drive them out; that would amount to wishing to restore the country but instead hastening its destruction."

(iv) "Your country must not be afraid of having no opportunity for independence, but must only be afraid of not having people of ability to take advantage of the opportunity. When Germany and France declare war against each other, that will be the golden opportunity for your country's independence."

---

5. According to AM, the translation was to and from Cantonese.

A few days later, I asked Liang to introduce me to some Japanese politicians, as I wished to fulfill my purpose of obtaining aid. Liang promised me that about the middle decade of the Fifth Month he would take me to see Count Ōkuma [Shigenobu]. The Count had served twice as prime minister, having distinguished himself by his contribution to the Meiji Restoration, and was currently a leader of the Progressive Party *(Shimpo-tō)*.[6] When the time came, I went to see Liang; he said to me: "If one wishes to see Ōkuma, one should first see Viscount Inukai Tsuyoshi. This man was formerly minister of Education and is currently the president of the Progressive Party. He is Ōkuma's right-hand man.[7] Among Japan's party politicians *(dân-đảng)* these two are the most influential."

That very day Liang took the two of us to Tokyo. We met Inukai first; then, through him, we met Count Ōkuma. At the meeting between hosts and visitors, everyone was extremely cordial. When our conversation touched on the question of aid, Inukai asked me: "With regard to your request for help—have you secured authorization from a leader of your country? If the country is a monarchy, this should be a member of the royal family. Have you considered that yet?" I answered "Yes," and from my pocket I took out a travel permit for the Marquis Cường-Để to show him.[8] Inukai said: "You had better bring this man out of your country, or else he may fall into the enemy's hands." I said we had thought about that.

---

6. Count Ōkuma (1838–1922) was one of the most prominent politicians of the Meiji and Taishō eras in Japan, serving twice as prime minister and several times in the cabinet. He was also the founder of Waseda University. He is remembered as a modernizer and an upholder of democratic principles.

7. Viscount Inukai (1855–1932) was a longtime party politician during the Meiji, Taishō, and early Shōwa eras. He had a particular interest in Chinese affairs and supported Sun Yat-sen during his years of exile in Japan. Having become prime minister in 1931, he was assassinated in the course of an incident provoked by extreme right-wing army officers.

8. AM adds that the permit was issued by the *résident-supérieur*, and that at this point Phan also showed Inukai a picture of Prince Cảnh.

At that point, a discussion took place for a while among the three men, Ōkuma, Inukai, and Liang; then they told me: "It is possible to assist you in the name of the party, but this is not the time to give you military assistance. These days, the setting for conflict is not just a problem between Japan and France but actually the problem of rivalry between Europe and Asia. If Japan wished to assist your country, then she would have to open hostilities with France. Once hostilities were opened between Japan and France, then it is likely that conflict would be ignited worldwide. At present, Japan does not have enough power to stand against the whole of Europe. Could you possibly be patient and await your opportunity?" I replied: "If it were possible for me to be patient, then why should I cry for help at the court of Ch'in?"

Ōkuma then said: "Now that you have come here, I have realized for the first time that the Vietnamese, like those in India, Poland, Egypt, and the Philippines, have lost the independence of their country; but nowhere else are things so gloomy. You should rally the intellectuals inside your country and send many abroad, so that their ears and eyes may be opened to new things. Regardless of where they went or what work they pursued, they could all breathe new, fresh air, and their spirit would not have to suffer from suffocation. This would be an immediate measure to save your country."

Inukai went on to ask me: "Have you organized a revolutionary party?" At that moment I felt so ashamed I wished to die, knowing that there was not yet any real revolutionary party in our country. Reluctantly, however, I replied: "An organization there is, but its influence is negligible, as if it did not exist." Ōkuma then said: "You might bring the members of your group here to Japan; our country would take in all of you; in case you wished to live in our country, we would provide accommodation for you, giving you the treatment accorded to foreign guests; you need have no concern about your subsistence, since chivalry and respect for patriotism are special traits of our Japanese people."

When Ōkuma said that, he looked quite full of pride. Feeling ashamed, I replied: "We have come here across the waves of the boundless ocean only because we are seeking a way to save the people in our country from death. If it had been simply to obtain an easy life while our people remain in hell, and to forget about them completely, then why should you bother to respect such persons?" Liang, sitting next to me, took a pen and wrote to Ōkuma on a piece of paper: "This man deserves great respect."

Madame Inukai, who was sitting nearby at the time, took a fan and asked me to inscribe some characters on it. I wrote down: *That the wind blows through all the Four Directions is thanks only to your great work.*[9]

Also among the people sitting there was Kashiwabara Buntarō, a member of the Japanese House of Representatives.[10] Having read all the papers of the conversation between the other three and myself, he said: "Today, as I watched all of you, I felt as if I were reading a tale of the ancient heroes in a novel, since you are the first Vietnamese who has come to the Land of the Rising Sun to meet with our men in high positions." On hearing that, I was smitten with sorrow, thinking of the lack of foresight on the part of our people; yet the measures adopted by the French to put our people in confinement had really been extremely ingenious.

Our discussion commenced at noon and did not come to an end until the late afternoon. This was the first time that I met with the Japanese.

---

9. In Sino-Vietnamese, *Tứ phương phong động duy nãi chi hưu;* a compliment made by Emperor Shun to his minister of Justice, Kao Yao. From the *Shu ching* (Books of Historical Documents), Book II, "The Counsels of the Great Yu." *Hưu* in this case means *mỹ*, i.e., "excellence."

10. Kashiwabara (1869–1936) served for four terms in the House of Representatives. He became one of the founders of the Tōa Shōgyō Gakkō (East Asian Commercial School) and the Tōa Dōbun Shoin, among other educational institutions. His care and concern for the Vietnamese students led them to call him and his wife "Otōsan" (Papa) and "Okāsan" (Mama).

LIANG CH'I-CH'AO invited me to his home again to lay out a plan of action on my behalf. Our dialogue through brush-conversation was detailed and exhaustive. A summary of it is as follows: "Our country and your country, through geography and history, for more than two thousand years have had very close relations, like brothers. How could an elder brother sit and watch his younger brother dying without saving him? Unfortunately, our mandarins have been people who care for nothing but their stomachs.[11] My heart is aching. I have done my best to think, and at present there are only two plans that I can offer you:

(i) To use impassioned and heart-rending writings to describe the tragedy of the loss of your country and to expose to the world France's baneful scheme to annihilate the people of your country. This is a plan to use the medium of diplomacy.

(ii) You might now return to your country, or send writings back to your country, to urge many of the youth to come overseas for study in order to revitalize the people's spirit and enlighten the people's mind. This is also a key plan.

Apart from the above two plans, you must endure hardships, taste bitterness,[12] and hold back your anger while you wait for the right time. When our country becomes stronger it will surely engage in war against the outsiders, and the first shot will be fired at France. Since your country adjoins our border, the two railways that connect Vietnam with Kwangsi and Yunnan are truly crucial concerns that our men of high purpose and prudence could never forget for a single instant. It is best for you to wait."

In that moment, the horizons of my consciousness and vision suddenly broadened. I became painfully aware that up to that time my ideas and my actions had all been thoughtless and imprudent. Thereupon I began to write the book *Việt-Nam vong-quốc-sử* (The

---

11. Literally, "people who eat meat."

12. In Sino-Vietnamese, *ngọa-tân thường-đảm*, literally "sleep on pine boughs, taste gall."

to print it; Liang agreed. In about ten days' time the book was in print. I went to see Liang to let him know that I was returning home. It was in the last decade of the Sixth Month in the Year of the Snake [the end of July 1905].

I LEFT TĂNG-BẠT-HỔ behind in Yokohama, and returned to our country together with Đặng-Tử-Kính, carrying several dozen copies of *The History of the Loss of Vietnam*.[13] My purpose was twofold: (i) to make arrangements to bring the Marquis out of the country, and (ii) to dispatch a number of promising youths who would blaze the trail for the students we would secretly send abroad. Sending out students would certainly call for funds, and raising funds would certainly require the Marquis to go abroad. Thus the plan I had at the time to make use of his name was actually not all that inspiring.

Early in the Seventh Month in the Year of the Snake [early August 1905], I left Yokohama, arriving at Hong Kong in the middle decade of the month. The boat on which Lý Tuệ was working arrived also. He had made a secret plan for me to stow away on board. I returned to Hải-phòng and stayed there one night.[14] After shaving my beard and changing my clothes, tying a white cotton band around my head in the fashion of a merchant of Bắc-Kỳ, I embarked on a steamer to go to Nam-định. By the time the boat arrived, it was getting dark. Making use of the night, I walked to Đốc-biện Khổng[-Định-Trạch]'s house. I reported to him the details of my journey to Japan, and asked him to look for some promising youths in Bắc-Kỳ. I stayed at Khổng's house for several days, sending someone to Quảng-nam to report secretly to Tiểu-La [Nguyễn Thành].

I then disguised myself and took a train to return to Nghệ-an. When

---

13. AM and CT give the figure of fifty copies.

14. AM and CT give the place where he stayed as the house of Phan Thiệu, Tăng-Bạt-Hổ's adopted son.

I then disguised myself and took a train to return to Nghệ-an. When the train arrived at Ninh-bình, I met the provincial governor *(tuần-phủ)*,[15] who told me that the authorities had ordered a strict search for me to be made in all localities, and warned me to be careful. Therefore I quickly got off the train before it reached Thanh-hóa, and walked for three days and nights until I arrived in Hà-tĩnh Province.

I stayed at a comrade's house[16] and invited Ngư-Hải [Đặng-Thái-Thân] to come and discuss the business of conducting the Marquis out of the country. Ngư-Hải, not wishing me to go in to the imperial capital [Huế], stopped me from doing so. I then promised to meet Thai-Sơn [Đặng-Nguyên-Cẩn] on a small boat on the Lam River [in Nghệ-an]. I showed him various sheets of paper written in Liang's hand. When Thai-Sơn had read what Liang had written, including the plan to organize [the overseas Chinese][17] secretly in support of Vietnam, he said to me: "We should make use of the movement to set up associations of cultivators, merchants, and students within the country to give our people a sense of organization, so that later it may be easier to carry out our activities. On this matter, Tập-Xuyên [Ngô-Đức-Kế] and others should be consulted." I strongly endorsed this suggestion. The Triều-Dương Thương-Quán (Morning Sun Chamber of Commerce) and those associations of farmers and students later set up in various places owed their existence to this idea.

I then secretly stayed on in the Nghệ-Tĩnh area to meet with members of the movement. Our consensus on the plan to send people abroad to study can be summarized as follows:

(i) The qualifications for the selected youths were that they should be intelligent, studious, patient in hardship and persevering in adversity, and able to remain firmly determined and unshaken by circumstances.

---

15. AM gives the name of the governor as Mr. Đoàn; CT gives the full name, Đoàn Triển.
16. AM describes it as Mr. Đặng's house; CT as Đặng-Văn-Bá's house.
17. AM adds this term explicitly.

(ii) The arrangements for expenditures were to be made in concert with both the peaceful-action group and the militant-action group.[18]

(iii) The persons who were to act as escorts should be carefully selected and absolutely trustworthy.

(iv) To forestall infiltrators and the leaking of information, all correspondence and reports should use a special mark, and if possible it would be better yet to use invisible ink.

After these arrangements had been made, I again left for Bắc-Kỳ in the last decade of the Seventh Month [late August 1905], using the old route via Hải-phòng to leave the country. Accompanying me were Nguyễn-Thức-Canh of Đông-chu (who was the son of my teacher Đông-Khê and had been a student in Germany), [Nguyễn Điển] of Cao-điền, and [Lê Khiết] of Thanh-hóa.[19] Ngư-Hải saw me off to Hải-phòng. I entrusted the business of bringing the Marquis out of the country to Tiểu-La. [Đặng-]Tử-Kính again traveled with me to Japan.

IN THE FIRST DECADE of the Eighth Month [September 1905], we arrived in Kwangtung. I visited Liu Yung-fu, and incidentally met the former military commander *(tán-lý)* of Tam-tuyên,[20] Nguyễn[-Thiện-]Thuật. Liu at that time was already in his seventies, but in appearance still alert and hale. When in our conversation reference was made to the French, he promptly banged the table, saying: *"Tả! Tả! Tả!"* ("Down with them! Down! Down!") I then recalled that at the time when French soldiers twice attacked Hanoi, had it not been for the army under Liu, our people would not have had a single drop of blood left to wash the enemy's neck. Alas! How is it possible not to call him

---

18. According to CT, the "peaceful-action group" comprised those who would raise funds through production and trade or donations; the "militant-action group" would resort to coercion to persuade the wealthy to contribute.

19. The names in square brackets are not found in the original text; Nguyễn Điển is mentioned explicitly in CT and GB, Lê Khiết only in CT.

20. Comprising the Sơn-tây, Hưng-hóa, and Tuyên-quang areas.

a hero? From that time on, my penchant for hero worship made me instinctively Liu's ardent admirer.

The military commander Nguyễn also did one thing that in itself would suffice to make him a teacher of others. He had been addicted to opium for more than ten years. At that time, he was being supported by Liu. His funds were quite ample and his smoking habit had become even more severe. When we came to see him and showed him the program of the Vietnam Modernization Association and the *History of the Loss of Vietnam*, he was smoking. Suddenly, he pushed away his pillow, rose up, and took all his smoking utensils and smashed them to pieces, saying in a loud voice: "If younger people can act the way you do, how can I go on living with black rice?"[21] He immediately quit smoking, and until the end of his life not even one more puff entered his mouth.

In later days his eldest son, [Cả] Thân,[22] was struck by a bullet and died for our country in battle under Đề Thám [Hoàng-Hoa-Thám]. The middle son, [Hai] Thường, was involved in the New Movement and was sent into exile to Côn-lôn (Poulo Condore) until his death.[23] Thường's younger brother, [Nguyễn-Thiện-]Kế, was sent to Poulo Condore when he was only seventeen years old. Nguyễn-Thiện-Tổ, Nguyễn[-Thiện-]Thuật's eldest grandson in the direct line, studied at the Peking Military Academy and during his career after graduation was promoted all the way up to the rank of colonel, but eventually he contracted lung disease and died, his promise unfulfilled. At the time when I was arrested [1925], Nguyễn[-Thiện-]Thuật was still in good health; I do not know how he is now.

I stayed on with Liu and Nguyễn for about a month, mainly waiting for news from the Marquis. Having come to realize that he would not be able to leave before the end of the year, I decided to conduct the three young men on to Japan.

---

21. A reference to opium.

22. A nickname meaning "the eldest" Thân. His real name was Nguyễn Tuyển.

23. According to AM and CT, Thường was shot to death.

IT WAS IN THE first decade of the Ninth Month [end of September/early October 1905]. I again went to Yokohama and took the three young men for an interview with Liang. Hardly had we sat down when Liang asked me about the business of dispatching students. I replied: "I have discussed this business with my comrades at home, but the greatest difficulty is funding. The children of the rich do not dare to go beyond the gate of their house, but the genteel-poor youth have their legs tied because they have no money." I then pointed to my companions and said: "I tried my best for several months but recruited only these three men."

Liang, having pondered for a while, said to me: "You might put something in writing to rally those in your country with their heart in the right place. Putting together bits and pieces of fur will make up an overcoat. That is the way you might resolve the problem of funding." I too thought that there was no other way better than this. I then drafted a piece entitled *Khuyến quốc-dân tư-trợ du-học văn* (An Appeal to My Fellow Countrymen to Provide Financial Support for Overseas Studies), which began with the following sentence:

> Alas! Gazing westward from the far side of the Ocean,[24] looking eastward from the Mekong River, what has become of our country, her mountains and rivers?[25]

When the manuscript was completed, I showed it to Liang; he generously undertook the printing, gratis.

MORE THAN THREE thousand copies were produced, but they had not yet been sent out when six young men from Bắc-Kỳ arrived all at once. First of all there were Lương-Lập-Nham of Hanoi and his younger

24. I.e., from Japan; in the original, *Đại dương tây vọng*. In the versions of AM, CT, and TQP (followed by GB), this sentence begins with the words *Côn-lôn Bắc vọng*, "Gazing northward from Poulo Condore."

25. Phan's grief over the loss of Vietnam's independence is expressed by his use of the words *vọng*, "gazing," and *cố*, "looking," which imply nostalgia and longing.

brother Lương-Nghi-Khanh; they were sons of Lương-Văn-Can.[26]
Then there were *Tú-tài* Nguyễn-Hải-Thần, Nguyễn Điển of Hà-đông,
and two others. All had secretly made their way overseas. On their
arrival in Yokohama they had not a penny left in their pockets. They
all came to look for me at my lodgings in Yokohama. Originally I had
rented only low-class quarters big enough for three persons. Now the
visitors had abruptly increased the number of persons by nine, but no
supply of funds had yet arrived. All of a sudden my lodgings were full
of people but empty of money—a difficult situation.

Tăng-Bạt-Hổ arranged on my behalf that I might go to a Cantonese
commercial store to obtain rice and firewood on credit, while he would
work his passage on a Western ship back to Kwangtung to see Liu, to
borrow some urgently needed money to send to me. Then he would
secretly take with him a few thousand copies of *An Appeal to My
Fellow Countrymen to Provide Financial Support for Overseas Studies*
and clandestinely reenter our country. Đặng-Tử-Kính, as well, would
accompany Tăng to launch big campaigns in Trung-Kỳ and Bắc-Kỳ.

In the last decade of the Ninth Month [October 1905], the two of
them left Yokohama. I and the nine others who remained had two meals
a day of coarse rice with some salt and a few cups of tea. Our small
house was crowded; we mutually relied on each other to survive. It was
then the beginning of winter. The snow came pouring down; the cold
wind cut to the bone. Our hands and feet were freezing. Yet as it was
the first time any of us had been out of our country, we had not prepared
for the cold at all. Our clothes were thin and our food was scanty. We
made a great effort to stand firm against hunger and cold. Fortunately,
Liang's place had a library with an abundance of books that we could
borrow to read day or night to keep ourselves more or less entertained.
Giving each other mutual support, the young men all stood up well
under hardship, and none showed any signs of it outwardly.

---

26. Lương-Lập-Nham (1890–1917) was also later known as Lương-Ngọc-Quyến.
His father Lương-Văn-Can (1854–1927) was a *cử-nhân* and the headmaster of the
Đông-Kinh Private School.

Most admirable was Lương-Lập-Nham with his irrepressible behavior, talking away cheerfully all the time, showing his big-hearted outlook. Seeing how desperate the situation was and how difficult it would be to survive, he indignantly said: "If this is not the time to go in for playing the flute,[27] then how long are we going to wait?" He then walked all day long on an empty stomach to make his way from Yokohama to Tokyo. That night he turned in to sleep in the doorway of a police station. The police questioned him in Japanese. In a state of blank incomprehension, he did not know what to answer. When they made a search, they found his pockets to be empty. They suspected him of being feeble-minded. When brush-conversation began, however, then at last it emerged that he was a young man from our country. The Japanese police were astonished, and supplied him with the money to go back to Yokohama by train.

Having received this money, which would buy him meals for several days, Lương did not go home, but instead went around to visit the lodgings of various Chinese students in Tokyo. By sheer chance he found the office of the *Min-pao*, the organ of China's revolutionary party. The managing editor was Chang Tai-yen and the editor-in-chief was Chang Chi.[28] Both of them were founding members of the revolutionary party. Lương made his way into the office and explained his current situation to Chang Tai-yen and Chang Chi. They felt very sorry about it. They hired him as their third-rank clerk, and told him to return to Yokohama and bring back his friends in the same plight, as they would take on a number of them.

Lương then returned home. As soon as he entered the door he gave a big laugh and said to me: "Uncle! Begging works!" He then left his brother Nghị-Khanh at my house and, together with two men from his village, parted from me and set off for Tokyo to take room and board at the *Min-pao* and study the Japanese language while waiting for news from home in the South.

---

27. I.e., begging. For the origin of this expression, see below, p. 127, n. 62.

28. At present they are eminent figures in the Peking government. [Author's note.]

Around this time I composed quite a few poems depicting our situation as it then was, one of which read as follows:

Solitary geese, lone steeds—nine brothers,
to each other bound;
O'er ten thousand seas, a thousand mountains,
shall their names resound!

Things went on like that for two months. Then it happened that a man from the Chinese revolutionary party called Tang Ch'ue-tun, seeing us in such a pitiful situation, said to console us: "Among the Chinese revolutionaries we hold the secret of success to be: 'Fear not hunger, fear not death, fear not cold, fear not poverty.' If you are able to live up to this, you will certainly achieve your goal one day." Tang in addition wrote a letter to recommend me to Chuang Yun-kuan, the military governor of Kwangsi. Chuang, who had been appointed by the Ch'ing government to train new recruits in Lungchow at the border of Kwangsi, was a native of Kiangsu and a former classmate of Tang's. After more than a month an answering letter came from Chuang, which said: "The servility of the Vietnamese is irremediable; there is no medicine that can help. Even if they have one or two men of high purpose, it will be impossible to do anything." Tang brought it to show to me, and told me with a sigh: "Chuang's military post in Lungchow adjoins the Vietnamese border, and he is perfectly acquainted with the situation of your countrymen. That is why he said this." At that point I was so sorrowful and indignant that I could not control myself; all I could do was wipe my tears in solitude. But even in this discouraging, sad, and desperate situation, there were nonetheless one or two things that should be put on record.

BEFORE TĂNG-BẠT-HỒ returned to our country, he and I went to Liang's house to bid farewell. Liang said: "The people of Yunnan are gnashing their teeth in fury because the rights over the Yunnan railway are in the hands of the French. At present there are quite a few Yunnanese students in Japan, and those who are enrolled in the Shimbu Gakkō[29] are quite public spirited. Once they complete their studies and go back home they will dedicate themselves to the profession of arms.[30] In the future, when you launch your undertaking, you will probably obtain a great deal of help from Yunnan. You ought to establish contacts with them now, planning your moves on the chessboard in advance." Liang then wrote down the three characters *Yin Cheng-hsien*, gave the note to me, and said: "This man is the most outstanding of all; as for the others, you can obtain introductions to them through him." I took the note, thinking of going to Tokyo to look for Yin, but when I asked for Yin's address, Liang did not know it; all he knew was that he was a student at the Shimbu Gakkō.

The following day, Tăng and I emptied our pockets and gathered together the few silver coins that we had to pay for the trip to Tokyo. When we arrived at the Tokyo railway station and got off the train, I called a rickshaw. When the rickshaw man asked where I would like to go, I showed him the piece of notepaper, but he looked very perplexed because no address was indicated, and neither of us could converse in Japanese. This rickshaw man called over one of his colleagues, who pulled up his rickshaw in front of me and then wrote down: "This man is not very proficient in literary Chinese *(kambun)*. He has therefore entrusted you to me. I am versed in literary Chinese. If you want to go anywhere, you can write it down and I shall be able to take you there." Having said that, he asked the two of us to get on his rickshaw. When we arrived at the Shimbu Gakkō, we asked for Yin, but were told that Yin had already left the academy. At the time, he was staying in a Japanese lodging house, waiting to enter the cadet corps for military training in the following year. The rickshaw man at that point looked nonplussed, bowed his head, and pondered for a while. A little later,

---

29. The Shimbu Gakkō (Academy for the Promotion of Martial Spirit) was established by the Japanese General Staff in 1903 as a specialized preparatory school for youths who wished to enter the Rikugun Shikan Gakkō (Military Academy), then the leading institution for officer training in Japan.

30. Literally, "fling themselves into the land of guns and cannons."

he pulled the rickshaw to the side of the street and said to me: "Please wait here. I am going to look for the address of your friend and I shall be back."

Tokyo being of such a vast size, with a total number of lodging houses that must be not less than ten thousand, one could imagine how difficult it must be for a Japanese rickshaw man to look at random for the address of a foreign student from China. At the outset I expected that the rickshaw man would share the same propensity to sharp practice as the rickshaw pullers in our country; I therefore worried about not having enough money to pay the rickshaw fare. I stood and waited from two o'clock until five o'clock; then I saw him coming back in jubilation and waving to the two of us to get on the rickshaw. After an hour's ride we arrived at a lodging house and saw a horizontal board hanging in front of the gate, on which the names and nationalities of the lodgers were inscribed. There were names like *Mr. So-and-so, Yunnanese, a foreign student from China.* I began to realize that it would be simple to search for a lodger.

I then asked the rickshaw man the fare, and he asked only for twenty-five cents. I was dumbfounded. I took from my pocket a silver coin and gave it to him to recompense him for what he had done. He refused to accept it and wrote, saying: " According to the regulations of the Home Ministry, the price from the station to this house is only that much. Since you are foreigners who were attracted to come here by Japanese civilization, I welcome you accordingly; it was not because I was looking for money that I brought you here. Were you to overpay me, it would mean that you thought little of Japanese people." As I saw those words, I felt overwhelmed with admiration. Alas! The mental level of our country's people, when one looks at this Japanese rickshaw man, would make one want to die of shame!

ONCE I HAD MET Yin, he introduced me to other Yunnanese students. Yang Chen-hung and Chao Shen were among those I became acquainted with at this time. That later on I became a member of the editorial board of *Yunnan Tsa-chih* (The Yunnan Review) can also be traced back to what took place at this time.

One day Inukai Tsuyoshi wrote a letter inviting me to his home to give me an introduction to Sun Yat-sen.[31] Sun, the great leader of the Chinese revolutionary party, at the time had just returned to Japan from the United States. He was staying in Yokohama to organize the Chinese T'ung-meng-hui (United League). Inukai said to me: " Your country's independence can only take place after the Chinese revolutionary party has succeeded. Between that party and you, ' the same affliction makes mutual affection.' You ought to see this man to prepare for your future moves."

The following day, I carried Inukai's name card, along with his letter of introduction, to the Shiwadō in Yokohama to meet Sun. It was past eight o'clock in the evening. Sun brought out brush and paper and discussed revolutionary affairs with me. Sun, who had already read my *History of the Loss of Vietnam*, knew that in my thinking I had not yet abandoned monarchical ideas; therefore, he scathingly denounced the hypocrisy of the constitutional monarchist party, on account of which he wished the Vietnamese to join the Chinese revolutionary party. When the Chinese revolutionary party succeeded, then it would use all its power to help the oppressed countries of Asia to achieve independence. Vietnam would be first on the list. In reply, I said that I recognized that the democratic republican system was ideal, but the main thrust of my argument was that, on the contrary, I wished the Chinese revolutionary party first to help Vietnam; when Vietnam became independent, then it would invite the Chinese revolutionary party to use the northern part of Vietnam as a base of operations to move into Kwangsi and Kwangtung, and finally take over central

31. Sun Yat-sen (1866–1925), leader of the Chinese republican revolution who became for a short time provisional president of the Chinese Republic in 1912; his later years were devoted to the revitalization of the Kuomintang Party. He went to Japan in 1897 and conducted his activities from there for the next ten years. In spite of his connections with leading Japanese politicians such as Inukai, he was asked to leave in 1907, some two years before the same fate overtook Phan and the Marquis.

China. The argument back and forth between Sun and me dragged on for several hours; at twelve o'clock I bade farewell, and Sun promised to meet me again for more discussion some other evening.

Several days later I went back to the Shiwadō to see Sun again. We reopened the subjects that had been discussed on the earlier evening. Sun and I agreed that we had both been in the wrong. I did not really know the inner workings of the Chinese revolutionary party, nor did Sun know the real situation of the Vietnamese revolutionary party. The discussion between us, though each knew what the other wanted, had been after all like groping in the dark but not grasping the essentials. Later on, however, at times when our movement ran into an emergency, it was thanks to the contacts secured through these two evenings of discussion that we received great assistance from the Chinese revolutionaries.

When Sun Yat-sen died of liver cancer in Peking, I wrote a two-stanza poem in his memory, which read:

> *The threefold right of peoples was your standard,*
> > *The threefold right of peoples was your Way.*
> *To me, at Yokohama's Shiwadō, twice over,*
> > *Your brush spoke truly for a future day.*
>
> *All people under Heaven you rejoiced in;*
> > *All people under Heaven you held dear.*
> *For you, long years oppressed by empire's minions,*
> > *For you I shed a final, painful tear.*

What is stated above was indeed true.

FROM THE YEAR of the Horse, the eighteenth year of the reign of Thành-Thái [1906], to the autumn of the Year of the Monkey [1908] is the period of my life with which I feel most satisfied, for the reason that from the time that I was born until then, the plans I made had never gone more smoothly than during this time.

In the second decade of the First Month [February 1906], I received a letter from Tăng-Bạt-Hổ saying that Ngư-Hải [Đặng-Thái-Thân] had taken the Marquis out of the country on the first day of the First Month of this year, and they might arrive in Hong Kong by the end of the month. In haste, I got my luggage ready and headed to Hong Kong to receive them. Just a few days after I arrived in Hong Kong, the Marquis duly showed up, accompanied by Đặng-Tử-Kính. This was because Ngư-Hải had traveled with the Marquis only as far as Hải-phòng; from Hải-phòng to Hong Kong, Đặng-Tử-Kính was his only escort.

When I met the Marquis, we talked about the situation in our country, then settled into lodgings at the Kuang-cheng-shing, a store owned by a Cantonese merchant.[32] The owner of the store was named Yang. He was a merchant, but one who treasured right-eousness. When I was in Yokohama I had met his nephew, who introduced Yang to us. Yang held our cause in high esteem and volunteered to provide hospitality to us in his home whenever we were in Hong Kong. Each time we came to Hong Kong, Tăng-Bạt-Hổ and I invariably stayed there. He never took any payment, even though our stay lasted weeks or months. Later, when we fell on hard times, we borrowed money from Yang, and Yang never showed any sign of regret.[33] Were one to seek for such conduct among our country's merchants, it really would be terribly difficult to find!

I toured around Hong Kong for several days. By chance I met a Cantonese man called Chuan who introduced me at the German Consulate in Hong Kong. That day marked the beginning of my contact with the Germans. The relations in later years between

---

32. According to GB (p. 62), who consulted the records of the French *Sûreté* in Indo-china, this firm was run by Kang Yu-wei, and later engaged in the transfer of funds for Cường-Để, notably in 1913. Whether the business was directly managed by Kang Yu-wei is, however, doubtful.

33. In the AM version (p. 69), Phan indicates that the borrowing was done when the Marquis was with him.

members of our movement and the Germans arose largely from this occasion.[34]

In the first decade of the Second Month [end of February/early March 1906], the Marquis and I went to Canton to visit Nguyễn-Thiện-Thuật, who was staying at the home of Liu Yung-fu in Shaho. It was then that the program of the Vietnam Modernization Association was committed to print. When the Association was secretly organized by Tiểu-La and me back at home, the program was conveyed by word of mouth from one person to another and recorded mentally—there was no written program. Now that the Marquis and I had gone abroad and were about to dispatch people to return home to launch a great movement, it would have been impossible not to have a written program. Moreover, both Nguyễn-Thiện-Thuật and Liu Yung-fu also supported the idea of printing it. The program contained just three broad articles and six detailed clauses. The gist of it was that Vietnam should be restored to independence and a constitutional monarchy set up. As only a few hundred copies were printed, it would be easy enough to carry them home surreptitiously. However, this program was already declared null and void in the Tenth Month of the Year of the Boar [November/December 1911], the Association also being renamed *Việt-Nam Quang-Phục-Hội* (Vietnam Restoration League),[35] so that it is not recapitulated in detail here.

AFTER STAYING AT Liu's house for several days, I received some very welcome news, namely that Tây-Hồ Phan-Châu-Trinh had by that time left our country. In the last decade of the Second Month [late

---

34. Using the records of the French *Sûreté*, GB (p. 63 n.) identified the German Consul ("Vorestch") as the person who helped Cường-Đề to print letters of credit in 1912.

35. *Quang-Phục-Hội* was the Vietnamese equivalent of Sun Yat-sen's *Kuang-fu-hui*. It should be noted that this was shortly after the Chinese Revolution in October 1911; Phan apparently hoped to achieve a comparable success by following Sun's example. The new League was founded in March 1912; see below, p. 191.

March/early April 1906], Tây-Hồ arrived in Hong Kong. Hearing that I
had gone to Kwangtung, he immediately set out for Nguyễn and Liu's
place. In a short robe and torn shoes and with his hair dishevelled,
he looked like a common laborer; he had purposely disguised himself as a cook on the boat in order to travel, with the secret help,
once again, of Lý Tuệ. When he saw us at Liu's house, he laughed
out loud before saying anything. I shook his hand. Our joy was
indescribable.

I presently showed him *An Appeal to My Fellow Countrymen
to Provide Financial Support for Overseas Studies*. He commended
it highly. When he saw the program of the Vietnam Modernization
Association, however, he made no comment, only saying: "I really
wish to go to see Japan once; then I shall return to our country
immediately afterwards." It seems that at that time, deep in his heart, he
already had a different aspiration. He and I kept company in Kwangtung for more than ten days. Every day when we talked about the
affairs of our country, he singled out for bitter reproach the wicked
conduct of the monarchs, the enemies of the people. He ground
his teeth when talking about the ruler of the day, who was bringing calamity to the country and disaster to the people; as much as
to say that if the system of monarchical autocracy were not abolished, simply restoring the country's independence would bring no
happiness.

The Marquis, who was sitting nearby, became very excited. Thereupon he wrote out a letter of admonition for himself; at the end of the
letter he signed himself "Enemy of the People," then "Cường-Đề."[36]
The letter was printed in several hundred copies altogether; I asked Lý
Tuệ to take them secretly back into our country. I also called on Đặng-
Tử-Kính to return home to collaborate with Tăng-Bạt-Hồ, dividing the
regions of the country between them—one to go to the South, the other

---

36. In the original, *Dân tặc hậu Cường-Đề*. TQP, GB, and CT translate this as
"Cường-Đề, the heir of the enemy of the people." Although such an interpretation
is possible, the translation given here seems more likely.

to the North, to distribute the aforementioned documents. They were to give top priority to two things: promoting the dispatch of students abroad and collecting donations for their school fees.

When these arrangements had been made, the Marquis and I left for Japan, accompanied by Tây-Hồ [Phan-Châu-Trinh]. In the second decade of the Third Month we moved into Bính-Ngọ-Hiên (Year-of-the-Horse House) in Yokohama. Bính-Ngọ-Hiên was a small center, the first to be established by our Đông-Độ (Sail East) movement.[37] By that time, Tăng-Bạt-Hồ had made his way back into our country and forwarded to us several hundred piasters; in addition, the Marquis had also brought with him quite a substantial sum of money. We made use of this to rent a two-story Japanese house with ample space and to hire a Japanese to teach our youth spoken and written Japanese. We called the place Bính-Ngọ-Hiên because it was then the Year of the Horse, and *Bính-Ngọ* implied an allusion, with bright auspices *(ly-minh)*, to our country in the South.[38]

---

37. This is the first time in the autobiography that Phan describes his movement by this term, which the Chinese and Vietnamese around the turn of the twentieth century commonly used to refer to a boat trip to Japan. " Đông-Du " (Go East), the term now popularly used for it, gained currency only after 1945, according to Nguyễn-Khắc-Kham, "Discrepancies between *Ngục-Trung-Thư* and *Phan-Bội-Châu Niên-Biểu*," in Vĩnh Sính, ed., *Phan-Bội-Châu and the Đông-Du Movement* (New Haven, Yale International and Area Studies, 1988), 44n.

38. In the Vietnamese calendar, modeled after the Chinese, the name of each year consists of two components, the first designating one of the Ten Heavenly Stems, and the second one of the Twelve Earthly Branches. In Bính-Ngọ (in Chinese, *Ping-wu*), *Bính* is the third of the Stems, referring to the South and Fire; *Ngọ* is the seventh of the Branches, referring to the South and Noon. Of the Eight Diagrams *(Bát-quái*, in Chinese *Pa-kua)* used in divination, *Ly,* like *Bính,* refers to the South and Brightness, as well as Fire and Separation or Parting. Phan is obviously playing on words when he follows *Bính-Ngọ* with *ly-minh,* as both imply " South " and " bright," i.e., " auspicious." Phan seems not to have recalled, in his eagerness to find a name that would symbolize a promising future, that according to Chinese tradition *Ping-wu* was one of the two most notoriously unlucky years in the calendrical cycle. (The other one was Đinh-mùi, in Chinese *Ting-wei,* i.e., the Year of the Sheep, *wei,* combined with the fourth Stem, *ting).* Curiously enough, when in 1945 the Trần-Trọng-Kim government was searching for a motif for a national flag, the design of the diagram for *Ly*

Upon my arrival, I immediately dispatched a letter to Inukai Tsuyoshi to ask him about the matter of school admission for our young men. Inukai consulted with three of his colleagues about this.

One was the Marquis Hosokawa [Morishige], then principal of the Tōa Dōbun Shoin (Common East Asian Culture Institute);[39] another was Fukushima Yasumasa, an army general who was then chief of the General Staff and director of the Shimbu Gakkō;[40] and the third was Nezu Hajime, an army major who was then the secretary-general of the Tōa Dōbun Kai (Common East Asian Culture Society).[41] Inukai also

---

was adopted with a slight modification. In his memoirs, Trần-Trọng-Kim recalled that at the time, there were those who opposed this design because *Ly* included among its connotations "Fire" and "Parting," suggesting warfare and an unhappy future for the country. Trần-Trọng-Kim was nevertheless adamant in his choice. (*Một cơn gió bụi* [A Whirl of Dust] [Saigon: Vĩnh Sơn, 1969], 61.) His flag continued in use in the South throughout the period when Vietnam was partitioned (1954–1975).

39. Hosokawa Morishige (1868–1914), a descendant of the famed Hosokawa family, went to England to study in 1885 and to France in 1887; in 1893 he was appointed a member of the House of Peers. He served with distinction in the Sino-Japanese and Russo-Japanese wars. The Common East Asian Culture Institute in Tokyo was established in 1902 by the Common East Asian Culture Society (see n. 41, below) to provide preparatory courses for Chinese students who could then go on to higher education in Japan. It was abolished with the Society in 1945.

40. In the course of a colorful military and diplomatic career, Fukushima Yasumasa (1852–1919) spent time in India and Germany before achieving the status of a national hero by traveling alone on horseback from Berlin to Vladivostok over a period of 440 days (1892–1893), gathering much information of value for military intelligence about conditions in Russia. He was military attaché at the Japanese consulate in Korea before and during the Sino-Japanese War, commanded the Japanese troops dispatched to China during the Boxer Rebellion, and served with conspicuous merit as a staff officer in the Russo-Japanese War. He became vice-chief of the General Staff in 1908 (not chief, as Phan describes him) and was promoted to the rank of general in 1914. On the Shimbu Gakkō, see above, p. 99.

41. Nezu Hajime (1860–1927), after early retirement following an outstanding career as an artillery officer, in order to further the interests of Japan in her relations with China co-founded the Nisshin Bōeki Kenkyūjo (Research Institute for Sino-Japanese Trade), where many young men were trained. The Common East Asian Culture Society was founded by the politician Konoe Atsumaro (1863–1904) in 1898 to foster Pan-Asianist sentiments among the Chinese and Japanese through promoting their

asked his protégé and right-hand man, Kashiwabara Buntarō, to act as liaison among the above.

After only a little more than ten days' time, the admission of our students had been arranged. Admitted to the Shimbu Gakkō were two students from Bắc-Kỳ and one student from Trung-Kỳ, namely Lương-Lập-Nham, Trần-Hữu-Công, and Nguyễn Điển.[42] One was admitted to the [Tokyo] Dōbun Shoin,[43] namely Lương-Nghị-Khanh. Six other students did not possess the qualifications and therefore could not enter.

In the first decade of the Fourth Month [late May/early June 1906], I sent the students to Tokyo to enter school. Tây-Hồ accompanied me to Tokyo to pay a visit of inspection to the schools and other showplaces of Japanese politics and education. He said to me: "The level of their people is so high, and the level of our people is so low! How could we not become slaves? That some students now can enter Japanese schools has been your great achievement. Please stay on in Tokyo to take a quiet rest and devote yourself to writing, and not to making appeals for combat against the French. You should only call for 'popular rights and popular enlightenment.'[44] Once popular rights have been achieved, then we can think about other things."[45]

---

shared cultural traditions, in particular the use of Chinese script. In 1899 the Society established a school in Nanking (moved to Shanghai in 1901 following the Boxer Rebellion), and in 1902 another school, the Common East Asian Culture Institute, in Tokyo (see n. 39, above); it also issued numerous publications. During the 1930s and early 1940s, the Society became an influential promoter of Japan's expansionist drive on the Asian continent. It was abolished in 1945.

42. Lương, alias Lương-Ngọc-Quyến, who died in the Thái-nguyên uprising; Trần, alias Trần-Thức-Canh. [Author's note.] — AM, CT, and TQP add: "Nguyễn Điển now has submitted to the French." [Translators' note.]

43. A junior high school. [Author's note.] — It was approximately equivalent to a senior high school of the present day. [Translators' note.]

44. In Sino-Vietnamese, *Dân-quyền dân-trí.*

45. This is the principle adhered to by Tây-Hồ throughout his life. [Note added in HTK, probably by the copyist.]

Thereafter, over more than ten days, he and I debated time and again, and our opinions were diametrically opposed. That is to say, he wished to overthrow the monarchy in order to create a basis for the promotion of popular rights; I, on the contrary, maintained that first the foreign enemy should be driven out, and after our nation's independence was restored we could talk about other things. My plan was to make use of the monarchy, which he opposed absolutely. His plan was to raise up the people to abolish the monarchy, with which I absolutely disagreed. In other words, he and I were pursuing one and the same goal, but our means were considerably different. He wished to start by relying on the French to abolish the monarchy, but I wished to start by driving out the French to restore Vietnam—that was the difference. However, even though his political view was the opposite of mine, he liked me personally a great deal and we roomed together for several weeks. Then all of a sudden he decided to return to our country.

By that time, I had introduced the Marquis to General Fukushima. Fukushima said to me: "According to diplomatic practice, when a member of your country's royal family does not possess a permit from the French government, our country cannot receive him openly; but he could mingle with the foreign youth and pretend to be a foreign student; then it would be all right." The Marquis thereupon left Yokohama for Tokyo to enter the Shimbu Gakkō. Among our five students at this school, only the Marquis paid the school fee; the remaining four all received Japanese support. This was indeed a clever arrangement by a civilized nation.

After the five had entered the school, there were only a few youths staying at Bính-Ngọ-Hiên to study spoken and written Japanese. I presently went to see Tây-Hồ off from Hong Kong. This was our last farewell. He said to me: "You should take care of yourself. The only person in whom the people in our country place their hope is you. The Marquis is utterly useless." I respectfully acquiesced. Over and over, I promised to meet him again, and asked him to tell Thai-Sơn [Đặng-Nguyên-Cẩn], Thạnh-Bình [Huỳnh-Thúc-Kháng], Tập-Xuyên

[Ngô-Đức-Kế], and others to do their best to promote popular enlightenment and put together associations to gain more support for our new movement.

BY THAT TIME, it was the middle decade of the Fifth Month [July 1906]. At that very point, two youths from Quảng-nam who had just left our country met me in Hong Kong. I received from them a personal letter from Tiểu-La describing the state of the movement in our country, which gave the impression that it was expanding. I then took the two youths to Japan, so that they could stay at Bính-Ngọ-Hiên.

I wrote Part I of *Hải-ngoại huyết-thư* (A Letter from Overseas Written in Blood). When it was completed, I awaited an opportunity to send it back to Vietnam. Seeing the Marquis, who had returned to Yokohama for the summer vacation, I said to him: "Our students, though not many, still comprise those from both Trung-Kỳ and Bắc-Kỳ. It cannot be said that this is without significance. The only thing is, one can hardly find a soul from Nam-Kỳ. We should arrange to do something about this in short order. In launching our movement in Nam-Kỳ, in order to be effective, we should certainly make use of the people's sentiment of nostalgia for the old days. Now, you are a direct descendant of the founder of the dynasty, and you yourself have gone overseas. It would be a good idea to draw up an appeal, and send people back to Nam-Kỳ to rally the youth and impel them to go overseas to study. To use the rich resources of Nam-Kỳ to nourish the talents from Trung-Kỳ and Bắc-Kỳ as well is an excellent plan." The Marquis urged me to act on this idea immediately.

I thus wrote *Kính cáo toàn quốc phụ lão văn* (An Appeal Respectfully Addressed to the Elders throughout Our Country). When it was completed I asked Lý Tuệ to carry it on his boat from Hong Kong back to Tăng-Bạt-Hổ and Đặng-Tử-Kính for distribution in Nam-Kỳ and Trung-Kỳ; in Bắc-Kỳ distribution would be carried out by Nguyễn-Hải-Thần. In the appeal, there was a passage that read:

[The French colonialists] maintain our emperor but empty our country. This is a way to deceive public opinion on the Five Continents. They occupy our land and colonize it. They massacre thousands of people mercilessly . . . . Even though there were kings whose determination was like that of Kou-chien and Shao-k'ang, nevertheless the clouds gather and the rain pours down; how could they struggle against natural calamities? Even though there were people whose loyalty was like that of Shen Pao-tzu and Chu-ko Liang,[46] the pity of it is that the sea has dried up and the mountains are parched; where could there be a place for them to display their talents?

A glance at this appeal instantly shows how very exalted were my expectations of the Vietnamese court and its mandarins, and how bitterly I resented the evil [French colonial] government.[47]

As it happened, when I visited Liang Ch'i-ch'ao he was writing *I-ta-li san-chieh chuan* (Biographies of the Three Heroes of Italy). He showed it to me, and I became a great admirer of Mazzini, as in the account of him there were these words: "Education and insurrection should go hand in hand," which filled me with enthusiasm.

---

46. Shao-k'ang, an emperor of the Hsia dynasty, by dogged perseverance managed to restore this dynasty after forty years of eclipse, reigning for twenty years from 2079 B.C. See the *Shih chi,* book II. Chu-ko Liang (181–234), also known as Wu-hou, was the talented and faithful minister of Liu Pei, founder of the Minor Han dynasty. For Kou-ch'ien, see below, p. 184, n. 122; for Shen Pao-tzu, above, p. 73, n. 24.

47. All the translated texts include some extra words at the beginning of the quotation, which are not found in the texts in literary Chinese (HXH and HTK): "The Marquis Cường-Đế, the direct descendant of the Crown Prince Anh-Duệ (commonly known as Prince Cảnh), respectfully makes the following declaration to the elders throughout the nation: ' . . . The French colonialists establish a hypocritical protectorate . . . .' " Also, there are minor variations in the text of the quotation. For example, HXH and HTK read *vân truần vũ kiện,* "the clouds gather and the rain pours down." The common form of this idiom is *vân truần vũ tập.* AM, followed by CT, reads *phong cuồng vũ sậu,* "the heaven rages and the rain roars." The text of the *Appeal* included in *Phan-Bội-Châu toàn tập* (Phan-Bội-Châu's Collected Works) edited by Chương Thâu (Huế: Thuận Hóa, 1990), II, 78, based upon the recollection of an old man, reads *vân truần thủy kiện,* "the clouds gather and the water pours down," much closer to the reading of HXH and HTK. No original copy of the *Appeal* seems to have survived.

Accordingly, on the one hand I would encourage students to go overseas, and on the other hand I would promote revolutionary ideas and activities among our people.

I then wrote a sequel to the first part of the *Letter from Overseas Written in Blood*. When this was completed it was entitled *Tục Hải-ngoại huyết-thư* (A Sequel to the Letter from Overseas Written in Blood), and was sent back home. Lê [Đại] translated it into *quốc-ngữ* and distributed it all over the country. The first part began like this: "Our fellow countrymen are strange, very strange indeed. Have they realized that there is a problem?" The sequel commenced as follows:

> *Not long ago I sent home*
> *My words written in blood and tears.*
> *As I cast my eyes over the Five Continents,*
> *There has been neither wind nor rain–*
> *I am profoundly saddened.*

In the first part I bitterly exposed the poisonous policy of extermination by the foreigners, which consists of the following:

(i) open exploitation, i.e., imposing heavy taxes and forced labor and a hundred kinds of hardship in order to extract the nourishment of our people;

(ii) covert methods, i.e., using the façade of their sham civilization and sham education to destroy surreptitiously our people's spirit and extinguish their knowledge and sensibility.

The sequel in its first paragraph bitterly exposed the three main reasons for the loss of our country:

(i) the sovereign ignores the people;

(ii) the mandarins ignore the people; and

(iii) the people ignore their country.

The [modern Vietnamese] translation reads like this:

> *Một là vua, việc dân chẳng biết,*
> *Hai là quan chẳng biết gì dân.*

> *Ba là dân chỉ biết dân,*
> *Mặc quân với quốc, mặc thần với ai.*

— First, the king does not know the affairs of the people.
— Second, the mandarins know nothing about the people.
— Third, the people only care for themselves; they ignore the king, the country, and the mandarins.

This section reiterates a pathetic and poignant appeal. The middle section sets out in detail our strategy for saving Vietnam from extinction, making a fervent appeal to our people's feelings of patriotism and hatred toward the enemy. Its principal theme can be summed up in the idea of "bringing the whole country into one accord," which is broken down into ten categories:

  (i)   bringing the wealthy into one accord;
 (ii)   bringing the mandarins in office into one accord;
 (iii) bringing the children of the great families into one accord;
 (iv)   bringing the Christian population into one accord;
  (v)   bringing those serving in the army and the navy into one accord;
 (vi)   bringing all the parties into one accord;
 (vii) bringing the interpreters, clerks, and servants of the French into one accord;
(viii) bringing the women into one accord;
 (ix)   bringing the children of families massacred by the enemy into one accord;
  (x)   bringing the overseas students into one accord.

Throughout the ten categories of this section, the translation of Lê [Đại] succeeded in conveying powerfully the pathetic sentiments of the original. The passage on bringing the parties together, for example, reads [in the original text]:

> *As the stench of the wind smites his face,*
> *The forlorn hero feels helpless.*

> *Indignation fills his soul. Here is his vow:*
> *Heaven and Earth, bear witness to my heart!* [48]

When this book had been printed, I returned to Hong Kong again, to find a way to send it clandestinely back home and to receive the comrades who had just come overseas. It was then that I met Vũ-Mẫn-Kiến from Hanoi, along with Dương-Tự-Nguyên and Nguyễn-Thái-Bạt [alias Nguyễn-Phong-Di], who were newly arrived in Hong Kong. I asked two of them to stay over in Hong Kong and wait for the boat [on which Lý Tuệ worked] to take the books clandestinely to Vietnam.[49] The fact that this book was widely circulated in our country was largely attributable to Vũ-Mẫn-Kiến and Nguyễn-Thái-Bạt.

In Hong Kong at that time we set up a small meeting place. About four or five of our students were studying English there. The number of the overseas Vietnamese was very small; they were employees of the French and their total number was slightly more than forty. Among them there were three or four interpreters or clerks; the rest were cooks and houseboys. I met these people personally and, not without using the most vehement persuasion, tried to win them over. Among them there were one or two who were passionately moved and readily listened to me. I then founded an organization called *Việt-Nam Thương-Đoàn Công-Hội* (Vietnamese Commercial Association), to collect money in order to do business for the common benefit and to inculcate in our overseas Vietnamese the idea of solidarity for the

---

48. AM and CT give this passage in both Sino-Vietnamese and modern Vietnamese. TQP gives it only in modern Vietnamese. The modern Vietnamese, a vigorous free paraphrase of the original, may be rendered into English as follows:

> *The stench of the wind is hard for the nose to take.*
> *With a sword at your hip, how can you stand idly by?*
> *Indignant blood fills your heart.*
> *O brothers! Let us draw forth our swords!*
> *Here is Heaven, here is Earth, here are we.*
> *Unity of such a kind is true unity.*

49. AM identifies the boat as that of Lý Tuệ.

common interest. When the Association was founded, a clerk, Phạm-Văn-Tân, was nominated as its president. Phạm, from Nam-Kỳ, was well versed in English and French and had a fair idea of the world situation. His monarchical sentiments went particularly deep, that being a characteristic of the people from Nam-Kỳ.

When the Commercial Association was first established, the overseas Vietnamese in Hong Kong participated in it with alacrity. Even the Vietnamese who were working as sailors on French warships also made contributions to the Association. For some time its prospects looked very hopeful; but within a year, an interpreter for the French consulate,[50] who was an old hand at informing, reported to the governor-general in Hanoi that our association was a revolutionary body. The French authorities requested the governor of Hong Kong to order us peremptorily to dissolve. The Association therefore died prematurely. Alas! Our people without a country could find no place where they were free from the affliction of being oppressed by the right of brute force.[51]

THAT YEAR I SPENT the autumn and winter traveling back and forth between Yokohama and Hong Kong, Japan being the headquarters of the overseas students and Hong Kong being the channel for contacts between our country and outside. I had no alternative but to look after both places.

In the last decade of the Eleventh Month [January 1907], thinking that the number of overseas students was still very small and that there had been silence about revolutionary activities inside our country for some time, I began to feel a gnawing anxiety. I wanted to return to our country to take my part in the activities of the movement, but unfortunately there were no funds for travel. Luckily, just at

---

50. AM gives his name as Nhung.

51. In Sino-Vietnamese, *cường-quyền*; in Chinese, *ch'iang-ch'üan*—a key term often used in Chinese and Vietnamese writings at the beginning of the twentieth century to refer to the imperialist powers.

that time five youths arrived from Nam-định. There were Đặng-Xung-Hồng, Đặng-Tử-Mẫn, Đặng-Quốc-Kiều—the youngest of the five—and two others. The three mentioned above were likeable young men of good parts. The most passionate and energetic was Đặng-Tử-Mẫn. Đặng-Tử-Mẫn would in later days risk his life courageously for the cause of the revolution. After their arrival in Hong Kong, our local agent, Vũ-Mẫn-Kiến, took four of them to Japan and brought them to Yokohama to meet me. They delivered to me more than one thousand piasters for the movement. My travel plans were thus decided.

I estimated that this journey would require four or five months before I could return to Japan. The purpose of the journey was threefold:

(i) to make use of the occasion to reconnoiter the entire border of Kwangtung and Kwangsi contiguous with our country. Through examining this whole area I could plan a route to return to our country in later days;

(ii) from the border of Kwangsi, to pay a personal visit to the Phồn-xương guerrilla post for a meeting with Hoàng-Hoa-Thám to persuade him to join our revolutionary movement, because I had been unable to meet him before;

(iii) to make secret contacts with important personages in the movement in Trung-Kỳ and political activists in Bắc-Kỳ, in order to draw up together a plan of action for the revolution.

When my plan had been decided on, I set aside three hundred piasters[52] for travel expenses, leaving the remainder to support the studies of the young men at Bính-Ngọ-Hiên.

In the first decade of the Twelfth Month [14–23 January 1907], I went to Tokyo to bid farewell to the Marquis and the students who were enrolled in institutions there. On the same day, I set out for Kwangtung. I went directly to Liu Yung-fu's residence to meet with Nguyễn-Thiện-Thuật and let him know of my plan of going back to Vietnam.

52. AM (p. 81) gives "five hundred."

He personally saw me as far as Chinchow; there he introduced me to one of his former followers, called Tiền Đức. Tiền Đức had been originally a notorious pirate, styling himself "Supreme Commander of the Vanguard" *(Tiền-quân đô-thống)*. Later he threw in his lot with the Cần-Vương movement as a provincial commander-in-chief *(đề-đốc)*. After the collapse of the movement, he followed Liu Yung-fu and Nguyễn-Thiện-Thuật and retreated into China. He was not a man to be bound by convention. Once in China, he went back to his old trade and became the chief of a band of outlaws in the two Kwangs.

Nguyễn-Thiện-Thuật now said to me: "Along the border of the two Kwangs, the areas adjoining our country are full of dens of bandits. We must rely on this man as a guide to make it possible to pass through, because the bandits hold him in respect." I then discussed the matter with Tiền Đức, and he was entirely agreeable. In that way I ran the border of the two Kwangs; though the journey took more than a month, it was safe and without untoward incident. Tiền Đức was indeed my benefactor. Although he was one of the leading outlaws in the two Kwangs, whenever he met any Vietnamese coming or going he always did his best to protect them. His way of saying things was full of spirit and quite out of the ordinary: "It is better to be the comb of a cock than the tail of a water buffalo." As he traveled with me along the way, I deferred to him as being my elder, yet he still treated me with the courtesy accorded to a teacher. Looking back on this now, I am deeply moved.

When I first arrived in Kwangtung from Japan, I met two comrades from Bình-sơn, in Quảng-ngãi Province, who had just come from inside our country. I saw that they were persons endowed with passion and courage, and thus could be entrusted to shoulder important responsibilities. I thereupon said to them: "The aim of our present undertaking is revolution. But in order to bring about revolution, there must certainly be people inside the country to carry on the movement. Indeed, their importance is even double that of the students overseas, because the students overseas are cultivating the ability to construct, but the ability to destroy cannot possibly be looked for only from the students overseas." Both of them agreed enthusiastically to return to our country to work for the movement. I then took out some of the books I had written lately, such as *The History of the Loss of Vietnam, The New Vietnam, A Letter Written in Blood from Overseas,* etc., and *An Appeal Respectfully Addressed to the Elders* by the Marquis, and asked them to use them as materials for promoting the movement inside our country. The two accompanied me as far as Chinchow; there they parted from me to take a sailing ship heading for Tunghsing.

Tiền Đức and I, however, bade farewell to Nguyễn-Thiện-Thuật and followed the route west from Chinchow, passing through Hsiang-tzuchow and Hsiatzuchow to Taip'ing across the Kwangsi border. The commander of this district was Ch'en Shih-hua, a surviving member of the movement led by Hung Hsiu-ch'üan and Yang Hsü-ch'ing.[53] Ch'en had secretly made his way into our country to become a stalwart commander in the Black Flag army. Later he submitted to the Ch'ing authorities, and in view of his achievements in suppressing the local bandits was appointed commander of the Kwangsi border. He had great sympathy for the Vietnamese. As he had heard of me by reputation, on seeing Tiền Đức and me he was enormously pleased. Ch'en said: "I still have followers remaining inside Vietnam. Many of them have come into close contact with Hoàng-Hoa-Thám." I told him of my plan to go back to Vietnam to meet Hoàng; he willingly made the preparations for my journey, providing me with a travel permit and bodyguards; in addition he gave me a letter of introduction to his former lieutenant Lương-Tam-Kỳ. Lương originally had been a Vietnamese bandit;[54] now he had become one of the leading gentry *(hào mục)* in Thái-nguyên Province.

I rested for a few days in Taip'ing, then took to the road again. Out of concern for the bandits along the road, Ch'en specially dispatched

53. The Taip'ing Rebellion of 1850–1866.
54. AM and CT indicate that Lương worked for the Ngô Côn group. This information, however, is not included in the original text.

an officer with ten picked soldiers, fully armed, to escort the two of us through Lungchow and P'inghsiang to Ch'ennankuan. Ch'ennankuan is the frontier post, across from the town of Văn-uyên in Lạng-sơn Province in our country, where the Chinese officials and soldiers are stationed. Travelers passing through the post had to show their travel permit to the post officials, who then provided them instead with a passport so that they might proceed. As I was about to cross the border at the post, Tiền Đức and the soldiers who had escorted me from Taip'ing bade farewell to me and went back. The only one who accompanied me was named Ho.

No sooner had we crossed the border into our country than we came up to a French military post. A French major was checking all travelers very thoroughly. I went into the French officer's room. Seeing the passports issued to us by the Chinese authorities, he took it for granted that Ho and I were Chinese, and did not ask any troublesome questions. Nevertheless, my height and my appearance were carefully recorded and I was asked to pay three piasters to obtain an entrance visa. I left the post and took a train from Đồng-đăng, getting off at Gia-lâm[55] to change to the line in the direction of Thái-nguyên.

As I APPROACHED the border of Thái-nguyên Province, I realized that Lương-Tam-Kỳ exercised no little sway in those parts. All the mountain provinces were full of merciless bandits and notorious outlaws who frightened everyone passing through; but when they saw us dressed in Chinese style they said to each other: "They are going to see the big bosses—we had better not touch them." I heard that Lương-Tam-Kỳ had long been the man whose word was law in the Cao-bằng and Thái-nguyên areas. The French, when they had just taken over Bắc-Kỳ, regarded Cao-bằng and Thái-nguyên as dangerous and inaccessible, and, wishing to win over Lương-Tam-Kỳ, they appointed him to be their grand plenipotentiary for pacification *(Chiêu-phủ đại-sứ)*.

---

55. A northeastern suburb of Hanoi.

For this reason the local people called him the " grand official " *(đại-quan).*[56] This made me feel sorry for our people who, being ignorant as well as timid, felt obliged not only to fear those who were strong like the French, but also to tremble before a rascal of a Chinese expatriate as if he were a tiger!

After a day's walk I arrived in Thái-nguyên Province, then walked for another day to get to Chợ Chu where Lương-Tam-Kỳ had his fort. Previously, Officer Ho had mentioned me to Lương. Knowing that I had an introduction from Commander Ch'en Shih-hua, Lương was very eager to show me around the fort. As far as the morale of the troops and strictness of discipline were concerned, his fort could not be compared to the fort of Hoàng-Hoa-Thám at Yên-thế. But its supplies were more plentiful and its manpower more numerous. Nonetheless, Hoàng was holding out in an independent territory, whereas Lương was in a dependent area. In terms of value they were by no means equal.

When I first met Lương, I had thought of making use of his military support; but after seeing him and talking to him, I gathered that he was devoid of any great long-range aspirations and was simply a conspicuous figure among the outlaws. Unless the influence of our movement expanded and we received support from outside, he would certainly not be of any help to us. Because of this I was smitten by a sense of disappointment.

In spite of my disappointment, however, there was one hopeful thing. I met comrade Trần-Đông-Anh, alias Trần Thiện, from Sơn-tây Province. Trần had secretly joined our movement at the outset. Now we met each other again at Lương's fort. Trần had also come here in an attempt to win over Lương. As soon as he saw me, Trần introduced me to a close friend of his called Đề Công. Đề Công to begin with had been a renowned commander in the Cần-Vương movement; his accumulated exploits led to his being promoted to provincial commander *(đề-đốc),* and he was on very good terms with

---

56. In colloquial Vietnamese, *quan lớn.*

Hoàng-Hoa-Thám. After the movement failed, there were many who surrendered to escape punishment; among them were those such as Đề Kiều and the like, who curried favor and were appointed as officials. Hoàng-Hoa-Thám and Đề Công were the only two who would not give in. Hoàng went to Bắc-giang; Đề Công headed to Thái-nguyên, but by some fast footwork Thái-nguyên had already been occupied. Đề Công and a dozen or so of his followers had no choice but to take to farming and hunting for a living, concealing themselves in the area within the sphere of influence of Lương-Tam-Kỳ. He was treated by Lương as a friend and colleague, and the lackeys of the French authorities did not bother to search for him, for the French regarded Thái-nguyên as stony ground.

Trần asked me to go to Đề Công's home. Our conversation lasted for quite a while. I was struck by his high forehead, generous chin, and piercing eyes. Once in a while he slapped his thigh, saying: "I wish I could get the chance to have my saber stained once again with blood from the enemy's head; then this life of mine would be complete." One day he confided to me: "It is a long time since I have ridden a horse. My legs are getting out of shape. If I had the money, I would buy a horse." I immediately presented him with fifteen silver piasters, thinking that if we had occasion to engage in combat, he would make a good commander.

SOME TIME AFTERWARD, he dispatched his eldest son to guide me along the mountain roads in the direction of Bắc-giang. After two days' walk we entered Yên-thế, passing through the Nhã-nam market to reach Fort Phồn-xương. I showed Hoàng-Hoa-Thám a secret token that had been given to me by Đề Công; Hoàng was absolutely delighted. He lodged me at the post where his son Cả Huỳnh resided. The following day he had water buffalo killed and rice wine set out and his lieutenants summoned to hold a feast in my honor. Once before I had entered the fort, but this was the first occasion for me to shake hands and have an intimate conversation with Hoàng.

I stayed over at the fort for more than ten days and obtained secret undertakings from Hoàng on several things, as follows:

(i) He (Hoàng) would participate in the Vietnam Modernization Association and recognize the Marquis as its president.

(ii) Those who had participated in the Cần-Vương movement in Trung-Kỳ and lost their base of operations would be taken on by Hoàng.

(iii) In the event that Trung-Kỳ launched a patriotic uprising, Hoàng would rise up likewise.

These were the three things that I asked of Hoàng. He in turn asked of me the following:

(i) In the event that fighting broke out at Fort Phồn-xương, Trung-Kỳ would rise to support it.

(ii) In the event of hostilities, outside assistance would be provided through the agency of the Vietnam Modernization Association.

(iii) In the event that Fort Phồn-xương was in need of military supplies, the movement would help it to the utmost.

When both parties were satisfied with the negotiations, Hoàng picked out for me a small hill at the back of his immense fort for those in the movement from Trung-Kỳ to use as a base. Some time afterward, Tùng-Nham, Hoàng Hành, and others arrived at the fort and set up a separate little camp known as Đồn Tú-Nghệ.[57] This was the result of our agreement at that time.

SEVERAL DAYS LATER, my secret colleague Đặng-Văn-Bá from Hà-tĩnh and I took leave of Hoàng and moved on to Bắc-ninh to visit a certain comrade at Nội-duệ village.[58] Soon Ngư-Hải and Dật-Trúc

---

57. *Đồn* means "post" or "camp." *Tú*, an abbreviated form of *tú-tài*, indicates those who had passed the lower level of regional examinations (usually translated into English as "baccalaureate"). *Nghệ* stands for Nghệ-an. Taken together they literally mean "the post of the baccalaureates from Nghệ-an."

a certain comrade at Nội-duệ village.[58] Soon Ngư-Hải and Dật-Trúc arrived and made a report on the latest developments. It was secretly agreed that the key members of the movement from Trung-Kỳ and Bắc-Kỳ would meet to discuss the plan of action of the Vietnam Modernization Association. Then it was decided that we should be divided into two groups:

(i) The peaceful-action group would be in charge of schools, speeches, publicity, etc.

(ii) The militant-action group would concentrate their activities on appealing to the military and gathering weaponry to be ready for action.

As for those responsible for traveling about to maintain liaison, Vũ-Hải-Thu [Nguyễn-Hải-Thần] would take care of Bắc-Kỳ and Đặng-Tử-Kính would take care of Trung-Kỳ; the venerable Hải-Côn [Ngư-Hải] would look after groups on either side, bearing on one pair of shoulders the burdens of South and North. From then on our fundraising on behalf of the overseas students outside the country and our program of activities inside the country were both reliably maintained. The influence of the revolutionary party was expanding little by little from day to day.

IN THE THREE YEARS of the Sheep, the Monkey, and the Cock [1907–1909], the Đông-Kinh Nghĩa-Thục (Đông-Kinh Private School) was created in Hanoi;[59] commercial and educational associations sprang up like a forest everywhere in Quảng-nam and Quảng-ngãi; there was an attempt at poisoning the military cadets in Hanoi; in Hà-tĩnh, Vũ Phấn, Nguyễn Truyền, and others projected an attack on the city. Regrettably, the time was not ripe and our wings were not fully fledged, or our plan of action leaked out before it could be realized, or things that

---

58. AM indicates that he was a holder of the *cử-nhân* degree, presumably the only one in the village at the time.

59. On this school, see the Introduction, p. 12, n. 6.

were almost accomplished nonetheless suddenly turned into failure. The result was that countless men of high purpose were cut down; innumerable patriotic folk sacrificed their blood.

> *Pray ask me not of painful things that happened yester-*
> > *year;*
> *My helpless rage, recalling them, is more than I can bear.*

Even if it were said to me that my return to Vietnam this time wrought only evil and no good, I could find no way to deny it.

In the first decade of the First Month of the Year of the Sheep [February 1907], I returned to Hanoi. After staying there only one day and one night, I happened to meet Tập-Xuyên [Ngô-Đức-Kế], who had just come in from Nghệ-an to see me. By that time the Triều-Dương trading house had been established in Nghệ-an; but when I heard that those in the shop were indulging in the habit of talking about revolutionary activities, I was very worried. That was because it is impossible to have talk and action at the same place and the same time with the same effect. I did mention this point to Tập-Xuyên, but it was too late.

The following day, after I had seen Tập-Xuyên, the comrades urged me to go back to Japan again. In view of the fact that things had then hardly progressed beyond the embryonic stage and our future prospects were still in the dim distance, and as none of them wished me to sacrifice myself in vain, they pressed me to leave. I eagerly desired to make a trip back to Nghệ-Tĩnh, but this was totally out of the question.

Thus in the second decade of the First Month [late February/early March 1907], I took the train from Bắc-ninh bound for Lạng-sơn. I got off the train at Đồng-đăng station. With shabby clothes and frayed hat, my hair cut and beard shaved, I disguised myself as a Chinese peddler. I made my way into the Văn-uyên market and mingled with the market people; in a matter of a few minutes I had turned into a man of Ch'ennankuan across the border. Accompanying me were

Lý-Văn-Sơn and Lưu-Ấm-Sinh.[60] We stayed over at P'inghsiang for one night. The following day we walked all day to Lungchow, where many expatriate Vietnamese lived, but more than half of them were working as houseboys or cooks for the French merchants and officials there. Moreover, there was a French consulate in the place. I therefore dared not stay over, but rather hired a trading boat that very evening to move on from Lungchow to Taip'ing County. But Ch'en Shih-hua, the military commander, transferred me to a different boat bound for Nanning; everything necessary for my trip was provided by Ch'en. This was a token of the sympathy that the Chinese had for us. When the boat arrived at Nanning I transferred to a steamboat bound for Wuchow, then to a British merchant ship going on to Hong Kong.

I ARRIVED AT Hong Kong in the last decade of the Second Month [early April 1907]. Lưu-Ấm-Sinh eagerly wished to leave for Japan. This was because he had undertaken his journey at that time, on the instructions of Tiểu-La and Ô-Da [Trình Hiền], specifically in order to have an audience with the Marquis and obtain some kind of statement from me that he could bring back to help reconcile differences of opinion at home. At the outset, Tiểu-La and I and others had lent our support to the Marquis mainly out of a desire to make use of royalty to rally the sentiments of the general populace. But our real objective was to expel the French.[61] Nominal though the aforementioned cause might

---

60. AM indicates that the former was a native of Bắc-ninh and the latter of Thừa-thiên. "Lưu-Ấm-Sinh" could refer to a student with the family name of Lưu who was attending a state college in the expectation of inheriting his father's official post; but it could simply be a personal name. GB assumes the first alternative, and therefore translates as "l'étudiant Lưu" or "jeune Lưu."

61. It is noticeable that political circumstances could influence the translations of this passage. AM, presumably because of the pressures of the colonial government of the day, read: "our real objective was to restore the nation." TQP, just after the first Indochina war against the French, translated instead: "our real objective was to expel the French enemy." GB, turning TQP's version into French, softened this into "nôtre objectif principal étant le départ des Français."

be [i.e., the restoration of the monarchy], after I had gone overseas quite a lot of people responded to it. But after Tây-Hồ [Phan-Châu-Trinh] returned from Japan, he vigorously championed the position of "Up with Democracy, Out with Monarchy" *(Tôn-dân bài-quân)*. He vehemently assailed the monarchy without questioning the French regime, advocating a policy of "Making Use of the French in the Quest for Progress" *(Ỷ Pháp cầu tiến bộ)*. Public opinion all of a sudden began to be perplexed, and the risk of strife within the movement was imminent. The journey of Lưu-Ấm-Sinh to Japan was on that account.

I immediately left Hong Kong for Tokyo. By that time, Bính-Ngọ-Hiên had moved to Tokyo. The students from Nam-định had all obtained instructors so as to learn spoken and written Japanese for admission to school. When they saw me, they were all very pleased. I tried to look happy too, but deep in my heart I felt as miserable as a tangled skein of jute, because I was worried about the internal conflict within the movement.

I presently took Lưu to have an interview with the Marquis, while I myself wrote a letter that I asked Lưu to take home in an effort to obtain the support of Tây-Hồ. In this letter were the words: "If the nation no longer exists, how can it possibly have a master?" *(Dân chi bất tồn, chủ ư hà hữu)*, specifically aimed at tempering Tây-Hồ's opinion. I also discussed the matter with the Marquis, saying: "If arguments for abolishing the monarchy come to be spread about very widely, public sentiment in Trung-Kỳ and Bắc-Kỳ will soon become disconcerted. If public opinion is not united, funds cannot be hoped for. We should now make use of some sort of publication, which someone can take back to Nam-Kỳ, to wage a campaign for the collection of funds, taking advantage of the nostalgia there for the monarchy. Once ample funds have come in, it should be possible to take other matters in hand. Otherwise I am afraid that [the movement in] Trung-Kỳ and Bắc-Kỳ may collapse." The Marquis emphatically agreed with this. He then asked me to compose *Ai cáo Nam-Kỳ phụ lão văn* (A Sorrowful Appeal to the Elders of Nam-Kỳ).

When this had been printed, I could find nothing left for me to do in Japan for the moment; but as the maritime service between Hong Kong and Saigon was extremely convenient, there was certainly a need for me to return to Hong Kong to set up a connection to Nam-Kỳ. In the first decade of the Fourth Month [May 1907], I went back with Lưu to Hong Kong. First of all, I gave Lưu all the documents he was to take home surreptitiously. I then devoted myself to making arrangements for a route down to Nam-Kỳ.

After our arrival in Hong Kong, young men from Trung-Kỳ began to turn up one after another. Altogether, there were seven. They were people who had come to study overseas—without having any money. At that point I felt a need to test whether or not the determination of these students was firm. I put a hard question to them, saying: "It is indeed commendable that you have enough determination to go abroad to study. But study certainly requires funds. Since your families are poor, they cannot possibly help you. As for funds from the general public, because the influence of our movement is still minimal, how can we possibly obtain such funds? Are you content to study in the face of adversities—for example, like Wu Tzu-hsü, who played the flute for a living, or like Chu Mai-chen, who used to fetch wood to sell? Those who have determination will choose some such way."[62]

Among these seven, there was Nguyễn-Thái-Bạt, who spontaneously asked to be allowed to go and beg in order to study. I gave him twenty-two silver piasters to use to pay his boat fare to go to Japan. With great determination, he accepted and bade farewell.

---

62. Wu Tzu-hsü, who lived in the Ch'un Ch'iu period (late sixth century B.C.), was a native of Ch'u; after his father was killed by the king of Ch'u, he went through the humiliation of playing the flute in the streets to support himself, thereby giving rise to the use of "playing the flute" to mean "begging." Eventually he played a key role in helping the king of Wu to conquer Ch'u. (*Shih Chi* 66.) Chu Mai-chen was born in Wu in the late first century B.C.; his family was poor, so he had to sell wood to maintain himself. Later, under Han Wu-ti, he became the governor of Kuai-ch'i, and eventually special adviser to the prime minister. (*Hsien Han-hsu* 64.)

Nguyễn-Văn-Câu [alias Nguyễn-Văn-Cu] was still a child;[63] he stayed on in Hong Kong to study English, and the remaining five waited for funds to proceed on to Japan. Alas for Nguyễn-Thái-Bạt! Seeking a way to pursue his studies, he had to traverse the endless heaving billows of the ocean all by himself, and to reconcile himself to the mortification of begging; how great was the resolve of Nguyễn-Thái-Bạt at that time! But later, the Nguyễn-Phong-Di who came first in the court examination for the doctorate *(Đình-nguyên)* was the same man —how deplorable that was![64]

At this point, having a few decades of free time, I wrote *Tân Việt-Nam* (The New Vietnam). This book could be broadly divided into two parts, the first part dealing with the ten deep satisfactions *(thập đại khoái)* and the second with the ten earnest aspirations *(thập đại nguyện)*. The book was printed in a thousand copies. I also undertook a translation of the *Sorrowful Appeal to the Elders of Nam-Kỳ* into Vietnamese demotic characters, the opening passage of which reads:

> *Six Provinces of Nam-Kỳ, undertaking of ten thousand*
> *years! Alas, what's left?*
> *Fog-shrouded fields and rivers—who is there cannot feel*
> *his heart bereft?*

This was printed in some thousands of copies. I planned to use them as materials for publicity in Nam-Kỳ.

At that time, there was a Catholic upper primary school in Hong Kong in which one of our youths from Nam-Kỳ was enrolled, named Trần-Văn-Tuyết, who was a son of Governor [Gilbert Trần-Chánh-] Chiếu of Saigon. I often used to go to Tuyết's hall of residence to

---

63. A grandson of Nguyễn-Thiện-Thuật, he was seven years old at that time. [Author's note.]

64. Nguyễn-Thái-Bạt changed his name to Nguyễn-Phong-Di and passed first in the *tiến-sĩ* examination in the very last competition, that of 1919, thereafter collaborating with the colonial government. His story is related in Đặng-Thai-Mai's memoirs. The bitterness of Phan's disappointment at this man's desertion of the movement after his return to Vietnam is a measure of the high expectations Phan had formed of him; this connection is not made clear by TQP.

stir up ideas of revenge and patriotism. On his part, a secretary named Phạm also encouraged him to support the Nguyễn monarchy. Tuyết sent my writings in prose and poetry to his father[65] and invited him to come over to Hong Kong just for a visit. Some decades afterward, Governor Chiếu arrived. Then, a few months later, Trần-Văn-Định, Bùi-Mộng-Vũ, and others, one after another, came to Japan. From that point on, the number of students from Nam-Kỳ began to increase.

In the third decade of the Fifth Month [early July 1907], there arrived three more young men from Bắc-Kỳ—Cao-Trúc-Hải, Phạm-Chấn-Yêm, and Đàm-Kỳ-Sinh—and two young men from Trung-Kỳ —Nguyễn-Quỳnh-Lâm and Phan-Bá-Ngọc; they all accompanied me on to Japan. Later, Cao fell ill and died in Yokohama, and Phạm fell ill and died in Hong Kong. Nguyễn-Quỳnh-Lâm died in battle during the second Chinese Revolution [1916]. Đàm-Kỳ-Sinh returned to our country to organize a campaign to raise funds; he was arrested and died in prison in Cao-bằng. Both these latter two deserve great respect.

AFTER I HAD returned to Japan, suddenly the tragic news reached me that Tăng-Bạt-Hổ had died. Since the time I had gone abroad, this was the first news of a real disaster. Tăng had returned to our country for two reasons: first because he saw the difficulty of our position in Japan, and secondly because he was concerned that there was no source from which to pay our school expenses; he had therefore planned to resolve these problems. Only a little more than a year after his return, the movement had quite considerable achievements to its credit. Thus during the Year of the Horse and the Year of the Sheep [1906–1907], the fact that expenses for schooling, travel, and day-to-day activities could be sustained was indeed due to work of the men of high purpose in Trung-Kỳ and Bắc-Kỳ, but the person who brought them all together was Tăng. In the spring of the Year of the Horse [1906], from

---

65. TQP translates this passage as if Phan had asked the young man Tuyết to send his writings to his father. The original text, followed by AM, gives the sense translated above.

Bắc-Kỳ he went throughout Thanh-hóa, Nghệ-an, Hà-tĩnh, and Quảng-bình, resting during the daytime and traveling at night. Physically and mentally exhausted, he arrived in the capital, Thuận-hóa [Huế], in the winter. He had intended to proceed farther south to Quảng-nam and Quảng-ngãi, and then on to Nam-Kỳ to make the campaign nationwide. Who would have expected Heaven to be so jealous that the undertaking could not be carried out as he wished? When he arrived at the home of Võ-Bá-Hạp in An-hòa, he became seriously ill. Võ rented a small boat so that he could stay at the mouth of the river, and took care of him day and night; but it was on this boat a few decades later that he breathed his last. Alas! It was thanks to him that I was able to travel overseas; yet he would never ask me, even once, to do any favor for him in return. His great aspiration was not achieved; his prospects were cut off. How cruel the Creator can be! Later on, when I wrote *Việt-Nam nghĩa-liệt sử* (The History of the Martyrs of Vietnam), it was not from personal favoritism that I placed the biography of Tăng-Bạt-Hổ at the beginning.

Tăng's death prompted me to write *Kỷ-niệm-lục* (A Record of Memories), in which I first recounted Tăng's biography, followed by that of Vương-Thúc-Quý, the son of Vương-Mậu-Tài. Vương[-Mậu-Tài][66] responded at the outset to the imperial proclamation of the Cần-Vương movement and became the local commander *(bang-biện)* of the patriotic forces; he died in action. Vương-Thúc-Quý fell heir to his father's aspiration, which remained unachieved when he died, a month after Tăng's death. In the last moments of his life, he wrote eight characters to Ngư-Hải [Đặng-Thái-Thân]:

> *With vengeance for my father yet undone,*
> *For nothing has my mortal course been run.*

Alas! How regrettable it was!

I had written *A Record of Memories* and was about to have it printed when it suddenly occurred to me that there had been heroic

---

66. AM refers to this man as Cố Bang ("Old Bang") from Kim-liên village.

figures in recent years whom I had known and whose names ought to be commemorated, such as Cao Thắng, Đội Hợp, and Quản Báo. Báo hurled himself into the fray with a dagger and killed the enemy commander Một Phiến to avenge his former master Cao Thắng. I collected their stories from beginning to end, roughly arranged them as a series of biographies, and called it *Sùng-bái giai-nhân* (A Tribute to Shining Lives).

At the end of the last page of *A Record of Memories*, there was an appendix added entitled " Khoái-văn nhất-tắc " (" Welcome News "), in which the welcome news was that Prefect *(Tri-huyện)* Lương had come overseas [to study]. Lương-Văn-Thành, who at the time was head of one of the prefectures, had hung up his seal, quitted his official post, and left the country to look around for us in Hong Kong or Yokohama. I did not know much about the motives behind this, but according to Nguyễn-Hải-Thần he was a man of high purpose. Because I urgently wanted to rally the incumbent officials to action, in what I wrote I overcomplimented Lương. Lương stayed in Hong Kong for only half a year; then his wife arrived to take him home. I regretted the mistake that I had made in writing "Welcome News," but it had already been printed and it was impossible to retrieve it for destruction. Through this I learned a good lesson: In dealing with a person or an event, one cannot believe someone else's word without having seen clearly for oneself; one cannot judge solely from the present without taking the past and the future into account. The Lương affair was indeed good medicine for me after I had cut my hands.

BY THE SEVENTH MONTH of that year [August/September 1907], the strength of the T'ung-meng-hui, China's revolutionary party, had increased greatly. Its periodicals bureau in Tokyo was producing several dozen publications, among which *Yunnan Tsa-chih* (The Yunnan Review) was the organ for those members of the party from Yunnan living in Japan. Thinking that one day in the future I should certainly be returning to Vietnam through Yunnan, I wished to obtain support from them in advance. I introduced myself to the editorial director, Chao Chi-chai, volunteering to become an editorial contributor. Such articles in this journal as " Ai-Yüeh tiao-T'ien " ("Lament for Vietnam and Dirge for Yunnan") and "Yüeh-wang ts'an-chang" ("The Sad State of Vietnam in Ruins ") were all written by me.[67] As a result, the members of the revolutionary party from Yunnan were highly sympathetic to our movement. At that time, however, because their strength was still minuscule, the only way they could support us was through their writings.

As I had more dealings with members of the Chinese revolutionary party, democratic ideas impinged on me more deeply day by day. Although I was restricted by our original plan and not able to speak out loud, from that time there was implanted in my heart the seed that would eventually give rise to change. I then wrote a book entitled *Hoàng-Phan-Thái* giving an account of the failure of the revolt of Hoàng-Đại-Hữu. In the book I pointed out in detail the wicked conduct of Emperor Tự-Đức. At that time Hoàng-Phan-Thái was regarded as guilty of disloyalty and high treason, but I wrote him up in a big way, calling him " the precursor of the revolution." That was because I wished to use this book to sound out the currents of opinion among the youth, and then I would come up with a plan to influence their ideas.

WHEN THIS BOOK had been printed, I received a letter from Hong Kong saying that several elders from Nam-Kỳ had arrived there who wished to see me urgently to discuss things, and had to return home as soon as possible. Because they had come to Hong Kong clandestinely, they could not stay there long, as any delay might cause problems. In the first decade of the Eighth Month [early September 1907], I left Yokohama carrying with me five books: *The New Vietnam, A Record of Memories, A Tribute to Shining Lives, Hoàng-Phan-Thái,* and the previously published *A Sorrowful Appeal to the Elders of Nam-Kỳ,* of

---

67. In Sino-Vietnamese, the titles read " Ai Việt điếu Điền " and " Việt-vong thảm-trạng."

which I still had several hundred copies. I put them in my suitcase and went off to Hong Kong.

When I arrived, the councillor *(hội-đồng)* of Mỹ-tho, the head of the township *(chánh-tổng)* of Cần-thơ, and the village official *(hương-chức)* of Long-hồ had been waiting for me for more than ten days. I went to their lodgings and handed over to them the various booklets for distribution. In addition, I particularly requested them to do two things: (i) to encourage students to come overseas; (ii) to collect donations for school fees. All gladly promised to do their best. They then immediately bade farewell to me and went home.

A few decades later, several dozen youths from Nam-Kỳ arrived; among them there were three children under ten years of age brought over by Trần-Văn-Định. These were Trần-Văn-An, Trần-Văn-Thư, and Hoàng-Vĩ-Hùng; they were the youngest among the overseas students. Seeing that those who had just arrived from Vietnam were not yet used to traveling, and that the permanent secretary of our organization in Hong Kong, Vũ-Mẫn-Kiến, could not possibly leave our office there for a moment, I personally took the group to Japan.

The number of the youths who had successively arrived from Nam-Kỳ amounted to more than forty. The youths from Trung-Kỳ and Bắc-Kỳ were more than sixty or seventy. All of them went together with me on a Japanese boat going to Yokohama. This was the biggest group from our country that ever set off for Japan; moreover, people from the Three Regions were all on the same boat, a wonderful thing indeed, which had never happened in previous history.

IN THE THIRD DECADE of the Eighth Month [late September/early October 1907], we arrived in Tokyo. At that time there were already more than a hundred persons at Bính-Ngọ-Hiên. Those who had arrived previously had already been learning the Japanese language for half a year and could move on to further study, yet those who had just arrived were all eager to start studying immediately; if they were expected to live anywhere but in the house, they would feel left out.

While I was frantically trying to arrange admission for the students, all sorts of troublesome problems came up:

(i) Our students who were enrolled in private academic institutions had programs and curricula that were not fully adequate, and there was no military training, which was contrary to the purpose of our studies. As for the national academic institutions, our students wished to enter them, but without having a certificate from the authorities, they could on no account be admitted.

(ii) Our students who had not studied the Japanese language would certainly need to practice Japanese, but in Japanese institutions there were no programs for learning the Japanese language. Without comprehending Japanese, how could they possibly study other subjects?

(iii) Our students' expenses made it necessary for us to have regular funding, but currently our finances had no firm basis and were wholly dependent on donations from home, which it would be unreasonable to hope would continue indefinitely.

None of these problems was easy to resolve. If we wished to resolve the first two problems, it would be impossible without asking for help from prominent Japanese.

For this reason I visited Inukai Tsuyoshi. Inukai took me to see General Fukushima to discuss measures to help the Vietnamese students. At the outset of the discussion I expressed our wish to increase the number of our students in the Shimbu Gakkō. Fukushima replied: "In my acquaintance with you gentlemen, strictly on an individual basis it is possible for me to show my good friendship. But in my capacity as Chief of the General Staff it is impossible to do so, because according to diplomatic practice the government of an imperial power certainly cannot overtly cooperate with a revolutionary party of another country. The admission of four of your students at the Shimbu Gakkō some time ago was already a great breach of that rule. To increase that number now is impossible, because this is an institution established by the state; to accept your students would certainly give the

French government an excuse to make a protest, which would cause trouble for the diplomacy of our government, and also would be of no benefit to you. A better course of action for you would be to seek support from the Tōa Dōbun Kai (Common East Asian Culture Society), because this is a society that has been organized by a political party. One political party may help another political party; there is no need for the government to ask questions. That is what would be best."

When Fukushima had made this statement, he looked at Inukai and asked: "The Vietnamese who have left their country [to come to Japan] are increasing in number day by day. What do you think will be the result?" Inukai replied: "The present prospect seems just fine, but we cannot tell if they are able to persevere and be patient for a long time or not."

Fukushima then said: "I am a military man. I shall only speak about strategic concerns. Should the Vietnamese go to war against France, the greater chance of winning would be with the Vietnamese. The reason is that Vietnam is a rather tropical land, and the people are acclimatized to heat. The French soldiers are people from a cold country. If the sky burns and the land is scorched, then the fighting power of the French would certainly be inferior to that of the Vietnamese. This possibility for winning comes from the Heaven-given climate *(thiên-thời)*. The dispatch of troops from Europe would necessarily be by sea; but in Vietnam the only military harbor which might be accessible for big battleships is the port of Cần-giờ. If one used a great fleet to blockade it, the route for the dispatch of troops from Europe would be cut off. This possibility for winning comes from geographical advantage *(địa-lợi)*. What is unknown as yet is only whether the people's heart *(nhân-tâm)* is there. If you [Vietnamese] can be patient and persevering, then one can hope for the restoration [of your independence]."

I said: "It is not that the people lack heart; it is only that they do not yet have sufficient strength, therefore they are not able to show it." Fukushima then said: "That is nothing to worry about. The people's heart is the greatest of forces. If one wishes to see what the people's heart is like, one should go by whether or not the people are able to endure hardship and withstand suffering. Japan was able to defeat Russia for many reasons, but the most important reason was that the Japanese were patient, and were able to endure hardship and withstand suffering. You must have read the Japanese newspapers and know that when the war against Russia ended in victory, every newspaper traced the cause of the victory to pickled radish." (Pickled radish is a most popular item among Japanese foods.) "What people said about that was not a joke. In our country the land is meager and the people are poor; supplies were extremely scarce and war requisitions extremely heavy for two years. Imagine if the Japanese soldiers had insisted on eating beef and drinking milk like the Russians—how could they possibly have held out? Only because they were satisfied with pickled radish and *soba* (dark noodles) could they score a victory at the end of the day."

At this point in the conversation, the maid brought in a plate of roasted sweet potatoes. Having invited me to partake, Fukushima took one first and ate all the skin; he then laughed and said to us: "We are military men; if we were squeamish about eating the skin, how could we eat the flesh of the enemy on the battlefield?"

Through our conversation at this time, a school curriculum was worked out comprising (i) specifically military studies and (ii) studies in general subjects. Both of the above were to be entrusted to the Common East Asian Culture Society, and the schooling was to take place in the Tōa Dōbun Shoin (Common East Asian Culture Institute), which would reserve a large area especially for our students.

In view of these arrangements, I was then introduced by Fukushima and Inukai to the chairman of the Society, Marquis Nabeshima, and its director, Marquis Hosokawa. These two were both formerly daimyō; now they were important members of the House of Peers. Two others were present as well: Nezu Hajime, secretary-general of the Society, and his secretary, Tsuneya Morikoto. They all agreed to do their best on our behalf.

The name of their school was Tōa Dōbun Shoin (Common East Asian Culture Institute).[68] In the Institute, five rooms were specially set aside to facilitate the studies of our students. The principal of the Institute, Kashiwabara Buntarō, was formerly Japan's vice-minister of education and currently a member of the House of Representatives. The instructor in charge of literature was Jū Tatsuya, who held a bachelor's degree from the Faculty of Letters of the Tokyo Imperial University. The instructor in charge of military science was Major Tamba [*sic*], who previously, while serving as a major, had taken part in the Russo-Japanese War, but by now had retired and assumed the rank of lieutenant-colonel in the Reserve Army.[69] The school day at the Institute was divided into two sessions, morning and afternoon. In the first half of the day, apart from the Japanese language, general subjects were taught, such as mathematics, geography, history, chemistry, physics, ethics, and so on. In the second half of the day military studies were taught, with particular attention paid to military drill.

Responsibilities were now settled: Programs and regulations within the Institute would be dealt with by the Japanese; matters outside the Institute would be dealt with by our people. Because of this, it was necessary for us to reorganize our own ranks. In addition to the main body of the Vietnam Modernization Association, we also organized an association called the Việt-Nam Công-Hiến-Hội (Vietnam Constitutional Association). While the Vietnam Modernization Association brought together all the members of the movement, the Vietnam Constitutional Association was an association specifically for the overseas students [in Japan].

---

68. In Sino-Vietnamese, *Đông-Á Đồng-Văn Thư-Viện*.

69. The person referred to is one Naniwada Noriyoshi; the name "Tamba" seems to have been given to him mistakenly by Phan because of a confusion with the first two characters of Naniwada's actual name. The only source for this individual's career appears to be the brief reference in Kuzuu Yoshihisa, *Tōa senkaku shishi kiden* (Spectacular Histories of Pioneering Men of High Purpose in East Asia) (Tokyo: Kokuryūkai, 1935), II, 820.

There were, all told, four committees in the Association: (i) the economic committee, (ii) the disciplinary committee, (iii) the external relations committee, and (iv) the secretariat. The president was the Marquis; the secretary-general, who was at the same time the director, was Phan-Bội-Châu. The membership of each of the four committees consisted of individuals selected from the Three Regions. Members of the economic committee were Đặng-Tử-Mẫn, Đặng-Bỉnh-Thành, and Phạm-Chấn-Yêm, who were in charge of keeping account of the revenues and overseeing the expenditures. Members of the disciplinary committee were Đàm-Kỳ-Sinh, Phan-Bá-Ngọc, and Hoàng-Quang-Thành, who were in charge of keeping track of the achievements and demerits of the students and making suggestions for commendations or penalties. Members of the external relations committee were Phan-Thế-Mỹ, Nguyễn-Thái-Bạt, Lương-Lập-Nham, and Lâm-Quảng-Trung,[70] who were in charge of dealing with foreigners and welcoming and sending off those from our country. Members of the secretariat were Hoàng-Trọng-Mậu, Đặng-Ngô-Lân, and Hoàng-Hưng, who were in charge of conserving and issuing all documents. In addition to the above committees, we also set up an inspection group to assess whether or not the members of the committees were doing their jobs as well as expected. Lương-Lập-Nham, Nguyễn Điển, and Trần-Hữu-Công were assigned for this task.

An accounting of the funds that had been forwarded from home at that time showed that Nam-Kỳ was at the top of the list and Trung-Kỳ was next, followed by Bắc-Kỳ. The total was more than ten thousand piasters, which was apportioned for three purposes: (i) to provide for the expenses of the students; (ii) to provide for the living expenses of the members of the movement not in school; (iii) to pay the common expenses on special occasions. For each student, the monthly allowance was eighteen piasters. For the president, the allowance was thirty-six piasters. For the secretary-general-cum-director, the allowance was twenty-four piasters. The members of the various committees did not

70. AM and TQP omit Lương-Lập-Nham's name.

receive any extra subsidy apart from their academic allowance for doing their assigned duties. When the members of the committees, even though they had been assigned to a regular duty, could not fulfill it owing to a busy study schedule, the secretary-general would carry it out on their behalf.

On Sunday every week there was a general meeting of all the members at once. We borrowed the Institute assembly hall to hold these sessions. First the president, then the secretary-general would deliver addresses of admonition to the students; following that, any member of the Association was free to speak. In this way, communication and a sense of solidarity were to be promoted. The above is an outline description of the Vietnam Constitutional Association.

The Vietnam Constitutional Association was established in the middle decade of the Ninth Month in the Year of the Sheep [October 1907]. All our youths were then admitted to the Institute. Thereafter, those newly arriving from home were sent straight to the Institute, because in the Institute we had special Japanese language classes. Once the Vietnam Constitutional Association had been set up, all the youths had a place to study and to live, and there was an appearance of quite good order. Every week without fail there were several days on which Major Tamba [*sic*] would take the youths out to the fields to do exercises in military drill. The fathers of the students from Nam-Kỳ who came to visit us all seemed delighted, but unfortunately, deep in my heart there were two things about which I was very anxious: (i) how to create a cohesive bond among the students; (ii) how to continue financial support.

As to the former, the people from the Three Regions up until then had not come into contact with each other; moreover, their temperaments and habits were quite dissimilar. Those from Nam-Kỳ tended to be forthright and honest but short tempered; in addition they could be strongly susceptible to material considerations. Those from Trung-Kỳ tended to be loyal and impetuous and liked adventure, but their

manners were crude and there was a feeling that it was hard for them
to blend in well. Those from Bắc-Kỳ were effusive in speech but fell
short in sincerity. Though among each of the groups there were excellent elements, for these streams to merge together was indeed difficult.
For more than a year I was acutely troubled, but I could not speak
out, and I feel painfully ashamed that my talent and virtue were so unequal to bringing about any improvement. Fortunately, from the winter
of the Year of the Sheep to the autumn of the Year of the Monkey
[1907–1908], the state of disunity had not as yet come to the surface.
During this period there was, so to speak, sufficient material to patch
up the holes; our achievements made up for our shortcomings. That
was thanks to the parents of our youths, through the influence of the
upbringing they had given them at home and the bountifulness of their
assistance, which was indeed enormous.

As to the latter source of anxiety, because our overseas finance
had no firm basis, we had to depend on donations from home, yet the
resources at home were terribly exiguous. The only funds for education
that were quite plentiful were those from Nam-Kỳ; thanks to that, we
could, as it were, draw out from them to top up the others. Therefore,
our attention was concentrated on campaigning for funds in Nam-Kỳ.
Among our students at the time, those from Nam-Kỳ were the most
numerous, and the fact was that we had to place our hope for support
on Nam-Kỳ.

From the beginning of the Tenth Month of the Year of the Sheep
until the Sixth Month of the Year of the Monkey [November 1907–July
1908], a succession of students entered school; altogether they numbered approximately two hundred. Of these, the students from Nam-
Kỳ were about one hundred, from Trung-Kỳ more than fifty, and from
Bắc-Kỳ more than forty. It was rumored that there were many more
still trying to follow in their footsteps. Had the path before us been
smooth and unobstructed, and had our support continued to increase
day by day, there is no telling how great the undertakings of the Vietnam Modernization Association and the achievements of the Vietnam

Constitutional Association might have been. But all of a sudden the students were to be dispersed; all of a sudden would come the order that the Marquis and I were to be expelled. The Vietnam Constitutional Association was thus brought to an end, and the Vietnam Modernization Association came to exist merely in name. The night-blooming cereus blossomed but for a moment;[71] the sickle moon was not to become a full orb as yet. The time was not prepared, and our human endeavors, also, were still inadequate.

Nonetheless, in this period there were several things that may well be recorded:

(i) the welcoming and sending off of the benevolent elders from Nam-Kỳ;

(ii) the welcoming of Mai-Lão-Bạng;

(iii) the welcoming of Nguyễn-Thượng-Hiền;

(iv) the generosity of Asaba Sakitarō of Japan;

(v) the first stage in our relations with Siam;

(vi) the brief drama of Trần-Đông-Phong, a man of high purpose who died a martyr for our country.

BEFORE THE FIRST MONTH of the Year of the Monkey [February/early March 1908], there had been many elders from Nam-Kỳ who, having received my *Appeal Respectfully Addressed to the Elders throughout the Country* and the Marquis's *A Sorrowful Appeal to the Elders of Nam-Kỳ*, had come overseas but only called at Hong Kong and then returned. But now there were several elders who came all the way to Japan, bringing many youths along with them. The most dedicated among these elders included Nguyễn-Thành-Hiến,[72] Trần-Văn-Định, and Hoàng-Công-Đán. I took them to the Institute to have

71. In Vietnamese *hoa đàm* or *ưu-đàm*, in Chinese *t'an-hua* or *yu-t'an; Hylocereus undatus*, also known as queen-of-the-night, a variety of flowering cactus with a stalk more than a meter (3.28 feet) in height, whose large and beautiful white flower appears only on one early evening during summer and withers before dawn.

72. Also known as Nguyễn-Thần-Hiến.

a look at the classrooms and the exercise ground for the students. They were all very pleased, and willingly undertook the task of collecting funds on their return home.

Around the middle decade of the First Month [February 1908], we gathered together all the students and held a farewell party for the elders. The elders from Nam-Kỳ were profoundly steeped in monarchical ideas and showed impeccable deference toward the Marquis. Their zeal in collecting funds sprang from their sincere feelings. Regrettably, in spite of their passionate devotion to the just cause, the way in which they conducted affairs was still extremely childish. At the beginning of the Fourth Month [early May 1908], those who had returned home from Japan sent a secret message to Tokyo through the Saigon post office. The message ran: "The people rallying to your just cause in Nam-Kỳ have collected more than ten thousand piasters,[73] but do not know how to transmit them. Would His Excellency and yourself be kind enough to instruct us what to do?"

Upon receiving this message, I was more alarmed than pleased, because I was afraid that the message had come under the eyes of the French. This news was not only empty of happiness but a harbinger of imminent calamity. But what, after all, was I to do? I had no other choice than to come up with a plan to look for a needle on the seabed. Thinking that there was no way for such a huge amount to be transmitted except through a bank, but that it would be impossible for a Vietnamese to arrange for its transmission, I hit upon the idea of asking for help from the Chinese revolutionary party. Fortunately, at that time Huang Hsing, one of its leading figures, happened to be staying in Japan. Huang Hsing and I had known each other previously. I went to see Huang to ask for his suggestions. Huang wrote a letter to authorize Feng Chi-yu, a member of the financial committee of the revolutionary party who was then in Saigon, to act on our behalf. Huang asked me to send someone back to our country to carry this letter to Feng and ask him to take care of the matter.

---

73. In TQP and GB the figure is inflated to two hundred thousand piasters.

The funds would be transmitted to Huang and Huang would transfer them to me.

Thus the plan was made; I thought it was the best one possible. Among the students from Nam-Kỳ I selected two persons, namely Hoàng-Quang-Thành and Đặng-Bỉnh-Thành. Đặng was well versed in the French language and familiar with Chinese characters, and possessed a calm and resolute temperament. Hoàng liked adventures and often volunteered to play the part of a man of action. These two were outstanding among the youth from Nam-Kỳ. Now that they had received the order to return home, they bore quite a grave responsibility, as it was expected that the first step toward solving the financial problems of the Vietnam Modernization Association would be achieved by their journey.

The two were smuggled onto a British ship to go back from Hong Kong to Saigon. But as soon as they arrived at the pier, the French officials made an extremely thorough check; the two were discovered, arrested, and escorted to the police station. All the documents they were carrying were confiscated, and they were condemned to three years' imprisonment.

Previously the French authorities had heard that a good number of youths had gone abroad; however, when they had questioned the youths' parents, all had adamantly replied that they were not aware of the whereabouts of their children. But now that Đặng and Hoàng had been arrested, the French authorities all at once became apprised of the details of the movement. It happened that, just prior to that time, Japan and France had concluded a treaty.[74] The diplomatic situation had thus been entirely changed; the Japanese would give in to whatever France demanded. One day the Japanese military police, on the order of the Ministry of Home Affairs, showed up at the Institute to find out the exact names and addresses of the students, and said: "On the request of the French Embassy, each student must write a letter home, to be sent through the Japanese police. Otherwise, he will be turned over to

---

74. The Franco-Japanese treaty was concluded on 10 July 1907.

the French Embassy." The Institute in an instant became a scene of panic.

Within a few decades, the students were receiving letters from their parents describing in detail the sufferings that they were undergoing in prison, and urging their children to return home immediately and submit to the authorities. At the outset, the youths from Nam-Kỳ had come overseas because they had been caught up in our movement, without any definite objective. Now that the movement was falling to pieces, they came to me to ask for money to return home. At first, I kept trying to talk them out of it and firmly refused to provide money, as I thought that if the students were dispersed, the result would be catastrophic for the state of affairs within our country.

This situation dragged on for several months. Then, in the Ninth Month of the Year of the Monkey [late September/October 1908], some of our students graduated from the Shimbu Gakkō.[75] The celebration party on their behalf was being organized when an order to disperse the students arrived. Greatly dismayed by the news, I hastened to ask for help from Inukai and Fukushima. They said to me: "This thing was done by order of the Ministries of Home Affairs and Foreign Affairs. We have no way to change it. But it is only a temporary measure. If the students disperse to the provinces and are prepared to lead a life of hardship while pursuing their studies, we may be able to come up with some means to restore the previous state of affairs." I went to the Institute to summon the students, asking them to come to my lodgings and discuss plans for them to stay on in Japan and work while pursuing their studies. But among the youth from Nam-Kỳ, everybody vehemently pleaded to return home, including some who burst into tears and some who became ill. There were only two students who did not want to go home, Hoàng [Hưng] and Nguyễn-Xương-Chi, and the three children.

---

75. TQP specifies that there were three who graduated: Lương-Lập-Nham, Trần-Hữu-Công, and Nguyễn Điển.

At that point there were two difficult problems. One was the expenses for sending students back, and the other was the expenses to provide for those who were staying on. The expenses of those staying on could be deferred for a little while, but the expenses for sending students back were of burning urgency. From the Sixth Month [late June/July 1908] up until that time, no funds had arrived from home, while the money saved by the Vietnam Constitutional Association had all been exhausted. Four or five thousand piasters were needed all at one time to cover travel overland and by ship; what an enormous difficulty! Having no other way, we explained the whole situation and asked for help from the key members of the Common East Asian Culture Society and the Association of Kwangsi-Yunnan Students in Japan. After about ten days of running around and crying for help, we received the best possible help from Inukai, which resulted in the Nippon Yūsen [Kabushikigaisha] (Japanese Steamship Company) donating one hundred tickets from Yokohama to Hong Kong, while Inukai himself gave two thousand piasters in cash. The funds for sending students home could be gradually paid back. I assembled all the students to announce that those who wished to return home would be supplied with funds.

EVENTUALLY, we had only five students from Nam-Kỳ who wished to stay on. Trần-Văn-Thư later graduated from Waseda University. Trần-Văn-An later went to Siam and died of tuberculosis. Hoàng-Vĩ-Hùng later entered the Peking Military Academy in China but died when he was about to graduate. Hoàng Hưng stayed on in Japan and worked in order to study for half a year; later he went to Hong Kong and strove with heart and soul to be a man of action. For manufacturing explosives, he was arrested by the British authorities, handed over to the French, and sent to Poulo Condore. As of now he has been returned to his village. Among the youth from Nam-Kỳ at that time, Hoàng Hưng was indeed like an eagle among sparrows. Nguyễn-Mạch-Chi [Nguyễn-Xương-Chi] later went to Hong Kong and accompanied the

Marquis on his journey to Europe; eventually he returned home, and I do not know his whereabouts now.

Among the students from Trung-Kỳ and Bắc-Kỳ who wished to remain, the most prominent were the following.

OF THOSE FROM Bắc-Kỳ, Đặng-Tử-Mẫn was the most dedicated individual among all the students from our country. He was a native of Nam-định. He stayed on in Japan and worked in order to study for about half a year. Then he was expelled from Japan. He went to China, roaming about in Hong Kong, Yunnan, Kwangsi, and Kwang-tung. He became acquainted with members of the Chinese revolutionary party and leaders of the outlaws, mixing in well wherever he went. On several occasions he was in command of insurrections on the border of Vietnam [with China]. Though he failed time after time, his chivalrous resolve only became firmer. In Hong Kong, while he was making smokeless gunpowder and explosives, some gunpowder went off and he was almost killed. Luckily, two of the fingers on his right hand still remained, and he was able to carry on as usual. Again in Hong Kong, he was imprisoned for six months for transporting arms. He also roamed about the border of Siam with the intention of entering Trung-Kỳ; regrettably, there were many French agents, and the power of the Vietnamese community in Siam was still weak, so that he was unable to fulfill his objective. He was often at my side. Once he had to beg for food in the countryside of Siam,[76] but he showed absolutely no sign of despair. Even though success eluded him, he was a true revolutionary in failure.

Cao-Trúc-Hải, a native of Hanoi, originally had attended a French medical school in order to pursue a career in medicine. He was quite well versed in French and had translated "A Journey to Yunnan" from the French for publication in the *Yunnan Review*. Following the dispersal of the students, he went to Yokohama to work as a clerk

---

76. AM and TQP add "for three days."

for a Western shop. Unfortunately, he caught smallpox and died in Yokohama. He was richly endowed with patience. At the time when he had just left the school, having no funds to live on and not being willing to return home, he worked for a Japanese inn as a cook. His noble desire was not fulfilled; Heaven did not grant him the blessing of a ripe old age. How regrettable it was!

Hoàng-Đình-Tuân, a native of Hanoi originally known as Nguyễn-Kế-Chi, went to Japan when he was fourteen years old. In the Institute's classes in spoken and written Japanese, he was the most brilliant student. When the school was closed he stayed on in Japan and for one year worked in order to study. He made the acquaintance of some Chinese students in Japan; the Chinese liked him and introduced him to the Chinese ambassador in Japan. He was naturalized as a person from Kwangsi and became a scholarship student. He passed the examination to enter Japanese high school, from which he graduated in five years. He then passed the examination to enter a Japanese teacher training college, from which he graduated with distinction. After that he went to China, taught at a Chinese high school in Peking, and in addition took charge of the *Journal* of the Peking chapter of the East Asia Common Culture Society as a member of the editorial board. He was both erudite and eloquent, highly proficient in the English and Japanese languages, and well versed in German and French.

Over a number of years, whenever I was in Peking, my contacts with the diplomatic circle owed much to his assistance. He was a close friend of the secretary of the Russian ambassador, Joffe,[77] and on the several occasions that I went to talk with Vorestch,[78] the consul at the German legation and a prominent figure among the diplomatic corps, he was my interpreter. Even though he was passionate and a

---

77. The Bolshevik politician Adolf Joffe (1883–1927) served as Soviet envoy in China in the years 1922 and 1923; he encouraged cooperation between the Communists and Sun Yat-sen's Nationalists.

78. This transliteration is the one given by GB. In the list of the diplomatic corps in China at this time, the German envoy extraordinary and minister plenipotentiary is identified as a Dr. Boyé.

firm character, his demeanor was extremely conciliatory; through weal and woe, through thick and thin, he always stood by his friends; in the midst of adversity and suffering he was always cheerful. Six years ago the Phan-Bá-Ngọc group used honeyed words to solicit him to return home to take up a teaching position at the École Normale; his brother, a *cử-nhân* graduate, also wrote him to urge him to return, but he refused everything. Regrettably, his physique was chronically weak; after staying in Peking for a long time, he could not withstand the chilly climate and died of tuberculosis two years before I was brought back home. With his death, diplomatic talent lost an experienced hand, and I lost a bosom friend. What a fate!

Lương-Lập-Nham, after the school was closed, went to China. As a graduate of the Shimbu Gakkō, he was admitted to the Canton School of Munitions, then entered the Peking Military Academy; on both occasions he was a scholarship student of the Chinese government. He possessed an audacious temperament. He was not much interested in other subjects, but when it came to military drill and tactics he was extremely keen and dedicated. His dream of being a mounted swordsman was something he could never forget even for one moment. Owing to his abundant spirit of adventure, when the European War was about to break out he often traveled back and forth to Hong Kong; he was arrested there by secret agents of the French and brought back to Hanoi, then transported to Thái-nguyên. During the seven-day Thái-nguyên uprising for the restoration of independence,[79] he was in the very vanguard. What has been said—"Having no martial spirit is a matter of concern; having no chance to display it is a matter of no concern"—indeed holds true when one looks at Lương.

---

79. This uprising began in the early morning of 31 August 1917; it involved the local militia and freed prisoners, led by Trịnh-Văn-Cấn (also known as Đội Cấn) and Lương-Lập-Nham. The rebels took control of Thái-nguyên for seven days, hoping that the army of the Vietnam Restoration League would come from Kwangtung to their aid. This did not occur, and they were crushed by French reinforcements from Hanoi. When the rebels withdrew to the jungle, Lương, who was partly crippled, committed suicide so as not to impede them.

Lương's brother was Lương-Nghị-Khanh. After the dispersal of the students, he worked in order to study for more than half a year. Through a recommendation from some Chinese, he was admitted to study as a government scholarship student at a Japanese school of technology. Later on, suffering from lung trouble, he decided to return home for treatment, but he was arrested in Hong Kong and brought back to Hanoi, then deported to Cambodia.[80]

Đàm-Kỳ-Sinh, alias Đàm-Quốc-Khí, when he first arrived in Japan, having realized that the current conditions for the students surely could not be maintained for very long, once said to me: "Our program should be on the one hand to look after education, but on the other hand to prepare for militant action, if we are to achieve success." With that I heartily agreed. Born into a good family, he was well versed in classical Chinese and had some understanding of French. His indignation and devotion were often displayed in his countenance and his language. When Bính-Ngọ-Hiên had just moved to Tokyo, though there were altogether more than sixty of us, he volunteered to carry out the cooking duties. We often jokingly called him the "Minister of Home Affairs." When there were things like dishwashing and cleaning to be done, he was happy to take care of them. When the order came that the students should be dispersed, he said angrily: "Even if you do not disperse us, we shall disperse ourselves. Being honest-to-goodness men of moral stature,[81] how could we possibly confine ourselves to brush and inkstone?" When the school was closed, while the rest of the students received living allowances or travel expenses, he alone refused to take a penny. Burning all of his Japanese books, he packed up only my *Letter from Overseas Written in Blood* and *The New Vietnam* and a few others, and cheerfully left Tokyo. By that time he was able to converse in Japanese. He went to a Japanese construction company and asked to work as a carpenter. His daily wage was six cents.

---

80. AM says that he was imprisoned on Poulo Condore.

81. Literally, "being, fair and square, men of seven-foot stature," an Asian expression to describe gentlemen who put their high principles into practice.

Dressing poorly and eating poorly, he managed to save some money after half a year, and presently went to a Japanese gun shop, secretly bought two revolvers, and returned to Vietnam.

At that time—it was the spring of the Year of the Cock [1909]—I had moved to Hong Kong; at Yên-thế [in Vietnam], Hoàng-Hoa-Thám was actively engaged in fighting against the French. Đàm carried my secret letter back to Nghệ-an to give to Ngư-Hải [Đặng-Thái-Thân], in the hope that our compatriots in the two regions of Trung-Kỳ and Bắc-Kỳ would simultaneously mount a large-scale uprising on behalf of Hoàng to distract the enemy's forces. However, as the financial situation was hopeless, military weapons were in short supply, and on top of that Ngư-Hải had by then died a martyr's death, Đàm felt that he had no recourse but to sacrifice himself. He and another comrade, carrying the two revolvers, set out to break into the residence of a notorious lackey of the enemy in an attempt to assassinate him. Before they could accomplish anything Đàm was arrested; sentenced to life imprisonment, he was transported up to Cao-bằng. When he was first imprisoned he tried to bite off his tongue to kill himself, but it was only after arriving in Cao-bằng that he obtained his wish. The day before he was arrested he sent me a secret letter that read: "The movement is suffering a setback; it is not possible to change the people's mind. I am going to look for Ngư-Hải in the other world." It is regrettable that when he was in Tokyo he did not disclose his real name. Even at that time he was cherishing unbeknownst the idea of sacrificing himself. That he was the son of a provincial surveillance commissioner[82] is all that I know.

OF THOSE FROM Trung-Kỳ, Lâm-Quảng-Trung was a native of Quảng-ngãi Province; his original name was Võ Quán. He stayed on working in order to study for half a year, then went to China and entered the Peking Military Academy; there he studied strategy and

---

82. In Vietnamese, *án-sát*; in Chinese, *an-ch'a*.

余自海外倦遊還來、身圖圖蒙國民遇愛幸保殘生、得與數十年形
離影絕之親朋同志、重敘舊緣、愛余者惡余者責望余者、知余與
不知余者、咸欲悉諳佩珠之歷史始末、嗟乎余之歷史百敗無一成之
歷史耳、流離奔播幾三十年、連坐之累、繫延郡國、黨錮之獄毒、
流回脆、每中夜撫心、仰天揮淚、踞跼二十餘載、慟頁鬚眉、翹望
無名之英雄、有如饑渴、夫古來閒新華故之交、掃溫澄清之役、

The first page of a manuscript in literary Chinese
(HTK) of Phan-Bôi-Châu's autobiography.

The Perfume River at Hué.

留別全國同胞

救國存種有志無才今竟與國民長辭罪甚知怒

即仰 廣南 新青年 阮遺君惠存

珠 訣語

Phan-Bội-Châu
in his last years,
in his boat on the
Perfume River.

The monument at the grave of Phan-Bội-Châu at Huế.

Thái-Thị-Huyên,
Phan-Bội-Châu's
wife.

Hanoi at the beginning of the twentieth century, a view showing the Metropole Hotel.

Tiểu-La Nguyễn Thành.

Marquis Cường-Đề as
a young man.

Lý Tuệ in later life, a photograph
with calligraphy by Phan-Bội-Châu.

Yokohama in
1905, with
decorations in
celebration of
the Japanese
victory over
Russia.

Liang Ch'i-ch'ao.

Count Ōkuma Shigenobu.

Viscount Inukai Tsuyoshi, photographed shortly
before his assassination.

Liu Yung-fu.

Sun Yat-sen (front row, fourth from left) and Miyazaki Tōten (back row, fifth from left) in a group photograph taken on Sun's return to Shanghai from France in 1911.

Tây-Hồ Phan-Châu-Trinh.

General Fukushima Yasumasa on his departure from Berlin to return to Japan through Siberia.

The border post between Vietnam and China at Lang-sơn.

Phan-Bôi-Châu in a photograph taken
about 1905.

Dr. Asaba Sakitarō.

The monument to Dr. Asaba. Phan-Bội-Châu is seated, second from right.

On the waterfront at Canton.

Members of the League for the Restoration of Vietnam in 1912.

Along the railway north of Hanoi, near the Chinese border.

Marquis Cường-Để in middle age.

Phan-Bội-Châu in
middle age.

Phạm-Hồng-Thái.

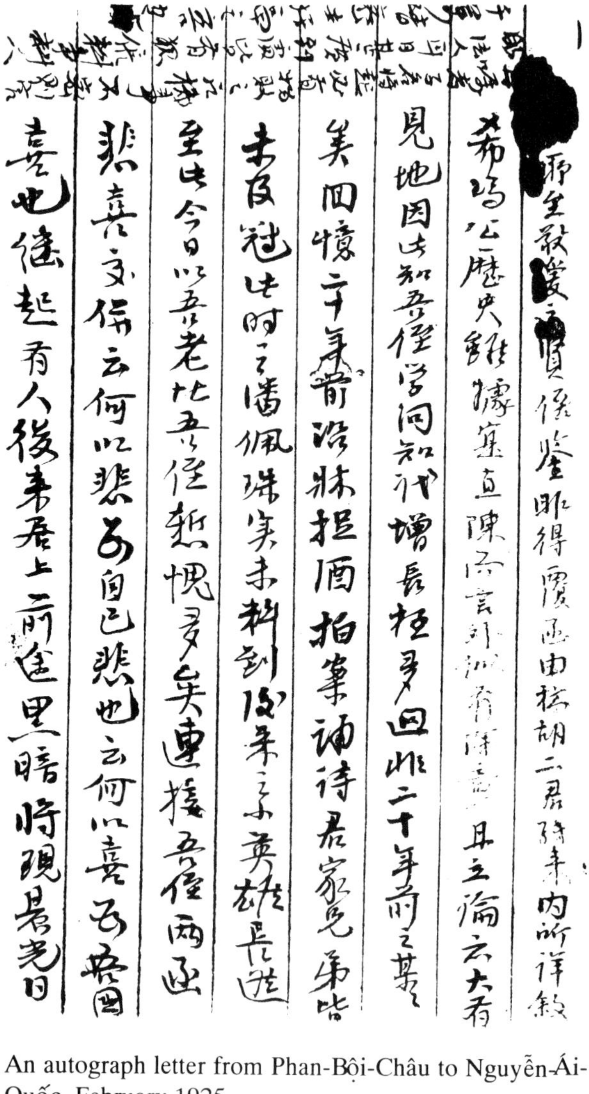

見地因此知吾儕學問知代增長枉尋回此二十年前之業

希馮公歷史雖爆墓立陳丙言外洲有陳言且立論云大有

那生教授賢侯鑒昨得覆函由拉胡二君歸來內所詳敘

美四憶平生前游昧招陌拍案誦詩君家兄弟皆

青氈此時之潘佩珠實未料到今年來英雄皆選

至此今日以吾老北五徑悲慨多矣連接五僅兩函

悲喜交併云何以悲自己悲也云何以喜不曾

喜也徒起有人後書春上前途黑暗時視昏光日

An autograph letter from Phan-Bội-Châu to Nguyễn-Ái-Quốc, February 1925.

The North Station in Shanghai.

did research on military science day and night, being determined to
hone his skills to the utmost. After his graduation, he asked President
Yüan Shih-k'ai to supply him with a travel allowance to make a re-
connaissance of the situation in the Kwangtung and Yunnan regions
along the Sino-Vietnamese border, as a first installment toward future
military operations. Yüan was pleased and approved his plan. Scaling
mountains and traversing streams, he exposed himself to the miasma
of the jungle for more than a year. In the Ninth Month of the Year of
the Ox [October 1913], he returned from Yunnan to Canton, stricken
with a serious brain fever. He stayed in hospital for several months, yet
his sickness only went from bad to worse. Lying on his bed, he became
infuriated that he could not die at the battlefront. He threw himself into
the Pearl River and took his own life. When I compiled his biography
I wrote the following poem in his praise:

> *When Ch'in asserted power supreme, Chung-lien felt*
> *mortal shame;*
> *Corruption at the court of Ch'u set Ch'ü P'ing's soul*
> *aflame.*
> *Unto the crystal stream did he those hallowed limbs*
> *commend;*
> *The river and the ocean have no boundary nor end.*[83]

Hoàng-Trọng-Mậu, whose original name was Nguyễn-Đức-Công,
was a native of Nghệ-an. He was well versed in classical Chinese and

---

83. Lu Chung-lien was an eloquent disputer from the State of Ch'i during the Warring States period. When the Ch'in army surrounded Hantan, capital of the State of
Chao, Hsin Yüan-yen of the State of Wei went to Chao and advised Chao to make
an alliance with Ch'in. This was reported to Lu Chung-lien, who said: "Should Ch'in
obtain the supreme power, I should go to the Eastern Sea and die there!" Hearing that,
Ch'in withdrew its troops. Ch'ü P'ing was the real name of Ch'ü Yüan of the State of
Ch'u during the Warring States period. He served King Huai-wang of Ch'u as a high
minister. The king's other ministers were jealous of him and he became isolated. To
enlighten the king, he wrote the famous poem *Li sao*. However, when Hsiang-wang,
son of Huai-wang, succeeded to the throne, he was sent into exile. Finally, holding a
rock, he jumped into a river and committed suicide on the fifth day of the Fifth Lunar
Month.

excelled in compositions in the set style of the mandarinate examination. When our movement began, he abandoned his studies for the examinations and used all his fortune to go overseas. He studied at the Institute for more than half a year, where his schoolwork surpassed that of his classmates. He immersed himself without respite in the various sciences and in Japanese composition. He also paid the utmost attention to military training. When the Institute was closed, he went to China, established contacts with those in the Chinese revolutionary party, and entered Lingnan College to master Mandarin like a native Chinese because he wished to prepare himself for admission to the Chinese army. At that time, Ts'ai Sung-po was training his new army in Kwangsi. Through the recommendation of Yang Ch'in-hung, the head of the Military Academy, Hoàng was admitted to the Chinese army and given military training. He showed special skill in shooting and battlefield maneuvers, for which he received praise from Ts'ai. After his graduation, he devoted himself to working out strategic plans for the revolution. When the Vietnam Restoration League was established, a book entitled *Quang-phục-quân phương-lược* (Strategic Directives for the Restoration Army) was published; half of this book was composed by him.

When the European War broke out, he could hardly wait for his military plans to be carried out. He traveled back and forth for several months between Yunnan and Kwangsi by himself, with a single horse and a revolver, heedless of wind and rain. Through his close contacts with Chinese officers and soldiers, he was able to gather several thousand men from Kwangtung and Kwangsi who were fairly well equipped with weapons. He intended to launch an attack on Lạng-sơn. At that time, he thought that his great undertaking was capable of accomplishment. Unexpectedly, China suddenly changed its diplomatic policy and declared war on Germany. The French thereupon asked China to cooperate and strictly punish our people. I myself was arrested by the Kwangtung government; on top of that, the Chinese soldiers recruited by Hoàng were dispersed. Then there was some good news, namely the Thái-nguyên uprising. He promptly planned an action in response to it. He took thirty men under his command and entered the Lạng-sơn border from Ch'ennankuan. He launched an ambush against a garrison, but it was a failure. He escaped to Kwangtung, planning to reenter Trung-Kỳ from the Siam border; but when he arrived in Hong Kong, he was arrested by a French agent and brought back to Hanoi to be imprisoned. French officials told him that if he submitted he would receive a pardon, but nonetheless he did not give in and was shot to death. It was he who wrote the commentary and the epilogue in my *Việt-Nam quốc-sử khảo* (A Study of Vietnamese History).

Trần-Hữu-Lực, whose original name was Nguyễn-Thức-Đường, a native of Nghệ-an, was the middle son of Đông-Khê, who was my teacher. For someone from a family who for generations had been Confucian scholars by tradition, his temperament was highly unusual, being that of a military man. When he was fifteen years old, he sneaked a look at my book *A New Booklet on the Ryūkyūs Written in Blood and Tears*. Thereafter he abandoned his plans to become an official and no longer studied to pass the mandarinate examinations, but instead associated himself with those who aspired to chivalrous adventures and practiced with baton and sword. It was he who stabbed the *cử-nhân* Nguyễn Điềm, a lackey of the enemy. To begin with, he did not intend to go abroad, but to stay home and plan for militant action. But after he killed Nguyễn Điềm, Ngư-Hải was concerned for his future and therefore pressed him to go abroad.

When he entered the Institute, he was wildly enthusiastic about military training. He wore a gun over his shoulder and bullets around his waist, reluctant to take them off even to eat or sleep. After the closure of the Institute, he stayed on, working in order to study. When the Marquis was expelled, he took it as an affront and wished to take some measure of revenge, but his comrades all persuaded him to refrain, so he gave up the idea and went to China. At that time, Ts'ai Sung-po was training his army in Kwangsi, and Kwangsi had a military academy. Together with Tiêu-Đẩu Nguyễn-Bá-Trác and Nguyễn-Thái-Bạt, he entered the academy and studied military command. When he was studying, he always showed as much fervor as if he were on the battlefield. After graduation, he went to Kwangtung and was promoted to sublieutenant in command of a company. When they carried out maneuvers, his troops all held him in awe.

At the time of the establishment of the Vietnam Restoration League, he volunteered to go to Siam to create a Restoration Army among the expatriate Vietnamese there, and to command a company himself. As the secretary-general of the Vietnam Restoration League, I appointed him to be the head of its branch in Siam. After his arrival in Siam, he traveled throughout the borders of Siam and Vietnam. Wherever there were expatriate Vietnamese, he did his best to recruit them into the League. The people who joined the League increased day by day, and funds to buy weaponry were also collected. The one thing that could not be decided on was when to enter Vietnam. At that point, Siam declared war on Germany, and the Siamese government, following the requests of the French, made a strict search for people in the Vietnamese revolutionary party. The French lackeys, Hùng from Bắc-Kỳ and a certain individual from Trung-Kỳ, did their utmost to track him down. When they caught him, he was handed over to the French authorities to be brought back to Hanoi. He was urged to submit, but he showed himself indomitable. Together with Hoàng-Trọng-Mậu, he was shot at the foot of Mount Bạch-mai. Before being executed, he composed a symmetrical verse in mourning for himself:

> *My country is already dead and gone;*
> *How then should I, her faithful son, live on?*
> *For ten years past I honed my sword's sharp edge,*
> *Whetted my dagger, in chivalric pledge*
> *To serve the honor of the motherland.*
> *The hour of success was not at hand;*
> *Came suddenly to grief my enterprise.*
> *Yet on the plain where the Nine Sources rise,*

> *Shall I, deploying hosts of spirits brave,*
> *Sustain the nation's army from the grave.*[84]

Nguyễn-Quỳnh-Lâm was a native of Hà-tĩnh. At the time when he went overseas he was only fifteen, yet his firm will, few words, and love of study were those of an adult. When the Institute was closed, he stayed on in Japan and worked in order to study for more than half a year. Then he went to China, and joined the army in Kwangtung to make himself familiar with battlefield drill. After leaving the military he studied how to manufacture explosives, and he was able to produce smokeless explosives and dynamite. He had extraordinary patience; no matter how great the difficulty, he never gave up. In the Year of the Cock [1909], on account of importing weaponry, he was arrested by the port police [at Hong Kong] and sent to prison for several months; but when the British authorities investigated his case and found that he was a member of the Vietnamese revolutionary movement, they freed him, because at that time the British authorities were still on friendly terms with us. He set about making friends in the Chinese nationalist party in order to secure its support in the future.

In the Year of the Ox [1913], the year of the Second Revolution [in China], he volunteered to enlist under Huang Ch'u-chiang's command. At that time Huang was defending Nanking, and appointed him to be a company commander. Always filled with enthusiasm, he regarded the battlefront with its rain of bullets and forest of bayonets as a land of pleasure. When Yüan Shih-k'ai launched an attack against Nanking and the city was about to fall, Huang fled immediately. The Chinese officers, who knew that Nguyễn was a Vietnamese partisan, advised him to escape, saying to him: "This has nothing to do with your cause. You had better protect your life so as to await your opportunity." He

---

84. The "plain of the Nine Sources" is a Chinese way of alluding to the world beyond the grave. The words *quốc-dân-quân,* "national army," in the original text and AM appear as *thiếu-niên-quân,* "youth army," in TQP, followed by GB. Although the reason for the change in TQP is unexplained, it may be observed that *quốc-dân-quân* could have been taken to imply "the army of the Quốc-Dân-Đảng" (the Nationalist Party).

indignantly rejoined: "People put me in charge of soldiers because they believed that I could dispatch the enemy. If, now that the enemy is in sight, I ran away, how could I dare to face them?" He then fought to the best of his ability. Struck by two bullets, one in the arm and one in the chest, he died right there on the battlefield. Previously, he had made attempts on several occasions to return home by way of Siam to investigate the situation in our country with a view to launching action, but all were blocked by the lackeys [of the French], and he barely managed to escape with his life. Alas! He was a true man of action, despite all his failures.

Lê-Cầu-Tinh was a native of Nghệ-an. He was a man of great skill. After the Institute was closed, he devoted himself to becoming a maker of arms. Using a Japanese gun as a model, he was able to produce a five-shot gun that was impossible to distinguish from one of those re-designed in the thirtieth year of the Meiji period [1897]. I was secretly transporting arms through Siam with the intention of sending them home. He made me a trunk with a secret compartment to contain the arms that even the customs officers were not able to discover. In the Year of the Rat [1912], with Đặng-Tử-Mẫn, he went to Siam to run our farm and died in an epidemic.

Đinh-Doãn-Tế and Phan-Lại-Lương were both natives of Nghệ-an. After the closure of the Institute, they worked in order to study for about one year. Đinh came from a middle-class family that used all its property to send him abroad. Later he set out for Siam, intending to take part in our activities there, but fell gravely ill before arriving at his destination, amidst the winds and rains of a place far from home, all by himself. The owner of the house, a former follower of Phan-Đình-Phùng called Lãnh Mục, was the only person who would come now and again to take care of him. Whenever he suffered an attack of fever and became delirious, he would call out: "Death to the enemy! Death to the enemy!" For a whole month he was confined to his sickbed and could not even sit up. When Đặng-Tử-Mẫn came to visit him, suddenly he sat up and talked about revolutionary matters for half an hour or so, then burst into a loud laugh and died. I was immensely saddened by his death. At the time, having reached the point of extreme destitution, I wrote the following symmetrical couplet in his memory:

> *I cannot live or die; no end can I discern*
> > *Of mourning for you; your affliction's mine.*
> *With you I went abroad; with whom shall I return?*
> > *My heart to untold sadness I resign.*

Phan was born into a family that had had a good literary reputation for generations. His father was a *cử-nhân* who held an official appointment as an instructor *(giáo-thụ)*. When our country lost its independence, he quitted his post and returned home. In the autumn of the nineteenth year of the reign of Thành-Thái [1907], Phan got married; but after being married for less than a month, he left his wife to go abroad. He was extremely diligent about his schoolwork. After the Institute was closed, he stayed on and worked under conditions of adversity. The winter cold in Japan being severe and his physical condition being that of a frail literary man, he contracted pneumonia. He went to China and died there in hospital. When he fell ill, out of concern that he might not be able to pull through, I very reluctantly encouraged him to return home to recuperate. He said firmly: "Better to die in a foreign land than surrounded by pigs and chickens." Being highly intelligent, after reading the old Chinese writings[85] just once, he never failed to comprehend them. What a pity it is that, owing to a frail constitution, he had to die prematurely! How important is good health![86]

IN THE SECOND MONTH of the Year of the Monkey [March 1908], as I was going through Hong Kong on my way to Siam, I happened to

---

85. TQP, followed by GB, for some reason expands this to say "Chinese and Japanese books."

86. The last three sentences of this paragraph are omitted by AM.

meet Mai-Lão-Bạng, who had just come from our country. Accompanying him was Lê-Dật-Trúc, who brought with him more than a dozen young students. Old Mai had been sent over by the whole Catholic church as the representative of the Catholics in the Vietnam Modernization Association. Up to that point, among the students who went abroad there had been no one from the church. After Old Mai's arrival, the church dispatched others abroad, among them Lê-Kim-Thanh, Lê-Hồng-Chung, Nguyễn-Mộ-Đơn, and Lưu-Yên-Đơn—several dozen people altogether. Among the seminarists, Kim-Thanh and Yên-Đơn were most outstanding. Yên-Đơn later changed his name to Lý-Trọng-Bá, obtained the status of a Chinese, and was selected to be an official scholarship student. Studying in Japan, this man graduated from a technical high school, then entered one of the imperial universities to study engineering and received a bachelor's degree in engineering.[87] The level of his proficiency in engineering was extremely high, but being unable to return to our country, he took employment with the [Chinese] national government. At present he is engaged in directing projects in China. How regrettable it is!

When Old Mai first arrived in Japan, out of the respect that I had for the Church, I gathered together all the students of the Institute and arranged a party to welcome him. He was passionately dedicated to mustering up support among the believers. Among his writings was a book entitled *Lão Bạng phổ khuyến thư* (A Public Appeal by Old Mai-Lão-Bạng), which had a resounding success. He later went to Siam, planning to return home, but on the demand of the French authorities the Siamese government detained him for four months. Upon being freed, he returned to Hong Kong; but at the request of the French the port authorities detained him for three months. Being freed again, he went to Kwangtung and was imprisoned, along with me, by Lung Chi-kuang, an adherent of Yüan Shih-k'ai, at the request of the French. In prison, to console him, I wrote a poem:

---

87. In a later passage, Phan again refers to Lý-Trọng-Bá and says that he had a doctorate in engineering.

In your career, time and again
You boldly skirted death's domain!
In riper years, undauntedly
You entered into prisons three!

After Lung died,[88] he was set free and went to Shanghai. On demand being made by the French to the British, the British handed him over to the French consulate. He was then brought back home and detained for some ten years more before being set free. His entire life was one of compassion for the sorry state of his fellow countrymen; he suffered every kind of sharp and bitter experience on countless occasions, but never gave up. He was a real disciple of Christ. Previously I had never had my photograph taken. It was only at the time when we welcomed him that he and I had our picture taken together. This photograph was later circulated in our country, and the French became able to recognize my likeness from then on.

IN THE SEVENTH MONTH of the Year of the Sheep [August/ September 1907], Emperor Thành-Thái was deposed by the French;[89] Mai-Sơn Nguyễn-Thượng-Hiền quitted his official position–he was at the time director of Education *(đốc-học)* of Nam-định—to go abroad. In the Fifth Month of the Year of the Monkey [June 1908], on my way back from Siam, I met him in Kwangtung and invited him to come to Japan. I sent a telegram in advance to the Institute asking the student body to send a delegation to Yokohama in the first decade of the Ninth Month to meet him. Upon our arrival in Tokyo, a welcoming party was held for him to meet with the students. At that time, the Common East Asian Culture Society had just remodeled the Institute for our students; its atmosphere was bright with promise. We were allowed to use the assembly hall of the new Institute to welcome him. He wrote an

88. TQP, followed by GB, corrects this to "after Lung fled."
89. The governor-general compelled Emperor Thành-Thái to abdicate on 3 September 1907.

inaugural address for the school and a long poem to encourage the neo-
phyte students,[90] as well as a book, *Hải-ngoại quy hồng* (The Geese
That Come from Abroad).[91] All of these were printed and sent back
home. Later, during the period of the European War, he shuttled back
and forth between Hong Kong, the two Kwangs, and Siam plotting an
uprising, but it all came to naught. In chagrin, he eventually retired to
a Buddhist temple. The Chinese Buddhist devotees relished his company. Could he not be called a Cheung Ssu-nan[92] or a Chu Shun-shui[93]
of our country?

IN THE TENTH MONTH of the Year of the Monkey [late October/
November 1908], the dispersal of the students had been completed and
the Vietnam Constitutional Association had collapsed. I realized that
it would be impossible to expect anything from Japan, and turned my
attention to the Chinese revolutionary movement and the peoples in the
world who shared the same sickness[94] with us.

90. AM adds that this poem was written in *quốc-ngữ*, and included the following
lines:
> *Fried rice is a delicious treat*
> *When foemen's flesh is used as meat!*
> *To make the soup taste really good*
> *Just flavor it with foemen's blood!*

91. AM adds another book, *Tang-hải lệ-đàm* (A Discussion in Tears of the Vicissitudes of Life).
92. The Chinese text reads "Cheung Ch'u-nan," but the reference is clearly to
Cheung Ssu-nan; both names are pronounced identically, as *Trịnh Sở-Nam*, in Sino-
Vietnamese. Cheung Ssu-nan, whose real name was Cheung Ssu-yao, lived during the
Sung dynasty in the thirteenth century. When the Sung were overthrown by the Yüan,
he retired to South China and became a symbol of loyalism.
93. Chu Shun-shui (1600–1682), whose real name was Chu Chih-yü, was loyal to the
Ming dynasty. When the Ming were overthrown by the Ch'ing in 1644, he went into
exile in Japan, where he eventually obtained the patronage of Tokugawa Mitsukuni,
daimyō of the Mito domain (now Ibaraki Prefecture). He strongly influenced Tokugawa Confucian thought, particularly that of the Mito school of historical studies,
which advocated imperial loyalism.
94. In Chinese, *t'ung-p'ing*; in Sino-Vietnamese, *đồng-bệnh*.

Previously, when I met Sun Chung-shan [Sun Yat-sen], he had introduced me to Miyazaki Tōten. Tōten was a Japanese adventurer[95] who was full of ideas for worldwide revolution. When I first met him, he said to me: "Your country certainly cannot bring down the French by your own strength. To seek assistance from friendly countries is not necessarily inappropriate. But how could it be that Japan would support you? Japanese politicians are by and large full of ambition but lacking in chivalry. You should encourage your youth to put their effort into studying the English, Russian, and German languages, making a lot of friends among the peoples of the world, and denouncing the foul crime of the French, so that the peoples of the world will be aware of it. The world certainly does not lack those who value humanitarianism and despise the right of brute force,[96] and those are the only people from whom you might actually get help." At the time, I did not really believe that, but now I have come to realize how true it was; this was the first time that the idea of world solidarity entered my mind.

Nevertheless, even if I had wished to travel to Europe and America it would have been impossible, as there was no money, and moreover I was not proficient in European languages, not unlike a man who is both blind and deaf to the world. In consequence, the plan of making contact with European and American personalities would have to wait for another time. As our first step, I thought we should begin by establishing contact with men of high purpose from other countries that had lost their independence, who could mutually support

95. In Japanese, *rōnin*. A number of Japanese civilians, who came to be known as *tairiku rōnin* ("continental adventurers"), were active during the nineteenth and early twentieth centuries in promoting Japanese interests in China, Korea, and Manchuria. Miyazaki Tōten (1871–1922) is particularly noted for his idealistic Pan-Asianism, which led him to support Sun Yat-sen and the Chinese revolutionary movement. For his own account of his career, see *My Thirty-Three Years' Dream: the Autobiography of Miyazaki Tōten*, translated with an introduction by Etō Shinkichi and Marius B. Jansen (Princeton, NJ: Princeton University Press, 1982).
96. For the significance of this term, see above, p. 115, n. 51.

each other and lead each of their peoples onto the stage of revolution. At the same time, we should concentrate on spreading the idea of revolution, so as to educate people even during the time when their independence was lost.

The problem that presented itself was that at that time I had no donation money coming from home, and my wallet had been cleaned out for ten days; the funds that we had managed to solicit for the students to buy tickets to return home had been used up. Thus expenses for food and lodging, expenses for outside activities, expenses of any other kind—all were unprovided for. A group of about ten of us comrades were gathered in our room, laughing about it to keep from crying, not knowing what to do.

> *Midst impassable mountains and torrents*
> *No way to emerge can be found—*
> *Lo! There, beneath sheltering willows,*
> *A village, with flowers around!*

By sheer chance we encountered a generous person; that was Asaba Sakitarō-sensei.[97] Asaba had been giving help to Nguyễn-Thái-Bạt ever since he met the latter begging on the street. At the time when the Vietnam Constitutional Association was established, Nguyễn found out about it by reading the newspaper. He asked Asaba if he might go to Tokyo to meet us. Asaba approved of his request, and even gave him the school expenses to enroll in the Dōbun Shoin. We were all deeply moved by his generosity. Now, seeing that we were in dire straits, the only thought that came to my mind was to ask him for help. But going to seek his help was not an easy thing to do. If we had not

---

97. Asaba Sakitarō (1867–1910), a medical doctor, was a native of Iwata, Shizuoka Prefecture. For further information on Asaba see, in Japanese, *Tōyū undō igo no Nihon to Betonamu no kankei* (Relations between Japan and Vietnam after the Đông-Du Movement), edited by Okakura Koshirō et al. (Tokyo: privately printed, 1982); in Vietnamese, "Phan-Bội-Châu and Asaba Sakitarō," in Vĩnh Sính, *Việt Nam và Nhật Bản trong thế giới Đông Á* (Vietnam and Japan in the East Asian World) (Ho Chi Minh City: Đại học Sư phạm, 1993).

known this generous person before, how should we have dared to make a request? But I discussed the idea with Nguyễn, and Nguyễn agreed with it, so I wrote a letter for him to deliver. Alas! We had done nothing to return Asaba's previous favor; how foolish to delude ourselves into going to his house to look for help again! Yet, beyond all expectation, my letter was sent out in the morning, and in the evening his check had already arrived. The check that he sent me was for seventeen hundred yen, and the letter enclosed in the envelope read: "For the moment, I have gathered together everything at home and come up only with this amount. I shall have more later. If you need more at once, please write to me quickly." It was just a few sentences without any air of condescension. I was at a dead end, yet this is what came to me. How overjoyed I was!

Having obtained the money, I immediately divided it into three parts. The greatest part was to cover expenses for outside activities; next came printing expenses, followed by food and lodging. After doing this, I hurried off to the Chinese revolutionary party and the Japanese *Heimin* Society.[98] First of all, we obtained support from Chang Ping-lin,[99] Chang Chi,[100] and Ch'ing Mei-chiu,[101] and then from Cho So-ang of Korea,[102] Đái of India, Heng of the

---

98. The *Heiminsha* (Society of Commoners) was founded by Sakai Toshihiko and Kōtoku Shūsui in 1903 and included both materialist and Christian Socialists. It was forced by the authorities to dissolve its formal organization in April 1907, but its members were still active when Phan made contact with them.

99. Chang Ping-lin (1868–1936), a scholar and anti-Manchu activist, edited the well known newspapers *Su-pao* and *Min-pao*.

100. Chang Chi (1882–1947), also an anti-Manchu activist and for a time editor of the *Min-pao*, was one of the few northern Chinese to achieve prominence in the Kuomintang.

101. TQP, followed by GB, mistakenly gives "Trương Kế Cảnh and Mai Cửu," instead of "Trương Kế and Cảnh Mai-Cửu."

102. This man lives in America and knows Nguyễn-Ái-Quốc. [Author's note.] — Cho So-ang (1887–?), fighter for Korean independence and politician, graduated from Meiji University in Japan, then returned to Korea. After the March First Movement (1919), he went into exile in Shanghai, where he participated in the establishment of the Korean Provisional Government. He was in charge of, among other things,

Philippines,[103] and several tens of comrades. In particular, Ōsugi Sakae, Sakai Toshihiko, Miyazaki Tōten, and more than ten Japanese indicated their emphatic endorsement.[104]

In the Tenth Month of the Year of the Monkey [late October/ November 1908], the Tōa Dōmei Kai (Society for East Asian Alliance) was founded.[105] Members from our country were Phan-Thị-Hán (my alias), Đặng-Tử-Mẫn,[106] Nguyễn-Quỳnh-Lâm, and more than ten others. This society was to become a basis for making contacts among East Asians; I placed quite a lot of hope in it. Then, however, I recalled the interdependency that China, especially the two Kwangs and Yunnan, had with our country. I thereupon hastened to make contact with students from those regions in order to found the Society for the Alliance of Yunnan, Kwangsi, and Vietnam.[107] The presidents of the

---

foreign affairs. In 1918, as the representative of Korea, he attended the Congress of World Socialist Parties in Geneva, and on the way back visited Britain, the U.S.S.R., and other countries. Returning to Korea after 1945, he participated in the National Convention; when the Korean War broke out, according to South Korean accounts, he was taken to the North, where his fate is unknown. [Translators' note.]

103. I have forgotten the romanized names of these two persons. [Author's note.]

104. Ōsugi and Sakai were leaders of the Japanese Socialists. [Author's note.] — Ōsugi Sakae (1885–1923), a native of Kagawa Prefecture, was a Japanese anarchist and the translator of Kropotkin into Japanese. Sakai Toshihiko (1890–1933), a native of Fukuoka Prefecture, was a Japanese Socialist, one of the founders of the Socialist newspaper *Heimin Shimbun*. Later he became the first chairman of the Japanese Communist Party. His *Autobiography* has been translated by Byron K. Marshall (Berkeley: University of California Press, 1992). [Translators' note.]

105. According to Shiraishi Masaya's carefully researched study, the Tōa Dōmei Kai was virtually identical with the Ashū Washinkai (Asian Friendship Association); the latter had been formed in the autumn of 1907. Shiraishi Masaya, "Phan-Bội-Châu in Japan," in *Phan-Bội-Châu and the Đông-Du Movement*, 72.

106. TQP, followed by GB, mistakenly reads "Đặng-Tử-Kính."

107. According to Shiraishi Masaya, if such a society of alliance between Yunnan, Kwangsi, Kwangtung, and Vietnam existed, it must have been formed in 1907. See his impressive study *Betonamu minzoku undō to Nihon, Ajia—Phan-Bội-Châu no kakumei shisō to taigai ishiki* (Vietnamese Nationalism and Its Relations with Japan and Asia—Phan-Bội-Châu's Ideas of Revolution and the World) (Tokyo: Gannandō, 1993), 410–478.

associations of students from Yunnan and Kwangsi, namely Chao Shen and Tseng Yan, both strongly approved of it. Ten days had not gone by before students from these two regions were flocking to join this Society. According to the constitution established for the Society, each constituent branch was to contribute funds to it; I therefore took 250 yen out of our funds as the contribution for the members from our country. This is how the funds we had solicited were used for outside activities during this period of time.

When it came to activities for promoting revolution inside our country, great importance was attached to printed materials. I thus had *A Letter from Overseas Written in Blood* reprinted in three different kinds of characters—in Chinese, in demotic script *(chữ Nôm)*, and in the modern romanized characters—for a total of three thousand copies. My book *Việt-Nam sử-khảo*[108] (A Study of Vietnamese History) was still being written; it had to be completed quickly and printed. Altogether this took about seven hundred yen. In addition, as Trần-Đông-Phong had just committed suicide, I compiled *Trần-Đông-Phong truyện* (The Life of Trần-Đông-Phong) and had it printed, in the expectation that as soon as I returned to Hong Kong the book could be sent back home. This is how the funds we had solicited were used for promotional activities during this period of time.

Owing to the fact that our enemy was strong and we ourselves were weak, our resources were slender, and our support had been cut off, all our planning of a hundred things was but a charade. It was only a few months after the creation of the Society for East Asian Alliance when it was finally dissolved by a peremptory order from the Japanese police authorities; the reason being that within the Society there were those who belonged to the British, French, and Korean revolutionary parties and the Japanese Socialist Party, so that the Japanese government strongly disliked it and the British and French governments added their pressure. As for the Society for the Alliance of Yunnan, Kwangsi, and

---

108. Correctly, *Việt-Nam quốc-sử-khảo*.

Vietnam, the Ch'ing government and the French connived in urging the Japanese government to issue an order putting it out of existence. The society was thus dissolved.[109] We came to realize that in this world of brute force, no society to promote justice and universal principles could possibly exist in the open!

The three thousand copies of the *Letter from Overseas Written in Blood* that had just been printed in the Year of the Monkey [1908] but were not yet distributed were confiscated by the Japanese authorities and burned in the front courtyard of the French Embassy in Japan. Fortunately, some ten minutes before the confiscation, surreptitious word was received from a secret friend and we were able to hide about a hundred and fifty copies in a different place.[110] Truly, the nemesis of writing is the strange hostility that follows upon it! This incident was of course a painful setback, but the cause of this setback was not unconnected with our earlier success. Supposing that previously Asaba had not generously emptied his purse to come to our aid, even if we had wanted to have a failure it would have been impossible.

BEFORE I LEFT Japan, I paid a visit to Asaba at his residence in Kōfutsu. As soon as I entered the house, Nguyễn-Thái-Bạt introduced me. Before I had even had a chance to express my gratitude to him, Asaba promptly shook my hand and led me inside. He invited me to drink while we had a talk; there was no air of worldly hauteur about him. The son of an army general, he had studied medicine and obtained a doctoral degree. He had opened a clinic, devoting himself to the treatment of poor patients. In the whole of his career he had never set foot in the political world. In his conversation with me he evinced a great

---

109. AM gives a fuller statement about this event: "When the Society had been established for just three months, Chang P'ing-lin and I were expelled by the Japanese. The Society was thus dissolved immediately."

110. AM indicates that the books were confiscated after they had been brought to Phan's boarding house, and the warning was given by Kashiwabara Buntarō.

dislike for the Japanese politicians; even for Ōkuma and Inukai he did not have much use. He said to me: "Their behavior to you is no more than a subtle maneuver in an intrigue among ambitious personages."

I bade him farewell and went to China. Ten years afterward, when I returned to Japan, he had passed away. I appreciated what he had done for us, but up to that time I had never had a chance to do anything in return. Feeling ashamed, as I had not expressed my gratitude to a friend of a lifetime, I set up a monument in his honor before his grave and had the following inscription carved upon it:

> *Impelled by the ordeal of our nation,*
> *we betook ourselves to the Land of the Rising Sun.*
> *Feeling sympathy for our aspirations,*
> *you succored us in our time of need*
> *without thought of having your favor returned.*
> *Verily you should be compared to the chivalrous men of old!*
> *Now that we have come back, you have passed away.*
> *Looking around the Four Directions, we fail to see a soul,*
> *only the immensity of the heaven and the sea.*
> *How can we express what is in our hearts?*
> *We hereby carve our sentiments in stone, as follows:*
> *"Your generosity is matchless in times past and present;*
> *your righteousness stands forth in lands far and near.*
> *What you gave us was boundless as the heaven;*
> *what we received was measureless as the sea.*
> *We have not fulfilled our aspiration,*
> *yet you have not tarried for us.*
> *Our hearts will grieve forever, world without end."*
> *Written by members of the Việt-Nam Quang-Phục-Hội*
> *(Vietnam Restoration League).*[111]

---

111. Writing roughly ten years after setting up this monument and forced to rely on memory alone, Phan gives a version of this inscription differing slightly from that to be found on the actual monument, which reads:

A glance at the business of setting up the monument for Asaba will be enough to give some insight into the high standards of the Japanese people. I therefore put it on record, as follows.

When I first arrived at Shizuoka, I made plans for the setting up of the monument. The material and the carving fee would be about one hundred piasters. In addition, the expenses for transportation and setting up would require more than another hundred piasters. There were only 120 piasters left in my wallet, not nearly enough to have the work finished. Nevertheless, as I had made a promise to the departed, I had to carry it out by all means.

MONUMENT DEDICATED TO ASABA SAKITARŌ.
Impelled by the ordeal of our nation,
we betook ourselves to the Land of the Rising Sun.
Feeling sympathy for our aspirations,
you succored us in our time of need
without thought of having your favor returned.
You are indeed a chivalrous man
unsurpassed then or now!
Alas! You are no longer with us;
we look around the heavens and the sea
but we fail to see a soul.
We hereby carve our sentiments in stone, as follows:
"Your generosity is matchless in times past and present;
your righteousness stands forth in lands far and near.
What you gave us was boundless as the heaven;
what we received was measureless as the sea.
We have not fulfilled our aspiration,
yet you have not tarried for us.
Our hearts will grieve forever, world without end."
In the spring of the Year of the Horse,
respectfully written by members of the
Việt-Nam Quang-Phục-Hội.
Carved by Ōsugi Kyokurei.

For further details see, in Vietnamese, Vĩnh Sính, *Việt Nam và Nhật Bản*, 198–201, and in Japanese, Okakura Koshirō et al., eds., *Tōyū undō igo no Nihon to Betonamu no kankei*, 122.

At that point I went together with Lý-Trọng-Bá to visit Asaba Kōtarō, the head of Asaba village, to let him know of my intention, and to tell him about Asaba Sakitarō's chivalrous assistance to us, as well as other events of the past. That is how I found out that Sakitarō had never ever told anyone about this. The village head was greatly moved; he strongly endorsed my idea and encouraged me to carry it out immediately. I said that at present our funds did not suffice, and asked to leave one hundred silver piasters with him as village head; I would then return to China to arrange for more funds and would come back to Japan to complete the project. The village head said to me: "If you are going to build a monument on behalf of a person from our village, we should help you to fulfill your aspiration. You do not have to go to all the trouble of voyaging there and back." I was extremely pleased. He invited me to stay over in his house and provided me with everything I needed. On the sixth day of that month, the village head took me to visit a primary school in the village. He told the students to invite their family members to gather on Sunday at the school ground to hear him give an address. (Because the constitution provides for local autonomy in Japan, the village head is the one who makes the important decisions in the administration of a village.)

When the day came, I accompanied the village head to the school, where the heads of families had all gathered. The village head stepped up to the platform and gave his speech. He first recounted the chivalrous works of Sakitarō; then he introduced Lý-Trọng-Bá and me to the village people. (Lý was a Vietnamese who had obtained a doctorate in engineering from a Japanese university.) The village head next said with spontaneous emotion:

> Humankind has managed to exist for a long time because it has the sentiment of mutual affection. Through his chivalry and fortitude Mr. Asaba was able to help people of another country, and by doing so has indeed implanted a good reputation for our village people! Can it be that among our village people he is the only true gentleman? Now Mr. Phan and Mr. Lý, braving the wind and the waves, have crossed ten thousand miles of

ocean to come here, without any disdain for our remote village, to build a monument to commemorate Mr. Asaba. They have shown a great sense of honor toward our village people. If we did not do anything to assist them, how could we possibly not feel ashamed? And not only for our village people, but indeed ashamed for the Japanese people also.

When his speech came to that point, the sound of the applause was like thunder.

From the crowd someone stood up and said: "We are inexperienced and ignorant; we wish only to follow the instructions of our village head." (This village was a farming village; there were many brave fellows in it, but few literary folk.) The village head went on again with his speech:

My opinion is that in the setting up of this monument we should only ask them to buy the stone and pay the carvers. But when it comes to transportation and setting up, we village people should regard it as our duty to help them to complete it. This is because to sacrifice the wages of our labor to complete this monument for a chivalrous man is indeed a Heaven-sent vocation for us Japanese people.

His speech was not yet finished when the cry of "Yes!" shook the whole school building.

Ten days later, the monument was completed. It was four and a half meters high [about fifteen feet], made of natural stone five centimeters thick [about two inches] and two meters wide [about six and a half feet]. The characters were as big as a child's palm. On the day the work was finished, the village people gathered to celebrate its completion, contributing the money to put on a banquet to entertain us and other visitors. All of this was arranged by the village head. I spent only a little more than a hundred piasters altogether. I earnestly wish our fellow countrymen to know about this chivalrous deed; there is no fear of its story being irrelevant.

ON THE SECOND DAY of the Fifth Month of the Year of the Monkey [31 May 1908], Trần-Đông-Phong, a student at the Institute from Nghệ-an, abruptly left the school and committed suicide. In his pocket there was a note in *quốc-ngữ* to the effect that although his family was wealthy, with a grain business worth millions, nevertheless lately for his expenses at the Institute he had had to rely entirely on the donations from Nam-Kỳ. He had written letters home several times to suggest that his father follow the example of Chang Liang in dedicating his fortune to the cause of his country,[112] but had received from his father no reply. It was unbearable for him, being the son of a wealthy family, to have to endure the shame of relying on others for his survival, and thus he would part with his life to make his resolution clear. All our fellow countrymen felt sad about his death. People from the Three Regions worked together to arrange his funeral. Lieutenant-Colonel Tamba [*sic*] of the Japanese Army, Kashiwabara Buntarō, a member of the House of Representatives, and others, together with the Chinese students in Japan, attended the funeral ceremony. The Japanese erected a marker in his honor at the head of his grave with the inscription:

> *The grave of Trần-Đông-Phong,*
> *a man of high purpose from Vietnam.*

IN THE SECOND MONTH of the Year of the Cock [February/March 1909], the Marquis and I were simultaneously expelled from Japan by the Japanese authorities. The Marquis had to leave within twenty-four hours and I within a week, without any appeal. This was because of the signing of the Franco-Japanese Treaty. At that point I thought mainly of China and Siam as my two possible destinations. The Marquis went

---

112. Chang Liang (d. 187 B.C.), from a family who had long been ministers of the Han state, after it was conquered by the Ch'in spent his entire patrimony in an unsuccessful attempt to assassinate the First Emperor. However, after Liu Pang founded the Former Han dynasty (unconnected with the Han state) in 202 B.C., Chang Liang was honored as one of the Three Heroes.

to Hong Kong and sent a secret letter to his most trusted people in Nam-Kỳ to arrange for a big fund for him to travel to Europe. I too went to Hong Kong, rented a little place to live along with Mai-Lão-Bạng and Lương-Lập-Nham, and sent a letter to Ngư-Hải to ask him to try to raise some money. My intention was that after receiving the money I would conduct the youth who had now been dispersed from the Institute to live and farm together in Siam, and use the occasion to establish contact with the expatriate Vietnamese in Siam.

Prior to that, in the spring and summer of the Year of the Monkey [1908], after the Vietnam Constitutional Association had been established and the students had been taken care of, I had given some thought to preparing for this diplomatically, and had made use of my spare time to pay a first visit to Siam, staying over in Bangkok. At that time the old king of Siam was the country's most enlightened leader;[113] he had previously traveled to Europe and possessed a statesman's vision. He was well aware of the interdependent relationship between Vietnam and Siam. Moreover, before leaving Japan I had obtained a letter of introduction from Ōkuma to Satō Yoshikichi, who had a doctorate in law and was currently legal adviser to a Siamese minister. Thanks to this previously arranged introduction, the king very gladly accepted my presence, and I was granted an audience with the minister of Foreign Affairs. I sometimes saw the princes and other members of the royal family. The princes treated me with special courtesy, in accordance with the wish of the king. Siam was a country in which the monarchy was greatly revered. The fact that she was able to maintain independence from the Great Powers in the twentieth century was due to the king alone. Neither her domestic nor her foreign policy were decided by any of his subjects. At this time I had a discussion about clearing land for cultivation with one of the princes, who agreed to give help. Afterward, Đặng-Tử-Kính, Đặng-Ngọ-Sinh

---

113. King Chulalongkorn (1853–1910), who assumed full control of Siam in 1873, was responsible for bringing about the modernization of his country and the revision of the unequal treaties forced on Siam by the European powers.

[Đặng-Thúc-Hứa], Hồ-Vĩnh-Long, and others arrived in Siam one after another to engage in farming. Everything that followed was due to the preliminary opening of communications with the Siamese through my journey at this time.

After my expulsion from Japan, I was thinking of renewing our previous good relations by going to Siam again, but suddenly I received news from home saying that Hoàng-Hoa-Thám of Yên-thế had launched an armed uprising and was achieving quite considerable success. Also, Tùng-Nham [Phạm-Văn-Ngôn] had just gone back from Fort Phồn-xương to Nghệ-an to arrange to take action in concert with Hoàng's move. I was very excited, and immediately wanted to procure men and arms to smuggle back to our country to aid Hoàng's troops. Đặng-Tử-Mẫn, Hoàng-Trọng-Mậu, and others also strongly supported that idea. The plan of traveling to Siam was thus postponed.

I THEN ASSEMBLED our comrades in Hong Kong, and while we were waiting for funds to arrive, I asked Đàm-Kỳ-Sinh to return home carrying a letter from me asking Ngư-Hải [Đặng-Thái-Thân] to make an assessment of the situation from various points of view, which he could report to me when he came back. In the Third Month of the same year Đặng-Ngọ-Sinh arrived in Hong Kong from home to see me, bringing with him two thousand five hundred piasters from Ngư-Hải. He described in detail the conditions at home; the militant group was all set to go into action but was short of arms; if it could obtain some arms, then there would be a possibility of transmitting more funds from home. When I heard that, I was wildly happy. I thereupon set about acquiring arms.

First of all, I gave Đặng-Tử-Mẫn and Đặng-Ngọ-Sinh two thousand one hundred piasters to travel to Japan and purchase arms. Previously, while in Japan, I had established contact with an arms shop called the Yamaguchi Shōten. Now I asked these two to go to that shop to purchase one hundred rifles of the model of the thirtieth year of the Meiji era. The price was two thousand piasters, that is to say, each rifle cost twenty piasters. This was the model of rifle used during the war against Russia. After Japan's victory, a new model was designed, and these rifles were considered old models. The chamber could hold five bullets, therefore another name for this rifle was "the five-round rifle." Because there were a lot of the old model rifles left, so as not to let them go to waste, the Ministry of the Army sold them to people in the trade, and the people in the trade likewise wanted to sell them as soon as possible. We bought one hundred rifles for cash and another four hundred on credit, making five hundred altogether. Extremely pleased to have acquired them, we followed a plan of Li Wei, a member of the Chinese revolutionary party, to smuggle them to Hong Kong and store them secretly in a small house. But at that point we were down to two hundred piasters in cash; moreover, we had no means of smuggling them back home.

I happened to have heard that there was a route that the Chinese revolutionary party had used many times to transport arms, starting from Singapore in the South Seas. So in the third decade of the Fifth Month of the Year of the Cock [July 1909], Đặng-Ngọ-Sinh and I went south to Singapore to see Ch'en Shu-nan, a member of the Chinese revolutionary party in Singapore. We had discussions over several evenings on how to smuggle arms. Ch'en said: "Up to this time there have been two ways by which our party has transported arms back home: first, by hiring [Western] merchant ships to land them in the Leased Territories, and second, by hiring Chinese merchant ships to land them in the interior." I thought that, in the case of our country, there was no possibility of hiring any Western ships; in addition, the ports in our country could not be used as our destinations. If we wished to smuggle into the interior, we should necessarily have to use Chinese merchant ships. These would be convenient to use, because Chinese merchant ships were large sailing craft that could moor at any point on the riverbank where there were no people around, and when the arms were unloaded, people from the interior could secretly come and pick them up.

A Chinese merchant with a large-scale business to whom Ch'en introduced me set a transport fee of more than two hundred piasters for each one hundred rifles; therefore, without more than a thousand piasters there would be no way to transport the five hundred rifles. This did not seem like a very practicable idea to me, because such a large sum of money would certainly not be easy to obtain; but I had to acquiesce nonetheless.

IN THE FIRST DECADE of the Sixth Month [July 1909], I left the South Seas, stopping en route in Siam with the idea of asking for help from the prince I mentioned previously. If the Siamese government did not object, the contraband could be disguised as merchandise to get past the customs. This seemed to me much the best expedient. On arriving in Bangkok, I asked for an audience with the prince. At the outset he agreed to lend his support, but after the matter had been discussed several times, the minister of Foreign Affairs was unalterably opposed to the idea, for fear lest the business should leak out and the cordial relations of France and Siam be seriously impaired, as it was quite out of line with diplomatic practice. I had no choice but to return to Hong Kong and lie low, merely waiting patiently for funds to arrive to carry out the plan of hiring a Chinese boat.

Just at that time, Đàm-Kỳ-Sinh arrived from our country. I was greatly disheartened by his news of misfortunes one on top of the other: Tùng-Nham had been arrested; old Mạnh-Thận had died in combat; Hoàng-Hoa-Thám's fighters had been pinned down and were looking for aid with the utmost urgency; Ngư-Hải was using all his persuasive powers, but the collection of a large sum of money was as yet only in the planning stage. The only thing that could give one hope was that the people's heart had not yet had the life totally crushed out of it; witness the fact that before Đàm left our country, the local militias *(lính tập)* in Nghệ-an and Hà-tĩnh, led by certain persons,[114] were planning an

---

114. AM gives their names: Quản Phấn and Đội Truyền.

assault on the city [of Hà-tĩnh]. If this could be brought off, our critical situation could be turned around.

On hearing this news, I urgently asked Đàm to go back to inform the militant-action group that arms had already been purchased; all that was needed now was money, and as soon as we received it, then the arms could be dispatched home. I also asked Đàm to entrust Ngư-Hải with secretly looking for a good, quiet location along the coastline of Trung-Kỳ,[115] and arranging for people to receive the arms. At any rate, as soon as the money arrived the arms would be sent immediately.

It was already the Eighth Month of the Year of the Cock [September/October 1909]. Đàm took my letter and went home, but still no funds arrived. Concerned as I was over the business of transporting the arms home, I felt a burning anxiety, because if the smuggled arms were stored too long, I was worried that the British police would find out about them, or that they would get rusty and be good for nothing. Moreover, if in the meantime Hoàng-Hoa-Thám's troops should be crushed, our right arm would have been broken; of what use could the arms be then? After some time there arrived the fateful news about Ngư-Hải, which staggered and stunned me as if I had been struck by a sword. I had to hold my breath to stop myself from shedding tears, reproaching Heaven for having turned its eyes away!

From the Year of the Monkey[116] [1908] up until now, all the news from home had been shocking and appalling. Yet the thing that brought me to the utmost desperation was the fateful news about Ngư-Hải. During the summer and autumn of the Year of the Monkey, the stalwart people in Trung-Kỳ who refused to pay taxes had been massacred. The martyrs in Bắc-Kỳ who had taken part in the poisoning incident had been sacrificed. The Đông-Kinh Private School and the other commercial and educational societies in Trung-Kỳ one after another had been brought to an end. Our dedicated comrades sometimes had died while imprisoned, at other times had been sent to suffer exile in the farthest

---

115. AM indicates that the location would be in either Nghệ-Tĩnh or Nam-Ngãi.
116. AM and TQP read: "From the autumn of the Year of the Monkey . . . ."

corner of the universe. There were not tears enough to shed for all. My body was still alive, but to no purpose. Truly this period was the time of my utmost despair and sorrow during those ten years.

In the middle decade of the Second Month of the Year of the Dog [late March 1910], I received a letter from Phạm-Mai-Lâm that read:

> On the first day of the Second Month of this year Ngư-Hải's home was surrounded.[117] Setting fire to all the documents that he had, he first used his pistol to shoot dead a French soldier; next he pointed the pistol at a local militiaman, saying: "I could kill you, but I won't kill someone of the same race." Finally he turned the pistol on himself, shot himself in the throat, and died.

This news was indeed the first arrow to give me a fatal wound. Previously I had heard that Tiểu-La had been arrested, but that other comrades, such as Nam-Xương [Thái Phiên], Ô-Da [Trình Hiền], Cửu Cai [Trần Hoành], and others, all so far survived. The Nghệ-Tĩnh area was still in the good hands of Ngư-Hải. Though the large sum of money had not yet arrived, still there had been some measure of hope. With Ngư-Hải dead, that hope was extinguished.

The arms stored in Hong Kong could not now be used for anything. Just at that time the Chinese revolutionary party was planning an attack on Canton and was secretly puchasing arms. When this came to the ears of our people, I obtained authorization from our comrades in Hong Kong to donate the arms to the revolutionary party; they were collected by men dispatched by Sun Shou-ping, Sun Yat-sen's elder brother. Altogether, there were 480 rifles, complete with bayonets and attachments and bullets. My thought was that this would create warm sentiments that might be reciprocated after the other party had been successful. It was a plan devised at my wits' end, but it was a good plan for all that. The remaining twenty rifles, twenty packs of bullets, and twenty bayonets were taken out and surreptitiously packed

---

117. AM adds: "The French had sent out both French and Vietnamese soldiers." TQP reads: "On the first day of the Second Month of this year (11 March 1910), the French enemy had sent out both French and Vietnamese soldiers."

as merchandise in a valise. A first-class tariff was paid to send them by
boat to Bangkok, with the notion that first-class goods might escape the
scrutiny of the customs police. But contrary to expectation, when the
arms arrived at the port, the customs police became suspicious because
the valise was too heavy. This rash and hazardous plan ended in failure,
and because of that [Nguyễn-]Quỳnh-Lâm was imprisoned for several
months.

DURING THE SPRING and summer of the Year of the Dog [1910], I
lay low in Canton, from time to time traveling to the harbor piers of
Hong Kong and Macao, carrying with me the remaining copies of my
various books and hawking them, revealing neither my first name nor
my family name, in my quest for a way to make a living. The banner
advertising the books read:

A cry written in blood and tears
by one engaged in revolution.
A valiant champion
has fallen on hard times;
your support will help him
to play the flute later.

These words were apropos, indeed.

At the time, the Chinese students and merchants among the passengers were highly charged with revolutionary ideas. Seeing me selling
my books, sometimes they bought them at a premium price. It was
a time when food and clothing were plentiful. Every day I left early
in the morning and returned in the evening. Some days I could sell
two or three piasters' worth. I would then forgather with two or three
comrades to drink like mad, getting spectacularly drunk.

Nguyễn-Quỳnh-Lâm had the most marvelous way of getting
drunk. He was romantic by nature, without a trace of vulgarity. Then
there was Lương-Lập-Nham, who at the outset did not like to drink
but by this time could imbibe with the best. The money we acquired

from our daily book sales was all used up on drink. One day when our bottle had been emptied, he realized that I still had some money in the wallet in my sleeve. He asked me to buy some more, but I pretended there was no money left. He took my wallet out and finding ten cents yelled loudly: "You should be killed, you old codger! Why are you so stingy that you won't get us more to drink?"

The funniest thing was that when the younger people went out to sell books, most of the time they came back empty-handed. It was only on the days when I went out to sell that two or three piasters would come in, sometimes even five or six piasters. That was because of my unkempt hair and shabby clothes and shoes. People felt sorry for me, and bought at a premium price. For three or four months on end, I mostly lived the life of an old man of letters selling books.

During this time, after I had had a few drinks, I composed quite a lot of poems, one of which was much praised by my great benefactress Chou Po-ling. Every time she met me, she recited it. The poem read:

> *Daily upon the balcony I lean,*
> *My gaze turned south, beyond what can be seen.*
>
> *A cloud, that with its burden cannot part*
> *Of pent-up raindrops—it is like my heart.*
>
> *A shower passes, leaving no more trace*
> *Than does a secret tear wiped from the face.*
>
> *The sun has set; the moon has hid her light;*
> *Far off the lonely geese have taken flight.*
>
> *Let fire descend, and burn my grief to naught!*
> *But fiercer wrath is all the tempest wrought.*
>
> *I view my likeness; contemplate each feature;*
> *And laugh in scorn at the pathetic creature.*
>
> *In such a state my countrymen now languish;*
> *How should I then complain of private anguish?*

OUR BENEFACTRESS CHOU was a native of Hsiangshan County in
Kwangtung Province. She was well versed in literary Chinese. Having been widowed when she was still young, she opened a private
school and taught pupils in order to find the means to bring up her
son. Chou T'ieh-sheng,[118] her son, was also a teacher by profession.
When he came across me selling books in the street, he took me home
to meet his mother, who by nature possessed a high-souled disposition
and loved to talk about the glorious exploits of the great men of olden
times. When she had met me and realized that I was a member of the
Vietnamese revolutionary movement, she was absolutely delighted and
full of approval, and said: " You are in dire straits at the moment. Do
not hesitate to come and stay at our house."

At that time we were at the very end of our resources and had no
money even to pay rent; so we went to her house to live as her guests.
Thus from that time, the home of Madame Chou of Huangsha in Shihu
became our abode. There was not a single person in our movement
who did not stay at this house. We supplied what we could toward the
expenses for food and lodging; whether the compensation was much
or little, she never minded. When our group had some urgent need, if
there was no money in the house, she would leave her clothes in pawn
to take care of it. Not only did she have a deep and solid sense of right-
eousness, her fortitude was also extraordinary. At one time we stored
dynamite and ammunition in the house; she was not a bit frightened.
Trần-Hữu-Lực [Nguyễn-Thức-Đường] and Đặng-Tử-Kính once borrowed her vegetable knife to kill a spy late at night. When she appeared
in the morning, she laughed and asked them: " Were you fellows
butchering a pig last night?" Even when her son was thrown into prison
for more than ten days by Lung Chi-kuang on account of me, she never
lost her composure. She treated us as a mother would treat her children.
This year she would be more than eighty years old. Her feelings toward
us have been the same from beginning to end.

---

118. In Sino-Vietnamese, *Chu Hiệp-Sinh*. All the modern Vietnamese translations
give his personal name as " Thiết-Sinh."

Once there were three [Vietnamese] men who had previously stayed at her house, but several years later betrayed the movement, gave in to the French, and came back to spy. They called at her house and took out a large sum of money to offer her. She engaged them in conversation and forced out of them where the money had come from. In a rage, she berated them: "Before, I let you stay here because I thought you were human beings. Now that you are running-dogs, how dare you still come to see me?" After that, those three men never darkened her doorway again.

In this world, the persons that you treasure most are often those you meet when you are in great adversity. So this was someone we always remember and shall never be able to forget. Her family name was Chou, her literary name was Po-ling, and she was a teacher who, according to the Cantonese practice, was addressed as *hsih-tai* (Madame Teacher), therefore she was known to us as "Madame Teacher Chou" *(Chou Hsih-tai).*

AT THE END OF the autumn in the Year of the Dog [1910], suddenly we received encouraging news in the midst of nothing but depression. At that time there arrived a sum of more than five hundred silver piasters. Part of this was brought over by Lý Tuệ in person; it had been entrusted to him by Lương-Lập-Nham. Part was brought over by a certain person from Quảng-nam; it had been dispatched by comrades in Nam-Xương.[119] I thus decided on the plan of moving to Siam. To begin with, taking two hundred piasters, I asked Đặng-Tử-Kính, Đặng-Tử-Mẫn, and Lê-Cầu-Tinh to travel to Siam in advance to make arrangements with respect to farming equipment.

It happened at this point that two men from Bắc-Kỳ arrived who had been sent on by Lương-Văn-Can. One was Dư-Tất-Đạt, who later changed his name to Trương-Quốc-Uy, studied at Peking Military Academy, and joined the ranks of the [Chinese] revolutionary army

---

119. Nam-Xương was the home town of Thái-Phiên Trần-Cao-Vân, and it may be assumed that he took the initiative in the fund-raising.

as an officer. At present he is still keeping busy in the area of Kwangsi and Kwangtung.

The other one was Lâm-Đức-Mậu. When he first arrived, I at once sent him to Canton to stay at Madame Chou's house and study Chinese. At the time our diplomatic strategy was mainly focused on Germany; I therefore directed him to enter the Chinese-German Middle School established by the Germans in order to learn how to speak and write German, so that he would be prepared for future activities. I had previously hoped to travel to Berlin, but there had been no one who could act as interpreter and no travel funds. My travel plan thus could not be realized. Now that I had Lâm, it was like hearing a human footstep when lost in the depths of the wild woods!

Lâm was proficient in French but had not learned to read Chinese yet. After he had stayed in Kwangtung for half a year, his Chinese had improved immensely. After he entered the school, his German and his Chinese both progressed splendidly, and at the end of one year, having achieved excellent grades, he was exempted from tuition as well as from fees for room and board. After three years, when he graduated from the school, the teachers and students in the school all thought so highly of him that he was made a teacher of the first grade. Then he was recommended to go on to Chingtao to study at the high school. Because he was so proficient in German, he became very well acquainted with the Germans there. One year after the outbreak of the European War, he left China to go to Bangkok, because there the consuls of Germany and Austria all knew Đặng-Tử-Mẫn and myself; Lâm was to be in charge of the diplomatic side of things in Siam.

However, half a year after his arrival in Siam, the diplomatic situation was suddenly reversed. Siam declared war on Germany, and the Siamese government acceded to the requests of the French to extradite Lâm back to Hanoi. At that time he was arrested together with another man, who was working as a teacher, named Nguyễn-Văn-Trung, a native of Nam-định. While being tortured, both men were steadfast and indomitable. The French soldiers used rifles to frighten them. Lâm was infuriated, and said: "We shall die as true Vietnamese; we have no wish to live as running-dogs. Even if we die, the German troops will come soon!" Eventually they were both executed by a firing squad; at the foot of Mount Bạch-mai is their grave!

Alas! When Lâm arrived in Siam, I had been put in prison in Kwangtung. He sent me a letter to console me that included the following lines: "If it is the will of Heaven to help our country, how can it be possible that you, Sir, will not return alive?" His eyes were sparkling; his countenance was especially engaging and attractive; his speech was incisive; his diplomatic talent was comparable to Hoàng-Đình-Tuân's. Our country had sore need of such talents, yet these two men died one after the other. How painful it is!

IN THE NINTH MONTH of the Year of the Dog [October/early November 1910], I again left Kwangtung for Siam, with the intention of following in the footsteps of Wu Tzu-ssu, who went to farm in the land of Pi.[120] Accompanying me there were four or five working-class people. To be buffeted by the wind and soaked by the rain, with one's feet in the rice paddy and one's hands in the mud, I thought would not be appropriate without people like this around, so I brought them along. Among them there was a man of whom something should be recorded.

This man was called Hai Phương; he did not know a single written character, but by nature had a high-souled disposition. When he was young, following some Frenchmen, he had gone to Hong Kong and learned the art of French cuisine quite proficiently. He was the cook at the French bank in Hong Kong. The money he had saved up was quite substantial. He was unmarried and lived by himself, but he

---

120. According to the story in the *Shih-chih*, book LXVI, Wu Tzu-ssu, whose real name was Wu Yüan, was a man of the State of Ch'u; when his father and elder brother were murdered by Prince P'ing, he fled to the Wu state and farmed until he was able to enter the service of the Wu state and return to Ch'u to take revenge. The land of Pi was remote and wild, and its name came to stand for any such place.

loved to entertain other Vietnamese and thus came to know of our movement. At the time when the Vietnamese Commercial Association was founded in Hong Kong, he gave the largest donation. Every month he contributed five piasters; he never failed to do so. When the talk came round to revolutionary affairs, he promptly expressed his strong desire to abandon his servile occupation to join the cause as a fighter. In the port, the Vietnamese working as houseboys or cooks numbered approximately several dozen; he would stir up their patriotic sentiments, and many of them were greatly influenced.

As I was about to go to farm in Siam I stopped off at Hong Kong to see him, and he was happy to accede to my request that he come along; he was even able to persuade two of his fellow workers to come as well. Later on, he went with Đặng-Tử-Kính to farm in Ban Cham.[121] Rising early in the morning, retiring late at night, with his feet in the paddy field regardless of cold or heat, he was nevertheless always tranquil and at ease. Compared to Hai Phương in Western clothes and shoes as a Western cook, what an extreme change! Ah! Some there were like him, who, once inspired by righteous indignation, would then entirely free themselves from the taint of worldly greed!

IN THE THIRD DECADE of the Ninth Month [late October/early November 1910], we arrived in Siam. At the outset I thought that from this time on I should be staying in Siam for the rest of my life, following the pattern of "ten years building up the people, ten years training them."[122] This was because I was deeply chagrined by the fact that

---

121. In Sino-Vietnamese, *Bạn Thầm*. Its location has been debated among different authors; some hold that it was in Kamburi, others suggest that it was in Phichit.

122. This expression comes from the story of Prince Kou-ch'ien of the State of Yüeh. Defeated by the forces of Wu in 494 B.C., during the Spring and Autumn period, the Prince asked Prince Fu-chai of Wu to accept him as a subject. The counselor Wu Tzu-ssu advised Fu-chai not to do so, on the grounds that Kou-ch'ien would take "ten years to build up the people and ten years to train them" and eventually would crush the State of Wu. Fu-chai disregarded the advice of his counselor, and by 473 Kou-ch'ien had indeed extinguished Wu. In Phan's modern Vietnamese version, the

ever since I had gone abroad, the enterprises I had undertaken had all been just like attempts by a little child to build a brick house. When I arrived, Ngọ-Sinh [Đặng-Thúc-Hứa], Đặng-Tử-Kính, Hồ-Vĩnh-Long, and others had already rented land from the Siamese to put up houses; on the whole, we were off to a good start.

I again had an audience with the Elder Prince whom I had met before, submitting the details of our present circumstances and the plan of our group to take up farming, and requesting covert support from the Siamese government. The Elder Prince was most agreeable, and called in his younger brother, who was a lieutenant-general in the army, to entrust the matter to him. The lieutenant-general undertook to do his best in this regard. He invited us to his residence and entertained us to dinner; his wife herself was our hostess at dinner. He promised us that each newly arrived person would be provided with a monthly food allowance of five baht.[123] Afterward, we could rely on the produce of our fields.

In addition, he dispatched people to assign us some farmland. The land was in a hilly district called Ban Cham, situated close to a big river; it was therefore convenient for drawing water, and as it was in the river delta, the soil was fertile and easy to work. It was distant about four days' walk from Bangkok. The farm implements were all supplied by the lieutenant-general. The buffalo that we needed for farming were borrowed from the neighboring village; the villagers accommodated our wishes and agreed to lend them out without reluctance. Those among the formerly dispersed students who were able to sustain hard labor all gathered there.

---

quotation begins with the words *thập-niên sinh-dưỡng* (ten years of recuperation); the translation above renders the original text, which reads (in Sino-Vietnamese) *thập-niên sinh-tụ*. See Yang Po-shun, *Ch'un-ch'iu Tso-chuan chü* (Commentaries on the Tradition of Tso) (Peking: Yüanliu Ch'upanshe, 1982), II, 1606–1607. TQP, followed by GB, substitutes for this sentence the following: "It was my opinion that this was the time to make a long-term plan; we should go into action only when necessary preparations had been carried out."

123. One Siamese baht is equivalent to eighty cents of French money. [Author's note.]

At that time I was fit neither for hoeing nor for plowing; nevertheless, with torn clothes and a frayed hat, I picked the vegetables and gathered the firewood, and thus I did my full share. I also composed three ballads, *Ái-quốc-ca, Ái-chủng-ca,* and *Ái-quần-ca* (On Love of the Country, On Love of the Race, On Love of the People). I rendered them into colloquial Vietnamese and taught our people to sing them. While they were tilling the land they would sing them in chorus, and as the sound of our united voices rose in the air, the Siamese passing by would stop and clap their hands. Truly an exquisite scene!

Among those who were farming, there was an old military man called Cố Khôn (Old Khôn), sturdy and brave, honest and bluff, looking every inch a warrior of the old school. Formerly, when in our country, he had taken the mandarinate examination in military affairs. In the reign of Kiến-Phúc, in the Year of the Monkey [1884], he received a licentiate in military affairs and was appointed head of a battalion. When the French took over Nghệ-an, he was named head of the local militia. Ngư-Hải made an appeal to him in the name of the just cause; bringing his arms along with him, he joined the movement. After Ngư-Hải came to grief, he took to the hills. Now, on hearing that I had come to Siam, he followed me there. His age was close to sixty but he was still as alert and vigorous as a young man. He was well versed in the martial arts. Whenever there was a pause from tilling the land, in the pure air of dawn or by the evening moonlight, he would instruct the youths in all the techniques of stick fighting and bare-handed combat, swordsmanship and pike handling. Thanks to him, our morale received a great boost.

OWING TO MY FAILURES of all kinds, I had decided to lie low and wait for the right time, seeing this as the best choice. Then suddenly, after scarcely a year, the Chinese revolutionary army rose up in Wuhan. The call for the restoration of China beat upon my ears like thunder. Because of that I changed my plan. In fact, the germination of the second stage of my failure started here.

In the Tenth Month of the Year of the Boar [November/December 1911], the Chinese revolutionary army captured Wuchang. In less than a month the entire country rose up in response. In less than three months the Manchu government was overthrown. The republican government was established in Nanking; this was indeed beyond my expectations. As the news reached me, my old action-loving temperament was rekindled. As yet I assumed that after the success of the revolutionary party, the Chinese government could not possibly be corrupt like the government in the old days. (Right there was where I made my mistake.) China would inevitably follow the example of Japan and become a Great Power, and the two countries, Japan and China, would concentrate all their forces on counteracting Europe. The hour of independence would then arrive not only for our Vietnam but also for India and the Philippines, one after the other.

I decided to return to China and to reenter Japan as well, to put forward a plan for *hợp-tung*.[124] As there was a slack time on the farm, I composed a booklet called *Liên-Á sô-ngôn* (A Modest Discourse about an Asian Alliance). The whole text came to some ten thousand characters; it boldly set forth the advantages of unity between China and Japan and the harm done by disunity between the two. When the booklet had been composed, I first sent it to my old acquaintances among the Chinese revolutionary party, congratulating them on their success and also hinting that I was thinking of returning to China. My old acquaintances, such as Chang Ping-lin, Ch'en Chi-mei, Hsia Ying-po, and others, all wrote me letters to encourage me to come back to China.

I ENTRUSTED the management of the farm to two persons, Đặng-Ngọ-Sinh and Đặng-Tử-Kính, who would direct the more than fifty

---

124. That is, rallying small states to counter big powers; a reference to the plan of Su Ch'in during the Warring States period of allying the six small states against the Ch'in state. In this case, what Phan wishes to propose is obviously an Asian alliance against the European powers.

comrades who stayed behind to carry on farming. Together with a number of the comrades, I went to Bangkok and visited Shao Fo-sheng, the editor of the *Hua-hsien Hsin-pao* (China-Siam News). Shao was the key man in the office of the Chinese revolutionary party in Siam. When he had seen the manuscript of my *Modest Discourse about an Asian Alliance*, he printed one thousand copies on my behalf. The overseas Japanese in Siam warmly welcomed this book, buying no fewer than three hundred copies. Of the remaining seven hundred copies, I distributed a few among the overseas Chinese, and all the rest I took along with me to China.

Accompanying me were Đặng-Tử-Mẫn, Nguyễn-Quỳnh-Lâm, and Đặng-Hồng-Phấn. When we arrived in Kwangtung, we stayed over at Madame Chou Hsih-tai's home. It was the Twelfth Month of the Year of the Boar [January/February 1912]. Nguyễn-Hải-Thần had just come from Vietnam, and members of the movement who had been scattered all over China, such as Đặng-Xung-Hồng, Lâm-Quảng-Trung, Hoàng-Trọng-Mậu, Trần-Hữu-Lực, and others, arrived in Kwangtung one after the other. From Nam-Kỳ came Nguyễn-Thành-Hiến; Hoàng Hưng and Đặng-Bỉnh-Thành also arrived from Siam afterward. All of them were looking toward the same goal that I was, namely to take advantage of the success of the Chinese revolution and make use of the agency of the Chinese to turn our situation around.

Nevertheless, in retrospect, this plan was after all highly impractical, because there was no functioning organization whatsoever inside our country but only a sham outward appearance of force, and everything depended on the foreigners. In neither the past nor the present, in neither the East nor the West, had there ever been a revolutionary party that was such a lot of beggars as we were. The trouble was, at that time there was no possibility for us to reenter our country, but we found it unbearable to stay abroad leading an easy life and letting time pass idly by. So there was nothing else we could do but come up with this less-than-satisfactory plan.

IN THE FIRST MONTH of the Year of the Rat [February/March 1912], Sun Yat-sen was elected provisional president of China.[125] With both his governor of Kwangtung, Hu Han-min, whom I had known since my time in Japan, and his governor of Shanghai, Ch'en Chi-mei, I was on the best of terms. The membership of our movement in Kwangtung was rising steadily, to as many as one hundred.

The Marquis, from Hong Kong, and Mai-Lão-Bạng, from Siam, both came to a meeting we convened. Our discussion was getting nowhere when suddenly Nguyễn-Trọng-Thường arrived from Hanoi. Reporting on the situation at home, he said: "The tide of success of the Chinese revolution has had an immense effect upon our country. The people are tremendously stirred up as compared to before. If first a voice were raised abroad, we need have no fear that morale would not revive inside our country." The people attending the meeting, on hearing this news, became very excited.

I then decided upon a plan of action. The first thing was to convene a general meeting to decide the guiding principle and political doctrine we should follow. This was necessary because not only had the students in Japan been dispersed and the Vietnam Constitutional Association been dissolved, but in our country bad things had been happening one after another, so that the members of our movement had been scattered and the plans of the Vietnam Modernization Association had become scrap paper. Now it would be impossible to resume the activities of our movement without reconstructing it.

As a first step we had to make a decision about our political doctrine, to settle the issue of what our country's national polity (*quốc-thể*) should be. As a second step we had to select delegates to send to the Three Regions to mobilize support. As a third step we had to make contact with the members of the Chinese revolutionary party and set up an agency to approach influential people to solicit aid,

125. Sun's election in fact took place at a revolutionary assembly on 30 December 1911; on 12 February 1912 the emperor's abdication rescript was published, allowing the republicans to take control. The next day Sun set out terms for his resignation in favor of Yüan Shih-k'ai, but he did not relinquish his powers until 1 April.

both in weaponry and provisions. This was because at that time the members of our movement were completely empty-handed; unless we could draw on outside resources, we should not have anything at all.

With that thought in mind, the first step was begun. In the first decade of the Second Month [late March 1912], we used the family temple of Liu Yung-fu in Shaho as the meeting place for a general congress of the entire movement. Members from all of the Three Regions attended. When the congress was convened, there was one issue that had to be resolved first: that was monarchy versus democracy.

EVER SINCE MY arrival in Japan, I had been studying the origins of revolutions in other countries and the advantages and disadvantages of various political systems. I was fascinated by the theories of Rousseau, Montesquieu, and others. Rousseau's *Contrat social* and Montesquieu's *De l'Esprit des Lois* I had read for the first time only after I went overseas. Moreover, as a result of my many contacts with Chinese comrades, monarchism had been relegated to the back of my mind. But I had not yet dared to proclaim the fact, because at the time when I went abroad I had upheld the banner of monarchy, and I wished to keep faith with the people at home. Had circumstances not changed, our means would not have had to change; but now that circumstances had altered greatly, I suddenly reached the point of making a proposal for democracy quite openly.

Đặng-Tử-Mẫn, Lương-Lập-Nham, and Hoàng-Trọng-Mậu were the first to endorse this. The rest of the comrades from Trung-Kỳ and Bắc-Kỳ all added their support. In opposition were the members from Nam-Kỳ, because among our fellow countrymen from this region there was an enormous faith in the Marquis, and their frame of mind could not be changed all of a sudden. The senior elder Hải-Dương [sic] Nguyễn-Thượng-Hiền, though he had no idea what democracy was, did reluctantly give his approval. The result was that the majority decided to move toward democracy, and to abolish the Vietnam Modernization Association and set up a new organization to replace it.

The Việt-Nam Quang-Phục-Hội (Vietnam Restoration League) was thus born at this time. I drafted an agenda for the League, which was presently approved by the members at the congress. The first clause stated that its objective was to restore Vietnam's independence and establish her as a democratic republic. This was the sole objective of the League.

Members of the League were assigned to three committees:

(i) The Committee on General Affairs. The president of the League, Cường-Để,[126] was the chairman, and the secretary-general, Sào-Nam [Phan-Bội-Châu], was the vice-chairman.

(ii) The Conference Committee, for which the Three Regions each selected one senior person who was well educated and well respected: Nguyễn-Thượng-Hiền from Bắc-Kỳ, Nguyễn-Thành-Hiến from Nam-Kỳ, and Phan-Bội-Châu from Trung-Kỳ.

(iii) The Executive Committee, which had ten members. Hoàng-Trọng-Mậu and Lương-Lập-Nham were in charge of Military Affairs. Mai-Lão-Bạng and Đặng-Tử-Mẫn were in charge of Economic Affairs. Lâm-Đức-Mậu and Đặng-Bỉnh-Thành were in charge of External Affairs. Phan-Bá-Ngọc and Nguyễn-Yến-Chiêu, who were respectively proficient in French and German as well as Chinese composition, were in charge of Cultural Affairs. Fan Kwei-chun (who later changed his name to Yang Chen-hai)[127] and Đinh-Tế-Dân were in charge of the Secretariat.

In addition to the members of the committees, three members were delegated to return home to mobilize support: Đặng-Bỉnh-Thành for Nam-Kỳ, Lâm-Quảng-Trung for Trung-Kỳ, and Đặng-Xung-Hồng for Bắc-Kỳ.

---

126. In view of the adherence of the congress to democracy, Phan here omits the title of marquis.

127. A native of Taiwan; in their Sino-Vietnamese forms, his names are Phan-Quý-Chuân and Dương-Trấn-Hải. His story will be told below, p. 195.

There were three locations where our members could meet. One was the family temple of the Liu in Shaho, which Liu Yung-fu had permitted us to use, and which could hold more than fifty. Another was Madame Chou's house in Huangsha, which could hold more than ten. Finally, there were scattered places in the homes of Chinese people and in the dormitories at various schools.

The most difficult thing to resolve was the financial question. The League had been set up; the executive members had been selected; the locations had been decided upon; but for the time being, the League[128] had not a penny in its funds. Even though the executive members of the League were accomplished chefs, there was nothing they could do without rice to cook. They spent all day in empty talk, or else in looking at each other and shedding tears. The financial question was the most urgent one, but there was no way to deal with it other than to raise support in our country and to beg for help abroad.

To begin with, small donations were solicited, to prepare the groundwork for asking for large donations. Liu Shih-fu of the I-hsin-she (Oneness of Heart Society) gave two hundred piasters.[129] Kuan Jen-fu, the commander of the militia, gave one hundred piasters. Hsia Ying-po and Teng Ching-ya gave one hundred piasters. I then set aside a small portion of these funds to use for the expenses for the three members to return home. The greater part was used for the expenses of printing various documents. The plan of action of the Vietnam Restoration League and the League's manifesto were both printed at that time and entrusted to the three members to take home for distribution. By now, Lý Tuệ had already been imprisoned. On the boat there was no secret friend of the movement, but it was inconvenient to carry large quantities of these documents by the land

---

128. Some modern Vietnamese translations, such as TQP, followed by GB, here read *chính phủ lâm thời*, "provisional government," instead of *lâm thời, Hội* . . . .

129. Liu was a scholar of extreme socialist views, who founded the I-hsin-she to put into practice his ideology. [Author's note.] — TQP translates this phrase as "to put communism into practice." In fact, Liu Shih-fu (1884–1915) was a well known Chinese anarchist. [Translators' note.]

route, so that of those that were dispatched very few actually reached their destination.

As to the funds raised in our country, from the Three Regions there were scarcely more than two thousand piasters altogether.[130] The current situation in our country can be pretty well judged from this— the difficulties of our movement were ten times greater, compared with what they had been before.

AS THE THREE MEMBERS left to return home, I set about raising support from abroad. In the last decade of the Second Month of the Year of the Rat [April 1912], I went up to Nanking to have an interview with Sun Yat-sen. I had the opportunity to attend the first session of the [Chinese] congress as an observer. The Nanking government had been in existence for little more than two months, but a government under Yüan Shih-k'ai was just about to replace it. Sun, in view of the gravity of the circumstances at that time, had ceded the presidency to Yüan. My arrival in Nanking coincided with the handing over of power from the former to the latter. The affairs of the government were as complicated as a tangle of cotton threads. Sun had no time to receive visitors; I managed to see and talk with him only for a few minutes. However, after that I was in and out to see Huang Hsing on several occasions.

When the discussion touched on the question of giving aid to us, Huang Hsing said to me: "It is undeniable that our country has a duty to give assistance to Vietnam, but the time is very premature. At present the only thing that we can suggest on your behalf is simply that you should select students to send to our schools or to our army camps, to prepare their talents and wait for the right opportunity. This should not take longer than ten years at the most. As far as this matter is concerned, we should be able to take care of

---

130. TQP, followed by GB, gives the amount as "more than three thousand," but this must obviously be an error because, as they indicate, " Đặng-Bỉnh-Thành brought out one thousand piasters from Nam-Kỳ, Lâm-Quảng-Trung three hundred from Trung-Kỳ, and Đặng-Xung-Hồng six hundred from Bắc-Kỳ."

every necessity. Other than this, we are not able to do anything on your behalf."

When I heard Huang Hsing's words I was very disappointed, because sending out students was something that we had tried before; but I reluctantly acquiesced. Huang then wrote a letter recommending me to the governor of Kwangtung, Hu Han-min, asking Hu to take care of the affairs of our students in Kwangtung, because Kwangtung borders on Vietnam, and in view of their close relationship there could be no better place to help our people than Kwangtung.

I left with Huang's letter and went to Shanghai to have an interview with its governor, Ch'en Chi-mei. Ch'en was a generous man with a high sense of righteous indignation. I had been on friendly terms with him previously; when he had been busily pursuing revolutionary activities, he and I had been in the same plight *(đồng-bệnh)*. Without standing on ceremony, I straightforwardly told him of our pressing situation and asked for his help. Already knowing what I had in mind, Ch'en without hesitation offered me four thousand piasters.

Also, I told him that we were about to dispatch people to return to our country to carry out militant action. At first Ch'en disagreed with this, saying that we had better start with education, as a people without education would not be able to succeed at insurrection. I said in reply: "In our country, educational authority is entirely wielded by foreigners; the schools that have been established provide only a servile education, private schools are prohibited, and students are not allowed to go overseas. In no matter of education do we have the slightest freedom. For our people, in the midst of deadly peril, insurrection is the only catalyst for educational reform." I then cited Mazzini's words, "Education and insurrection should go hand in hand," and ran through the details of our failures thus far, such as the Đông-Kinh Private School, the Quảng-nam Học-Hội (Quảng-nam Society for Education), and so on.

I repeated my explanation in detail over and over. Eventually Ch'en agreed with me completely; he provided me with thirty grenades for use in battle. The desire that I had come with was more or less appeased, and the favor that Ch'en had done was so engraved in my memory that it could never be forgotten. I thanked him and bade farewell, and returned to Kwangtung to get on with the work of the League. This was the moment when the rice was placed in the cooking pot and the smoke began to rise from the hearth.

AT THIS TIME there was an amusing episode that is worth recording. Previously some men of high purpose from Taiwan had organized a secret movement that attempted to raise the flag of revolution in Taiwan. The leader of this group was Yang Chen-hai.[131] Yang had been a student at the Taiwan College of Medicine and obtained the degree of Bachelor of Medicine. He was intelligent and quick witted, well versed in English and Japanese as well as Chinese, and deeply committed to revolutionary ideas. Because the plan of his group leaked out, he was captured and imprisoned by the Japanese authorities. Yang killed his guard and escaped to Shanghai. The Japanese authorities requested China to extradite him on a charge of murder; the Chinese officials in Shanghai did not dare give him shelter. Yang therefore changed his name and fled to Canton. There he happened to read the manifesto of the Vietnam Restoration League and various books I had written. Finally he asked to join our movement and disguised himself as a Vietnamese. In due course, he was selected as an executive member of the League on account of his talent in the conduct of affairs. Behold! The people of one country that had lost its independence gave protection to a man of another country that had also lost its independence. Was this not an extraordinary occurrence?

This story prompts me to recall the time when I got four of our students into the Shimbu Gakkō during my sojourn in Japan. The Indian revolutionary movement at that time had many of its members in Japan, but because their appearance was noticeably different

---

131. For his position in the League, see above, p. 191.

from that of the Chinese, they were not able to enroll in the military schools.[132] Their leader, Mr. Đế,[133] asked for help from our group and was willing to be identified as Vietnamese in order to be accepted by the Japanese authorities. This our group could not agree to. At the time, as Lu Ying-ting, a native of Kwangsi, was the commander of the Kwangsi army and the founder of the Army Academy, I wrote a letter to Lu to introduce Đế. Lu highly praised Đế's commendable aspirations, but tactfully refused to accommodate him. What a difficult situation, not to have enough strength at home and to have to rely on foreigners! Nevertheless, in the case of the members of our movement, there were those who were admitted to the Peking Military Academy, the Kwangsi Army Academy, and the Kwangtung Military College— they were all trained, educated, and looked after without the slightest regard to expense. How strong was the sentiment that the Chinese people felt for us!

THE SUMMER AND autumn of the Year of the Rat [1912] were the period that witnessed the birth of the Vietnam Restoration League. From the time when it attempted its first cry, it met only with various failures and not a single good success. Nonetheless, during its infancy there were some things that it managed to accomplish, trifling though they might be. Most noteworthy among them are the following:

1. The decision to adopt democracy. (An account of this has been given above.)

---

132. AM gives a fuller version of this sentence: "The Indian revolutionary movement at that time had quite a few of its members in Japan, but because of the Anglo-Japanese Treaty [of 1902], and in addition because their appearance was noticeably different from that of the Chinese, the Indians in the movement were not welcomed by Japan . . . ."

133. This is the Sino-Vietnamese version of this name given at this point by Phan-Bội-Châu, who previously used the form "Đái" (see above, p. 163). Without direct evidence, one cannot be certain of the spelling. On the general situation of Indian students in Japan at this time, see Birendra Prasad, *Indian Nationalism and Asia* (Delhi: B.R. Publishing Corporation, 1979), 45–47.

2. The creation for the first time of a national flag. Once the League had been established, it had to begin organizing its army. From the outset, there were many who had been students at military schools abroad. At the Peking Military Academy there had been Lương-Lập-Nham, Lâm-Quảng-Trung, Hồ-Hinh-Sơn, Hà-Đương-Nhân, Nguyễn-Thiệu-Tô, Đặng-Hồng-Phấn, Phan-Bá-Ngọc, and others.[134] At the Peking College of Munitions there had been Lưu-Khải-Hồng, Nguyễn-Yến-Chiêu, and others. At the Kwangsi Army Academy there had been Trần-Hữu-Lực, Nguyễn-Tiêu-Đẩu, Nguyễn-Thái-Bạt, and others. As for those such as Hoàng-Trọng-Mậu, Nguyễn-Quỳnh-Lâm, Đặng-Xung-Hồng, and Nguyễn-Hải-Thần, all of them had been in military bases for quite a while and had obtained on-the-spot military experience. If we had an army, we need have no concern lest there should be no commanders to look after it.

Once an army had been created, there would have to be an army standard *(quân-kỳ);* once there was an army standard, it would be impossible not to have a national flag *(quốc-kỳ).*[135] It is indeed strange that until then, our country had had only a banner for the emperors, but no national flag. This was the first time that a national flag had been designed. It used five stars joined together in the form of a cluster of pearls:

As our country consists of five large sectors *(đại-bộ),* this design was to symbolize the idea that these five large sectors are connected and

---

134. In the original text, the name of Phan-Bá-Ngọc is given only as Phan-Bá-Mỗ (literally "Phan-Bá-So-and-so"). AM omits Phan-Bá-Ngọc altogether and adds Trương-Quốc-Uy instead. It looks as if this was done purposely, because of the generally accepted view that Phan-Bá-Ngọc had eventually gone over to the French colonial cause.

135. A great piece of foolishness. [Author's note.]

unified. The flag colors used were red stars on a yellow ground for our national flag, and white stars on a red ground for our army standard. The yellow symbolized our race. The red symbolized the location of our country—the South belongs to "fire," and fire's color is red. White is the color of "metal" *(kim),* conveying the idea that the army standard was for use in battles.

3. The compilation of a book on strategy for the League's army. This book consisted of more than one hundred pages. Its cover carried a reproduction of our army's standard and our national flag. Its content was divided into five chapters: (1) the army's guiding doctrine and objectives; (2) its discipline; (3) its composition; (4) its officers and their salaries; (5) its plans of action. At the time Hoàng-Trọng-Mậu was the chairman of the Military Affairs Committee; thus he drafted the chapters of the book from the third on, to which I made only some slight editorial additions. The first and second chapters were written by myself.

4. The printing of scrip for the League's army. By that time I had come to see that the propaganda that it had been our policy to use up to that point had been nothing but empty words and a waste of effort, and that peaceful, gradual progress was only vanity and a daydream. To give examples, our sending students to Japan had indeed been like starting out to paint a tiger but ending up with the likeness of a dog,[136] and the Đông-Kinh Private School and the commercial associations, like a cocoon that a silkworm spins only to get tied up inside it. In my eyes, propaganda about such things as "gradual reform" was only rhetorical stuff of which I wished to hear no more. I cogitated day and night,[137] intent only on seeking an opportunity to carry out an armed revolution; in the event that it failed, at any rate I should have found a place to die. It would be impossible to realize such a great undertaking

---

136. *Họa-hổ bất-thành* or *họa-hổ loại-cẩu,* an expression from the "Ma Yüan chüan" in the *Hou-Han shu,* referring to a person who, without adequate training, tries to act like a great man but ends up looking foolish.

137. AM reads: "After the League was established, I cogitated day and night . . . ."

without having an economic base to rely on. But in order to have a sound economic base, first one has to have some financial resources. In the last stage of a losing chess game, the only thing to do was to stake everything on a single strike—even if we failed, it would be preferable to sitting and waiting to die. Thus, although we knew very well that it was futile, we tried our luck, so that afterward our sympathizers would learn from our example.

At the time there was a member of the Chinese revolutionary party in Kwangtung called Su Shao-lou, who had been a commander of the militia before it was dissolved. Previously, he had lived in our country and taken his army to enter Ch'ennankuan by way of Lạng-sơn. He was very familiar with all the affairs of the revolutionary party in the past and was a close friend of mine. To the Vietnam Restoration League he gave his fullest support. He thought up plans for us, and advised us to print scrip for the League's army[138] that could be distributed, on the one hand, in the area of Kwangtung and Kwangsi, and on the other hand, inside our country, and to dispatch people to different places to promote its wide use. If by good fortune we succeeded, then using actual gold to redeem it would be extremely easy. If unfortunately we did not succeed, then this would be a kind of trick to get money from people in a civilized manner.

I agreed with this and deputed Hoàng-Trọng-Mậu and Su to go and consult[139] those in the Chinese revolutionary party who had been familiar with this business, and we secretly printed four denominations of scrip. At the top of the obverse of each coupon there was a line reading *Scrip for the Army of the Vietnam Restoration League;* at the center was written in big characters the amount, FIVE YUAN, TEN YUAN, FIFTEEN YUAN, and TWENTY YUAN indicating the four denominations; at the four corners these figures were given in arabic numerals. On the reverse, in both Chinese characters and Vietnamese *quốc-ngữ* letters, was an inscription reading *This scrip is issued by the Army of*

---

138. A very childish game. [Author's note.]

139. AM reads: "to go to Hong Kong and consult . . . ."

the Provisional Government of the Vietnam Restoration League, with a value corresponding to the amount indicated. When the Republican government is officially established, it will be redeemed for twice its face value. Counterfeiting is prohibited. Violators will be severely punished. The signatory was Phan-Sào-Nam [Phan-Bội-Châu] and the comptroller was Hoàng-Trọng-Mậu. These coupons were exquisitely printed in photogravure, just like the Chinese paper money.

5. The establishment of the Chấn-Hoa Hưng-Á-Hội *(Association for the Revitalization of China and the Regeneration of Asia).* As the first and second steps of our plan described in the previous sections had been more or less accomplished, now we attempted to execute the third step, namely, to carry out an armed revolution. There were only two ways to approach this: within the country, by mobilizing the local militias, and outside the country, by relying on the assistance of the Chinese army—neither arms nor ammunition could be procured anywhere else than from the Chinese. For this reason, on the one hand I devoted myself to selecting and sending people back home to mount a campaign;[140] on the other hand I tried to establish a liaison office in China.

Comrades Su Shao-lou and Teng Ching-ya said to me: " Although a revolutionary enterprise should of course be based on actual resources, there are occasions when one can well make use of a false impression to bring it about. Of course, a false impression is only something you would use to start things off at the beginning; afterward, what you have to rely on is actual resources. As at present you gentlemen lack real strength, you should devise some means of giving a false impression. What you should do now is set up an office presenting an outward appearance that will attract people's attention, to give the Cantonese the idea that your group already has fulfilled five- or six-tenths of the content its program. This is an application of the feint *(hư giả thực chi)* in military tactics."

---

140. In this regard, we suffered a great setback; it is painful indeed to recount it. See the following section. [Author's note.]

I acted on their advice, which was along the lines I had in mind. Thanks to the money provided by Ch'en Chi-mei, I still had twelve hundred yuan left after spending two thousand eight hundred yuan on printing, external activities, travel, sending people back home, etc. Seven hundred yuan were set aside to cover special activities *(hành-động đặc-biệt)*—details of which will be given later—and five hundred yuan were exclusively reserved for the use of our liaison office with the Chinese. First I thought of the name of the Association for the Revitalization of China, then I drew up its plan of action and manifesto. I showed them to comrades Su Shao-lou and Teng Ching-ya; they both gave it their strong approval. The manifesto was quite long, so that it is impossible to transcribe it here in its entirety; I simply excerpt the main ideas as follows.

In the opening section, it affirmed:

> China is the largest country in size, the richest in resources, and the greatest in population in Asia. In addition, as the country with the oldest civilization in East Asia, undoubtedly it ought to act as the eldest brother *(huynh-trưởng)* of all Asia. In fulfillment of its responsibilities as the eldest brother of all Asia, it is China's unique mission to help the weak and small Asian countries to become independent.

In the next section, the manifesto bitterly criticized the Manchu dynasty, which had abandoned China's mission as eldest brother. In the central section, it stated explicitly:

> China's national shame is due to the atrophy of its foreign policy, and the cause of the atrophy of its foreign policy is to be found in its failure to uphold its national prestige. In order to uphold its national prestige, there is no other way for China than a foreign policy of excluding the Europeans *(bài Âu); to* exclude the Europeans, the first step is excluding the French and helping Vietnam, as this would provide a good pretext for waging war.[141]

---

141. AM adds: "because Vietnam is a tributary state *(thuộc-quốc)* of China."

Specific reasons were given in this section, the most important being:

> — The British had a powerful navy, which China did not possess. Therefore it was impossible to think of [opposing] Britain.

> — Japan had recently become Britain's ally, and moreover, it was a newly emerging power and its flame was spreading; not only that, it was a country of the same race and same culture *(đồng-văn đồng-chủng)*. Contact should be maintained, as with a friend.

> — So far as Germany was concerned, William II had the ambition to establish a hegemony over all Europe, pushing aside even Britain and France. Now if China began hostilities against France, the Germans would certainly show their support; at present, contact should be kept up with Germany to win its powerful assistance.

> — Russia and France were allies; if France were attacked, Russia would certainly help France, but if we had the support of Germany, Germany would be able to hold Russia in check. Moreover, within Russia the revolutionary tide was currently rising; for fear of domestic repercussions, Russia would not dare to act boldly abroad. Not only that, but Russia was still concerned about Japan, and would not venture to lay hands on China.

The above diplomatic circumstances were no cause for concern. From an economic and military point of view, should China aid Vietnam, then the chances of victory would certainly be on China's side. In the first place, Vietnam was geographically adjacent to Kwangtung and Kwangsi, the route for supplying provisions was extremely easy, and Chinese troops, once having crossed the border into Vietnam, could use the provisions of the enemy. Secondly, Vietnam was situated next to the tropical zone, but the French, coming from a country with a cold climate, could not fight a long war in the heat as well as the Chinese soldiers. Thirdly, China and Vietnam were next door to each other, but France was oceans away from Vietnam, which meant that in terms of supply routes, China had an advantage and France had a handicap. Fourthly, the number of French soldiers stationed in Vietnam was not large; in case of emergency they had to rely on Vietnamese soldiers. Once the Chinese entered Vietnam, the Vietnamese would turn their guns around to shoot the French.

At the end, the manifesto said:

> Before declaring war against France, China should give massive assistance to the Vietnamese revolutionary party, building up its strength over time so as to make it China's spearhead against France.

It concluded by stating that if China's national prestige were revitalized, then East Asia would become strong, and there was no better first step in this program than to help the Vietnamese gain independence. This was the main gist of the manifesto. When the plan of action and the manifesto had been printed and distributed, they received the endorsement of many well known Chinese.

I THEN RENTED a two-story Western-style house with more than ten rooms, which was partitioned off into three large sections, for thirty-six yuan a month. Once it was rented we set up a clinic; at the front gate hung a signboard with four golden characters reading ĐÔNG-BẰNG Y-XÃ (Medical Society of the Friends of East Asia). The person in charge of Western medicine was Yang Shen-hai, and the one in charge of Chinese medicine was Mai-Lão-Bạng. We created this as a setting that would attract people to come to us. The Medical Society occupied the section of the house at the front. The section in the middle was the office of the Association for the Revitalization of China. The inmost section was used solely as a meeting hall for the Vietnam Restoration League; it was elegant and dignified, brightly decorated with our flags and banners without any concealment. We finally had a decent external appearance, all of which was meant to have the effect of producing a "false impression."

At the time, there were many among the journalists in Canton who knew me well; they helped us by writing publicity. Within a month, there were Cantonese coming to me to ask to join the Revitalization Association, and their numbers were increasing day by day. I judged that the time was ripe; therefore, in the Seventh Month of the Year of the Rat [August/September 1912], we held the opening congress of the Association for the Revitalization of China and the Regeneration of Asia. Close to two hundred people attended the congress. Among the Chinese, the participants included renowned personalities from commercial and academic circles, regional military commanders, and elegant highborn ladies. The plan of action and the manifesto of the Association were read to obtain the assent of the majority; the members at the congress approved them both. Teng Ching-ya, a Cantonese, and I both made long speeches, by which the audience was quite moved.[142] The congress then elected the Cantonese Teng Ching-ya as president and the Vietnamese Phan-Sào-Nam as vice-president; the secretary-ship and other executive positions were filled by both Chinese and Vietnamese.

Next, the order in which things should be carried out was discussed. According to the procedure laid down in the plan of action, the first step was to assist Vietnam, the second step was to assist India and Burma, and the third step was to assist Korea. The ultimate objective was to revitalize China and regenerate Asia, but the cannon should roar first in Vietnam. At this point, Teng Ching-ya took the lead in making a proposal:

> It behooves us, as a means of supporting Vietnam, to buy the scrip of the Army of the Vietnam Restoration League. To accomplish anything it was essential to have funds, and the most feasible way to procure funds was to issue the army scrip. Now that the scrip has been issued, all our compatriots, Chinese and Vietnamese, should please buy it.[143]

---

142. According to AM, Lâm-Đức-Mậu was a third speaker at the congress.
143. This last sentence is added in AM.

Many of those at the congress supported this proposal. By the time the congress adjourned, one thousand yuan of scrip altogether had been sold, and all the money was handed over to me to use for the Vietnam Restoration League. In addition, we selected among the general membership those who were familiar with the Vietnamese situation and asked them to take an active part in the Revitalization Association, in order to accelerate the progress of the Association's work.

In the Eighth Month of the Year of the Rat [September/October 1912], we reconstituted the executive of the Vietnam Restoration League so that the Chinese could participate in that, too. Phan-Sào-Nam was elected as the secretary-general, Su Shao-lou, a Cantonese, as deputy secretary-general; Li Li,[144] a Cantonese, as minister of Financial Affairs, with Mai-Lão-Bạng as his deputy; Hoàng-Trọng-Mậu as minister of Military Affairs, with Teng Tung-sheng, a Cantonese, as his deputy; Yang Chen-hai, a Taiwanese, as minister of General Affairs, with Fan Chi-chun as his deputy;[145] and the secretary-general and the deputy secretary-general as minister and deputy minister, respectively, of External Affairs.

For the first time since the Vietnam Restoration League had been founded, it could hope to make some progress. Fortunately at the time the governor of Kwangtung, Ch'en Chiung-ming, was quite sympathetic with our revolutionary party, and thus did not interfere with our activities. We were able to act freely. Moreover, the number of people joining the League was increasing steadily, and the sale of the army scrip eventually reached several thousand yuan. Our expenses for travel for external activities could be well maintained at a level not so low as to reveal our actual state of poverty. The only trouble was that there were still innumerable obstacles in the way of carrying out an armed revolution, as there was no possibility of acquiring military equipment and supplies without a huge sum of money, but in order to obtain a

---

144. AM gives this name as Li Li-nan (in Sino-Vietnamese, Lê Lệ-Nam).

145. Previously Phan-Bội-Châu indicates that Yang Chen-hai and Fan Chi-chun were the same person; see above, p. 191.

huge sum of money, some incident would have to take place in our country that would have the greatest possible impact. I had no choice but to resort to the expedient of some drastic measure of violence.

IN RECOUNTING this stage of my history, I must indeed wipe my tears and suppress my anguish, because it is unbearable for me to write, yet it would be more unbearable not to write. In sacrificing our dedicated and devoted compatriots, we hoped to help resurrect the destiny of our country. We accepted the suffering of a few in our quest for the happiness of the majority. Lenin has said: "If we have to kill one in order to save two, we cannot forbear to do so."[146] Grievous circumstances were all around, and how difficult it was to foresee the right time to act! That I caused numbers of our compatriots to be sacrificed in vain was indeed my grave sin.

In the autumn of the Year of the Rat [1912], after the movement had been reconstituted into the Vietnam Restoration League, I met the three delegates who had just returned from our country. They all said: "A military campaign in our country cannot be effective unless there is some astounding, earth-shaking explosion, because people are merely in a hurry for an overnight success[147] and are incapable of entertaining a long-term plan." The reasons that each of them gave for this, and their advice about how to obtain funds, were also almost identical. I looked into the old fund for special activities; there were still seven hundred yuan left. The amount gained from the scrip that had been circulated, after deducting expenses for external activities, was five hundred yuan, so that there were twelve hundred yuan altogether. I gave three hundred yuan to Nguyễn-Hải-Thần and Nguyễn-Trọng-Thường to enter Bắc-Kỳ by way of Lạng-sơn; six hundred yuan and four grenades to Hà-Dương-Nhân and Đặng-Tử-Vũ to enter Trung-Kỳ by taking the route from Siam; two hundred yuan

146. AM omits this quotation.
147. Out of ignorance. [Author's note.]

and two grenades to Bùi-Chính-Lộ to enter Nam-Kỳ by taking the route from Siam.[148]

After all of them had departed for their respective destinations, I thought that the awl of Chang Tzu-fang [Chang Liang][149] and the pistol of An Chung-gŭn[150] would simultaneously strike in the Three Regions; should one of the leading politicians in the government of brute force be brought down, that would suffice to shake up the people's mind and to chill the heart of the enemy; its impact on our future collection of funds would be enormous. Alas! Who could have known that the result would be just the reverse? The grenades brought into Bắc-Kỳ were not used where they should have been, but instead to kill the governor *(tuần-vũ)* of Thái-bình Province, a French restaurateur, and two French officers. The grenades brought to Siam did not reach their destinations; Hà and Đặng spent more time than they were supposed to in Siam, and their grenades were uselessly thrown away. Bùi-Chính-Lộ, being easily excitable and shortsighted, killed a few insignificant running-dogs in Bangkok and sacrificed his precious life. All these were things I had not expected at all.

Afterward I reflected on these events and suffered great remorse; I felt that my ability to plan things and judge people fell far short of that of Tiểu-La [Nguyễn Thành]. Nevertheless, the above-mentioned events gave me a very good lesson. When I originally thought of the plan, I intended it to be a secret matter that should not be divulged. Only in casual conversation with our people I often sighed with regret, and complained that I felt ashamed that I could not act like Chang Tzu-fang or An Chung-gŭn, but only pray day and night for such people to appear in our country. Nguyễn-Hải-Thần, Hà-Đương-Nhân, and

---

148. AM for some reason omits to mention the grenades.

149. The weapon with which Chang Liang attempted to assassinate the First Emperor. Cf. above, p. 171, n. 112.

150. An Chung-gŭn (1878–1910), an officer of the Ŭibyŏng (Righteous Armies) who had been active in the Korean independence movement in Manchuria and Siberia, assassinated Itō Hirobumi, who was regarded by the Koreans as the architect of the Japanese annexation of Korea, on 26 October 1909.

Đặng-Tử-Vũ knew what I had in mind; I did not urge this plan upon them, it was they who enthusiastically volunteered. Nguyễn-Hải-Thần at the time of his departure composed this farewell poem:

> *My cherished dream of thirty years will now come true at last:*
> *To shine forth in the annals of four thousand long years past.*

His desire for fame was succinctly displayed in these words. Đặng-Tử-Vũ, in his turn, wrote the following farewell poem:

> *All my guarantees of credit I regardless cast away;*
> *I'll use the precious sword I bear, my life's debt to repay.*

It is abundantly clear from these lines that he had not entirely forgotten the love of gain. Those who still cherish fame and do not forget the love of gain cannot sacrifice themselves [for a righteous cause]. This is something that is easy to understand, but regrettably by that time the die had been cast and the situation could not be saved. Although I had foreseen this, it was difficult to devise any means to turn things around.

Through the lesson I received at this time, I came to realize that those who undertake a great risk for a righteous cause must be single-minded and detached, without a trace of desire for fame or love of gain, calmly self-possessed and persevering. They must have an un-shakable sense of righteous indignation in addition to spiritual strength and courage, and be endowed with extraordinary determination. If any one of these qualities is lacking, they certainly cannot succeed; or if they give in to persuasion or are coerced into acting, it will necessarily be an imposture that will not bring about a good result.

NONETHELESS, among this group of people there was Bùi-Chính-Lộ, whose sacrifice deserves respect. He went to Siam not on his own ini-tiative but at my request. Previously, when still in our country, he had worked together with Ngư-Hải for many years and had been the lat-ter's bosom companion and my trusted disciple.[151] When Ngư-Hải

---

151. He was therefore a student of Chinese studies. [Author's note.]

was still alive, he made five or six trips from Vietnam to Siam carrying money and documents, and contributed a great deal to the activities of the movement in Nghệ-an and Hà-tĩnh.[152] Following Ngư-Hải's sacrifice, being a keen member, he continued to travel back and forth for the cause. When his activities were disclosed he was arrested and sentenced to life imprisonment with forced labor. While he was in prison, several dozen prisoners died of an epidemic in the prison. He disguised himself as a prisoner dying of the epidemic and asked an accomplice to pretend to bury him. The prison guards did not dare to come close to the dead, so he escaped through this feigned burial. At once he went secretly to Nam-Kỳ and by way of Cambodia reached Siam, then proceeded to Kwangtung to see me.

At the time, I was conceiving the above-mentioned plan, but had no one who could be entrusted with going back to Nam-Kỳ. Knowing that he was familiar with the roads in Nam-Kỳ because he had passed through it, and moreover was a person who thought lightly of his life while cherishing righteousness, I asked him to undertake this task. Regrettably, in him a calm self-possession and sense of endurance had not fully matured, and so on account of a little anger he would ruin a great enterprise. Carrying the grenades to Bangkok, he was spotted by some running-dogs and trailed by them wherever he went. Unable to suppress his anger, he took out the grenades and threw the lot at them, killing two of the running-dogs. He was then arrested by the Siamese police, but before being handed over to the French, he took his own life. Alas! Using a shining pearl to shoot a sparrow, killing a snake with a precious sword! A real Chang Tzu-fang or An Chung-gŭn would not have done that! But I was also guilty of selecting the wrong person. When I was in prison in Kwangtung, I wrote *Tái sinh truyện* (The Story of a Resurrection) in his honor.

---

152. This sentence is placed at this point by TQP, followed by GB. In the original text it appears at the end of the paragraph.

THE GRENADES BROUGHT back to Bắc-Kỳ, according to the plan as originally conceived, were supposed to be set off on the day in the Eleventh Month when the results of the provincial examination were announced, as on that day all the administrative officials would be in attendance to confer caps and gowns [on the successful candidates]. In a departure from the intention of our plan, the grenades were not detonated at the gate of the examination site[153] but at a restaurant. Was it the prestige of Governor-General Sarraut[154] that was capable of warding off the explosion of the grenades? Alas! The great favor that Ch'en Chi-mei did on my behalf was distorted into a grave error. In the other world, having let down my good friend, what words shall I be able to find to justify myself?

In the Twelfth Month of the Year of the Rat [January/February 1913], the detonation of the grenades in Bắc-Kỳ reached Kwangtung, and that led to all sorts of difficulties rising up to confront me one after another. By and large, when a success happens, it may be followed by one or two more successes at the most; but when a failure happens, it is often followed by countless other failures. "Good fortune does not come twice; misfortune does not come singly"—with this saying I now have to agree.

On the basis of the grenades incident, the French had an excuse to present an accusation to the Chinese authorities, saying that our office was a den of murderers and Phan-Sào-Nam was the leader of these murderers. The French minister in Peking demanded that the Chinese authorities hand over the accused. Fortunately, the then president, Yüan Shih-k'ai, inwardly nurtured the great ambitions of a Napoleon or Alexander. The Marquis had come to Peking to ask

---

153. TQP indicates that this was the Nam-định examination site.

154. Albert Sarraut (1872–1962) was governor-general of Indochina from November 1911 to November 1913, and again from January 1917 to May 1919—the only person to serve twice in this office; he gained a reputation for his liberal attitude with respect to French colonial policy. In the course of his subsequent political career in France, he was minister for the Colonies (1920–1924 and 1932–1933) and premier (1933 and 1936).

for an audience with Yüan. Yüan asked Premier Tuan Ch'i-jui to see the Marquis on his behalf; Tuan gave the latter a cordial reception. Because I was an advocate of democracy, I was afraid that Yüan would not be happy to see me; all our diplomatic dealings with Yüan were entrusted to the Marquis, and the Marquis was treated with great courtesy by Yüan.

Tuan's words were as follows: "The president will one day punish the Europeans. His Excellency has often said to me that China has to demonstrate her power to the outside world. It will take five or six years at the most for China to prepare herself completely, and she will certainly use Vietnam as a proving ground." Our country's youth who received Chinese government scholarships to study at Peking were all well treated.

In line with the above, to all the French accusations the Yüan government returned a denial, saying that they were groundless. Thanks to that, the office of our movement in Kwangtung was able to postpone its last gasp. The value of the military scrip of the Vietnam Restoration League, however, dropped precipitously. This was because our activities inside our country had not made any impact, and our diplomatic difficulties outside our country made the speculative traders shrink back. If we sat back and did nothing, how would money come to us? Yet if we did something, but without success, money would dry up anyway. This was an impasse from which we could neither advance nor retreat.

IN THE SPRING of the Year of the Ox [1913], our movement held a meeting in Canton of the hundred members and more still there. We were like the remnant of an army that was being confronted by a powerful foe; if we advanced we might have a chance of survival, but if we retreated we should surely be exterminated. The reason for flying our flag and beating our drums to keep up a false impression, even though it would do no good to our overall prospects, was that it would serve as a means to help us in suing for a new lease on life. For this reason we still kept up our previous activities, taking risks in search of an opportunity.

At that time there was a ludicrous incident. With the problem of many people and no money, there was little comfort for us even for a single day. We had to resort to the kind of cheating that civilized people do. The Đông-Bằng Y-Xã (Medical Society of the Friends of East Asia) had formerly entered into commercial relations with a Japanese pharmaceutical company on a cash basis, which had won its trust. Moreover, Yang Chen-hai was so fluent in Japanese that this company was not aware that he was a member of the Vietnamese movement. We bought three hundred yuan of drugs on credit. Soon the Đông-Bằng Y-Xã was closed down, and there was no consolation for the Japanese company that suffered the loss.

The money collected from donations was all used for our comrades to travel here and there. Hoàng-Trọng-Mậu went to Kwangsi to establish contacts with the outlaws in Kweilin and the militiamen, who were all well armed and whose activities were like those of Ch'en Sheng and Wu Kuang.[155] Đặng-Tử-Mẫn, Hoàng Hưng, and Đặng-Bỉnh-Thành went to Hong Kong to set up a secret plant dedicated to manufacturing dynamite and grenades, in the hope of carrying out activities as before. Later, Hoàng-Trọng-Mậu was arrested; Nguyễn-Thành-Hiến, Hoàng Hưng, and Đặng-Bỉnh-Thành were all extradited to the French; Đặng-Tử-Mẫn lost three of his fingers and was put in prison. All sorts of calamities came upon us around this time. Trần-Hữu-Lực's trip to Siam attempting to bring in a few arms to Trung-Kỳ, Lương-Lập-Nham's secret return to Bắc-Kỳ, and Nguyễn-Yến-Chiêu's secret return to Nam-Kỳ were all risky ventures on behalf of our finances. These three were all arrested afterwards. Alas! How painful it was!

---

155. Ch'en Sheng and Wu Kuang were two men of humble background who organized a revolt against the tyranny of the First Emperor late in the third century B.C.

IN THE THIRD MONTH of the Year of the Ox [April/May 1913], Mai-Lão-Bạng and I were mainly looking after our office in Kwangtung. Some forty-five people still lived there, enduring hunger and thirst, just managing to survive each day. Yet we still wished to carry out our plan, flying the flag over an empty fortress. I thus compiled the details of the story of the poisoning incident in Hanoi and wrote *Hà-thành liệt-sĩ* (The History of the Martyrs of Hanoi). After the book had been printed by lithography, I asked Đỗ-Cơ-Quang to carry it back home and distribute it surreptitiously among the soldiers, to stir up the sentiments of the local militiamen in the hope that they would respond to Hoàng-Trọng-Mậu and Nguyễn-Thức-Canh upon their return to our country.

Who were the Hanoi martyrs? On the basis of what I had heard, they were Lê-Đình-Nhuận, Nguyễn-Trị-Bình, Đỗ-Đình-Nhân, Hai Hiên, and others, that is, those who had attempted in the Year of the Monkey [1908] to poison some French soldiers in order to capture their arms and attack Hanoi. The attempt was disclosed and ended in failure. They were indeed unsung heroes. In narrating their story, it would be impossible not to record the role of Đỗ-Cơ-Quang, whose story I have written in detail in *Việt-Nam nghĩa-liệt-sử* (The History of the Martyrs of Vietnam). Now I will excerpt it briefly, as follows.[156]

At the time of Đỗ-Cơ-Quang's first arrival in Kwangtung, the Vietnam Restoration League was on the rise. As it gradually declined and the roads back [to our country] from Kwangtung and Kwangsi were blocked, he asked me on his own initiative for a little travel money to return to Bắc-Kỳ by the Yunnan railway. Taking advantage of the occasion, I entrusted him with the task of raising support among the local militias.

When he first left our country, he was accompanied by a man named Nguyễn-Hắc-Sơn, who had supplied him with the funds to go

---

156. TQP, followed by GB, departs quite markedly from the original at this point, reading: "Now, in writing *Liệt-sĩ Hà-thành*, we needed only to make the style as elegant as possible in order to do homage to these martyrs, as well as to the unsung heroes."

abroad. He was not aware that this man was a spy. Hắc-Sơn stayed with Đỗ for about half a year; they took military training together at a camp in Nanking for about another half a year, sharing hardship and suffering. Đỗ trusted him completely. When Đỗ traveled to Yunnan, he took Hắc-Sơn along, as the latter had money that he had received from home to pay for the trip.

Đỗ was well versed in literary Chinese, and his writing in *quốc-ngữ* was excellent. He was also a moving speaker. At the time of his departure, he carried along with him a vast quantity of the publications of the Vietnam Restoration League. He mobilized a great deal of support [for the movement] among the Vietnamese living in Yunnan,[157] from the soldiers guarding the Yunnan-Vietnam railway to the interpreters and clerks, maids and cooks around the Mengtzu region. Altogether, some fifty persons joined the Vietnam Restoration League. Soon the European War broke out and he began to receive assistance from the German consulate in Mengtzu; thus his activities became even more effective.

Eventually, through the connivance of the soldiers guarding the railway, he secretly returned to Hanoi and surreptitiously established contact with the local militias; one of the battalion commanders clandestinely joined [the League]. The affair leaked out, and Đỗ was arrested. The battalion commander, as well as more than fifty expatriate Vietnamese in Yunnan who were implicated in the charges against him, with Ký Lan heading the list, were executed in Hokow. The French made use of such a punishment in order to intimidate other expatriate Vietnamese.

That from all the branches of the Vietnam Restoration League organized by Đỗ, not a soul managed to escape the net, was due to Hắc-Sơn's accomplishment as a spy. After Đỗ had been executed by beheading, Hắc-Sơn surrendered himself. He was acquitted, and was

---

157. AM is more specific: "from Hokow to the metropolis of Yunnan [i.e., Kunming]."

rewarded with an official rank.[158] Nguyễn-Hạ-Trường, the longtime spy who had dispatched Hắc-Sơn, was made a prefect. Alas! To massacre dozens of patriotic fellow countrymen for some petty official rank—what kind of heart would allow someone to do that, I cannot find words to say! I have heard that on the day of the executions, among the fifty victims, Ký Lan was the most outstanding and worthy of admiration. Regrettably, his life history is not known in any detail.

IN THE FOURTH MONTH of the Year of the Ox [May/June 1913], I was staying in Canton. I thought that, should the above-mentioned plans fail altogether, the more than forty people living with me, if they did not perish in the course of the revolution, would certainly die from hunger and cold. I thus radically changed my way of soliciting money. If I were to come right down to it, all our activities during those years outside our country were only a kind of begging in a civilized manner. At this point I suddenly thought of Chang Hui-tsuan, a native of Hunan, who during my years in Japan had been a classmate of our students at the Shimbu Gakkō. This man had a great sense of righteous indignation and was passionate about revolution. I had often met and talked with him. When the republican government was set up, he was appointed a divisional commander in Hunan. The governor of Hunan, T'an Yen-k'ai, was also a literary friend of mine.[159]

In the last decade of the Third Month [late April/early May 1913], with Lương-Lập-Nham for company, I went to Hunan to visit Commander Chang and to have an audience with T'an. When I arrived in Hunan and saw Chang, I showed him the manifesto of the Association for the Revitalization of China and the Regeneration

---

158. AM indicates that he received the eighth rank of officialdom *(bát-phẩm)*.

159. T'an Yen-k'ai (1879–1930) was a highly educated Confucian scholar who owed the military governorship of Hunan to the support of the constitutional monarchists, and the civilian governorship he combined with it to Yüan Shih-k'ai. He lost his position when he broke with Yüan, but survived to become one of the most prominent politicians of the Kuomintang.

of Asia, and its plan of activities. Chang was extremely pleased. He put on a welcoming banquet, introduced us to about a dozen of his colleagues including Ch'en Chia-yu, and said: "Within a period of ten days, we can collect and give you thirty thousand yuan as a loan."[160] On hearing this, we were wildly elated—we felt like jumping for joy!

Who could have expected that on the following day the situation would change so drastically? The Kuomintang military forces rose up against Yüan Shih-k'ai in the three provinces of Anhwei, Hupei, and Kiangsi. Being a province having close mutual relations [with these three], Hunan had no choice but to join in the battle. The important persons who had talked with us the evening before now had their hands full and had no time for the other things they had promised to do, merely offering us three hundred yuan as expenses to get us back to Kwangtung. How suddenly things change in the most unpredictable way! Even though ill fortune was working against us, this certainly also demonstrated that reliance on other people brings no good result. From now on would be the most sorrowful and miserable period of my life.

IN THE FIFTH MONTH of the Year of the Ox [June/July 1913], the Second Chinese Revolution reached Kwangtung. Ch'en Chiung-ming went on campaign to support Hunan. Lu Jung-t'ing and Lung Chi-kuang received orders from Yüan Shih-k'ai to suppress Ch'en; Ch'en fled from Kwangtung and Lung became its governor.[161] At the time,

160. TQP, followed by GB, translates: "Within a month, we shall arrange to give you twenty thousand yuan." He does not mention that the offer was of a loan. AM also gives twenty thousand yuan instead of thirty thousand yuan as in the original.
161. Ch'en Chiung-ming (1878–1933) had been governor of Kwangtung but was deposed by Yüan Shih-k'ai in 1913. He fought Lung Chi-kuang to regain his position and succeeded in returning to Canton in 1920, but was finally driven out five years later. Lung Chi-kuang (1860–1921), a native of Yunnan, was an early supporter of Yüan Shih-k'ai who had been military commander of Kwangsi in 1908 and Kwang-tung in 1911. Restored to his position in Kwangtung in 1914, he became deeply

Yüan was secretly aspiring to become emperor, and his foreign policy had become more pliable. With Ch'en's departure and Lung's arrival, the Kwangtung government's attitude to us was completely changed, quite different from before. The office of the Association that had been established in the Year of the Rat [1912] was quietly compelled to close down, owing to Lung's acute concern that it might be less than agreeable to the French. I returned to the residence of Madame Chou Hsiht'ai and rented a separate house from the German church in Honan as a lodging place for the members of the Association.

At that time, although a collision between France and Germany was not yet clearly evident, the diplomats in China already foresaw that it would occur sooner or later. As this had come to my ears, I rented the house from the Germans as a way of drawing closer to them. This plan was still in its formative stage when it was discovered by the expert hand of the police; the end result was that the wielders of brute force were able to block it in advance. This was also because we had no real strength of our own. Supposing that at this time we had had a few thousand yuan, I should have gone to Germany, saving myself from spending four years in prison as a revolutionary.

In the Seventh Month in the autumn of the Year of the Ox [August 1913], the governor-general of Indochina, Sarraut, went in person to Canton to negotiate directly with Governor Lung Chi-kuang about his request for the extradition of the key members of the Vietnamese revolutionary movement, namely Cường-Đề, Phan-Bội-Châu, and Mai-Lão-Bạng, who were under suspicion of murder in the Hanoi restaurant bombing incident. Governor Lung promised that he would

---

unpopular there, and after the death of Yüan in 1916 was transferred to Hainan Island, while his forces on the mainland suffered a defeat at the hands of Ch'en's army in October of that year. At the end of 1917, he launched an invasion of the mainland, but was defeated by Sun Yat-sen in January 1918, and took refuge in the French concession at Kwangchowwan until his death. Lu Jung-t'ing (1856–1927) was an ex-outlaw who rose by attaching himself to Lung, but broke with him in mid-1916, and though he tried to keep up connections with various factions in the following years, he was decisively defeated by Ch'en Chiung-ming in 1921.

arrest us, and when evidence had been collected, would have us extradited.

In the office of the governor of Kwangtung was the chief of the security police, named Kuan [Jen-fu], who secretly informed me of this and advised me to leave Kwangtung. At first I too thought that I should leave Kwangtung, but I felt a difficulty because there were still more than thirty comrades who were counting on me. If I were to leave immediately, this lot of beggars would have no leader, and there was no way for them to make a living. So I simply waited to acquire some money little by little; then I would disperse the comrades one by one, and after that I too would take flight to some place far away.

The Marquis being in Hong Kong at the time, I talked him into going with me to Europe, and asked him to return to Nam-Kỳ in person to collect a large sum of money, because where Nam-Kỳ was concerned, unless the Marquis went there in person, it would be impossible to obtain donations. The Marquis agreed. Around the Eighth or Ninth Month [September/October 1913], the Marquis took the risk of going to Nam-Kỳ, stayed there for only a little more than ten days,[162] and managed to gather together fifty thousand yuan.

As soon as the Marquis returned to Hong Kong, he was arrested and thrown into prison by the Hong Kong authorities, because when Governor-General Sarraut had visited Hong Kong he had asked for the Marquis's extradition, just as he had asked for my extradition in Kwangtung. The Marquis at once tried to escape. Fortunately, he had money in his pocket; he gave three thousand yuan to a British lawyer to bail him out. As soon as the Marquis was released, he hurriedly boarded a Japanese merchant ship bound for Europe. In his haste to escape from death, the Marquis failed to keep his appointment to meet me. Because of that, it became impossible to realize my plan of traveling to Europe, and soon I became a confined man.

---

162. AM reads "for three weeks."

IT WAS KUAN JEN-FU, a Cantonese who had previously known me well, who accepted two thousand yuan from the French to make a false accusation to Lung Chi-kuang that I had secretly formed a liaison with Ch'en Chiung-ming, and to advise Lung to hand me over to the French. Being a base fellow who would shrink from nothing, Lung had not yet handed me over to the French only because he was waiting to use me as a commodity for his own profit. Now, hearing that I had been secretly in contact with Ch'en, he saw this as the right time to finish me off.

Thus on the twenty-fourth day of the Twelfth Month of the Year of the Ox [19 January 1914], he arrested me and Mai-Lão-Bạng. We were fettered with handcuffs like common criminals. The residence of Madame Chou Hsih-t'ai where I was staying was immediately searched; fortunately, all the materials found were only memoranda and documents concerning the Vietnamese revolutionary movement, and none of them had anything to do with Ch'en's group. Madame Chou's son, Chou T'ieh-sheng, was also arrested and was under interrogation for fifteen days, but Lung found no connection whatsoever between our movement and Ch'en's group, and his suspicions were cleared up.

But Lung still wanted to keep us as a prize piece of merchandise. While on the one hand he detained me in a cell in the army prison, on the other hand, as a condition for my extradition, he requested that the French let him use the Yunnan-Vietnam railway to deploy his troops back to Yunnan.[163] My life at that point was in great danger, hanging by a thread.

Fortunately, the premier in the cabinet in Peking, Tuan Ch'i-jui,[164]

---

163. AM reads more specifically: "to deploy his troops to attack T'ang Chi-yao (Đường Kế-Nghiêu)." T'ang Chi-yao (1881–1927) had been a student at the Shimbu Gakkō, 1904–1907, and a follower of Sun Yat-sen. After the revolution of 1911 he became military governor of Yunnan. He was one of the commanders of the National Protection Army and obtained the post of governor of Yunnan.

164. Tuan Ch'i-jui (1865–1936) was a follower of Yüan Shih-k'ai who survived in power for some time after Yüan's death, being premier for most of the period April 1916–October 1918.

was a kindhearted and compassionate gentleman, who from the outset had done his best to protect us. Mai-Sơn Nguyễn-Thượng-Hiền at the time was residing in Peking. Đặng-Xung-Hồng and other comrades in Kwangtung quickly sent a telegram to Mai-Sơn urging him to ask for help from Tuan, who was concurrently acting as minister for the Army. Using his authority as minister for the Army, Tuan sent a telegram to Lung ordering him to take responsibility for the safety of the two of us, Mai-Lão-Bạng and me. Lung had no choice, but detained me in Mount Kuanyin prison, absolutely prohibiting my fellow countrymen from coming to visit me, and telling the French consulate, to keep them happy, that he had decided to execute me by beheading. Mai-Lão-Bạng was kept separately under surveillance at the police headquarters, as he was not considered an important criminal.

I was in prison four years altogether, from the Twelfth Month of the Year of the Ox to the Third Month of the Year of the Snake [January 1914–April/May 1917].[165] I was released only when Lung's army was defeated by the National Protection Army and he fled to Ch'iungchow.[166] Throughout those four years, I was altogether cut off from seeing the face of even one of my fellow countrymen, or yet from hearing the voice of any of them.

As I WAS QUITE well versed in Cantonese and Governor Lung was deeply hated by the Cantonese people, while in prison I made friends with a Cantonese, a cook called Liu Ya-san. I identified myself to him as a Cantonese. Everyone else working under Lung was from Yunnan,

165. For the dating of Phan's release from prison and his subsequent activities, see below, p. 227, n. 173. TQP gives the year as the Year of the Dragon [1916].

166. The National Protection Army (Hu-kuo-chün) was formed at the end of 1915 by a group of political and military leaders in southwest China who opposed Yüan Shih-k'ai in his bid to make himself emperor. Yüan gave up the idea of emperorship in March 1916 and died in June, but the Army continued to combat those who had supported him. Lung Chi-kuang withdrew to Ch'iungchow (another name for Hainan Island) in mid-1916, but it was not until January 1918 that his forces were finally routed and he himself forced to take flight.

and for this reason the relationship between Liu and me became very close. Once every few days I secretly asked him to call by Madame Chou Hsih-t'ai's residence, and thanks to that, news of my countrymen inside and outside of our country was surreptitiously carried into the prison. I composed quite a few poems, but now I remember only two poems in Vietnamese. The first:

> *No less am I chivalric, no less apt*
> > *At judging elegance among the best,*
> *Though flying from pursuit my strength is sapped,*
> > *And in a prison I have come to rest.*
>
> *A stranger everywhere, no sheltering home*
> > *I find within the Four Seas' endless span;*
> *On the Five Continents through which I roam,*
> > *I live in peril as a hunted man.*
>
> *That peace may be established as of old,*
> > *The people's lives with happiness be filled,*
> *With outspread arms my country I enfold;*
> > *I laugh aloud, that hatred may be stilled.*
>
> *As long as I have life, fast shall I stand*
> > *In my vocation high, my mission clear;*
> *Though dangers compass me on every hand,*
> > *My mind is single; nothing do I fear.*

The second:

> *It might be well if I had died, but I am still alive;*
> *What task am I supposed to do, as long as I survive?*
> *In Heaven there's no prison house to hold the gods and saints;*
> *On earth let's follow wind and cloud, that suffer no restraints.*
> *Enough to dry the Eastern Sea, one breath of eloquence;*
> *A sweep of one's two arms will clear the Northern Forest fence.*
> *My brethren, let us strive the more, though good results delay;*
> *Our work is for a thousand years, and not a single day!*

During my time in the prison, once in a while I managed to get hold of a jar of rice wine; I considered these to be my happiest moments. The tastiest delicacies to go with the wine were the literary morsels that proceeded from my soul. Altogether I composed the following: *Quốc-hồn-lục* (Records of the Spirit of Our Country), *Ngư-Hải-Ông biệt-truyện* (An Individual Biography of Ngư-Hải), *Tiểu-La Tiên-sinh biệt-truyện* (An Individual Biography of Tiểu-La), *Hoàng-Yên-Thế Tướng-quân biệt-truyện* (An Individual Biography of Commander Hoàng of Yên-Thế), *Tái-sinh-sinh truyện* (The Story of a Resurrection),[167] *Nhân-đạo-hồn* (The Humanitarian Spirit), *Trùng-Quang tâm-sử* (The Moving History of Trùng-Quang), and *Dự-ngu-sấm* (My Modest Prophecy). Six of the above were prose works.[168] [Then there were] *Hà-thành nhị-liệt-sĩ truyện* (A Short History of the Two Martyrs of Hanoi) and *Kiến-quốc hịch-văn* (An Appeal for the Rebuilding of Our Country; this last piece was written on the outbreak of the European War).[169] There were some other short works, the titles of which I do not remember.

BY THE SEVENTH MONTH of the Year of the Tiger [August/ September 1914], I had been inside the prison for eight months. Liu Ya-san often brought me newspapers and asked me to read them for him. One day I read a copy of the *Kuomin jihpao* (The People's Daily News) that carried a headline in big characters, "War Has Broken Out in Europe," and I thought that in our country at that point there would be an earth-shaking turn of events that would bring comfort and joy to those of us in prison. Who could have known that from that time onward, bad news would come thick and fast? This was because all those of passion and sincerity inside our country, driven by the impulse to seize this moment to fulfill their aspirations, with their brains on fire and

---

167. In his earlier reference to this book, Phan gave the title as *Tái-sinh-truyện*.

168. The other two were written in verse.

169. AM and TQP give the title as *Bình-Tây kiến-quốc hịch-văn* (An Appeal to Put Down the French and Rebuild Our Country).

their courage screwed up to the limit, rushed forth with wild leaps, thus allowing the manhunters to cut off their heads. My luck in not being killed is thanks only to Heaven.

The following is a brief list of the bad news that I heard while in prison:

(i) Lương-Lập-Nham was arrested in Hong Kong.

(ii) Trấn-Hữu-Lực was arrested in Siam.

(iii) Hoàng-Trọng-Mậu was unsuccessful in carrying out his plans in Kwangsi, went to Hong Kong, and was arrested.

(iv) Đỗ-Cơ-Quang was unsuccessful in carrying out his plans in Yunnan, returned to Hanoi, and died a martyr.

(v) Lâm-Đức-Mậu and Giáo Trung were arrested in Siam and brought back to Hanoi to be executed.

(vi) Nguyễn-Trọng-Thường went back to our country and was arrested.

(vii) Hoàng-Trọng-Mậu and Trần-Hữu-Lực died as martyrs on the same day.

(viii) The Duy-Tân incident occurred and Nam-Xương died a martyr.[170]

Nam-Xương was an alias of Thái Phiên, who worked ardently in the cause of our country and was skillful in dealing with finances and handling the conduct of affairs.[171] He worked together for many years with comrades Tiểu-La and Ngư-Hải. Around the Year of the Monkey and the Year of the Cock [1909–1910], when there were almost no comrades remaining inside our country, it was he alone who stood fast. At the time when Emperor Duy-Tân was removed from the throne

---

170. In 1916 Emperor Duy-Tân (reigned 1907–1916) conspired with two close associates to carry out a coup against the French. It was betrayed in advance and the Emperor was sent into exile, while his two fellow conspirators were executed.

171. Thái Phiên (1882–1916), from Quảng-nam Province, had been associated with Phan-Bội-Châu as one of the mainstays of the Đông-Du movement and a member of the Vietnam Restoration League.

because of his compassion for the people, Nam-Xương, as an important man behind the Emperor, was arrested and sentenced to death. (Several other men were also executed in connection with this incident.) It was my third year in prison when I heard the news. Alas! Bad news came scudding in the wake of the clouds; tides of wrath washed in with the waves of the sea.

After I had been in prison for some time, I abstained from food for seven days, wishing only to die. But it was on the seventh day that the news of the European War reached me, and I took heart and resumed eating. How was I to know that my grief befitted the actual state of affairs and my joy was merely illusory? In prison I composed a great many poems of a melancholy cast, which I cannot now recall; I remember only the following four lines:

I'm sorry, comrades, you're not here, and I the one long gone!
  My country I have lost; my soul will not depart from me.
In the battle to the finish, I survive and linger on,
  But in my dreams I follow you across the far-off sea.

DURING THESE FOUR years there was one affair in particular that should be recorded, so that my compatriots may derive a lesson from it. In the Ninth Month of the Year of the Hare [October/November 1915], while I was in prison, Liu Ya-san unexpectedly brought me a secret letter. Opening the letter, I recognized the handwriting of Đặng-Tử-Kính. Its content was more or less as follows. The two ministers of Germany and Austria in Siam had asked the Siamese about the Vietnamese revolutionary movement. They met a Siamese prince (in fact, the person who had previously met me and helped me with the business of the farm), who referred them to Đặng-Tử-Kính. When Đặng-Tử-Kính went to see them, they promised that they would do their best to help us but must see the leaders of our movement, and asked about the Marquis and myself. This is because the Siamese knew the Marquis and me, and the two ministers of Germany and Austria had also been informed of our names. (The Marquis had stayed in Siam for several months and made the acquaintance of many members of the Siamese royal family.)

Now that the Marquis was in Europe and I was in prison, Tử-Kính [wrote to] ask me what should be done. Seeing that Mai-Sơn [Nguyễn-Thượng-Hiền] had by then returned to Kwangtung from Peking, I thought of asking him to travel to Siam on our behalf. In my letter of reply to Tử-Kính, I mentioned this idea, and in a separate letter I provided an introduction for Mai-Sơn to the Siamese prince. I asked Tử-Kính to carry this letter [to Mai-Sơn] and to go back to Siam together with him to obtain an audience with the prince. Although Mai-Sơn had not been to Siam before, there should be no problem if he could travel with Tử-Kính. The following is the account related to me by Mai-Sơn and Tử-Kính after they had traveled to Siam.

As soon as Mai-Sơn arrived in Siam, he was introduced to the two ministers from Germany and Austria, who promised to meet him again the following day. The next day, when the two [Mai-Sơn and Tử-Kính] arrived at the gate of the German Consulate, an attendant was already waiting for them, and as soon as they saw their calling cards, the two ministers came right to the gate to shake hands with them, and took them for a stroll. On reaching a spot where there was no one else around, the German minister took out from his pocket a ten thousand yuan bill and handed it to Mai-Sơn and Tử-Kính, saying: "It would be premature for us to offer you assistance now, but this ten thousand yuan is a substitute for a cup of coffee on the occasion of our first acquaintance with people of your country. If you could bring about some kind of sensational incident within your country that would cause our governments to take notice, you would certainly obtain assistance from them. Indeed, if it did not amount to more than a few million yuan, how could it possibly be considered assistance? Now this small amount of money is our own idea, as a token of our ardent patriotism, and is not the idea of our governments."

Even though what has been described is a small incident, it is enough to give evidence of the way in which the Germans handle things—no putting on a show, no empty words, no rash commitments. Thus, right at the beginning, instead of waiting for us to make a request, they parted with a substantial sum of money. Moreover, where money was concerned, they assumed a most prudent attitude in only talking about it in a deserted place without any other people present. In addition, they made their promise of giving substantial support of a few million yuan only if there was an incident within our country that caused a sensation. This shows that they took the interests of their country seriously, and in establishing outside connections did not overlook the slightest matter. Alas! How many people are there in our country who could conduct things so well?

The two accepted the money and returned to Kwangtung, and our subsequent failures started from there. When the ten thousand yuan arrived in Kwangtung, the members of the movement divided the money three ways:

— one part was taken by Nguyễn-Mạnh-Hiếu to go to Tunghsing to launch an attack on Móng-cái;
— one part was taken by Mai-Sơn to go to Lungchou to launch an attack on Lạng-sơn;
— one part was set aside for Hoàng-Trọng-Mậu to launch an attack on Hà-khẩu (Hokow), because at the time Hoàng was still in Yunnan.

As the amount that was so divided was only ten thousand yuan, failure could have been predicted from the outset. Moreover, when one considers deeply the situation inside [the movement, it appears that] splitting our advance along several routes was only a secondary consideration. As a consequence, when the money was divided and a share was offered to Hoàng, he firmly refused to accept. The only thing that resulted was that Vũ-Đình-Mẫn[172] and Nguyễn-Hải-Thần took a mere

---

172. HXH reads " Vũ-Mẫn-Đình "; AM and TQP read " Vũ-Mẫn-Kiến."

few dozen men to carry out an attack against a French garrison near Lạng-sơn, causing injury to a person called Ba Môn, and the affair ended in total failure. Thereafter, Hoàng came back from Yunnan to Kwangsi, then went to Hong Kong in order to proceed to Siam, only to meet with all sorts of adversities until his death, for which this was one of the reasons. Alas! The spirit of faction in our counsels marred our endeavors and betrayed the interests of our country; it was a flowing poison that spread everywhere. From this we should derive a lesson.

IN THE YEAR OF the Snake, 1917, in the Third Month [April/ May], Lung Chi-kuang was defeated, and leaving Kwangtung, fled to Ch'iungchow. It was only at that point that I was released.[173] I did

---

173. There are chronological difficulties with Phan's narrative from the point at which he left prison to the point at which he returned from Yunnan to Hangchow. He gives the impression that his captivity ended at the time of the final rout of Lung Chi-kuang's army and the warlord's flight; but this took place only in early 1918, so Phan must have gained his freedom—how, he does not reveal, though his reference to Chang T'ien-min may afford a clue—during the previous period when his captor was on Hainan Island. (AM says that two hundred yuan were given to Phan on his release.) He had then spent somewhat more than three years in confinement, rather than a full four years, as he sometimes implies. Trần-Hữu-Công, who later accompanied Phan on his journey to Yunnan, in his memoirs gives the date of Phan's release as March 1917, slightly earlier than the date Phan indicates here. See Trần-Trọng-Khắc, *Năm mươi bốn năm hải ngoại* (My Fifty-Four Years Abroad) (Saigon: Tài-liệu lịch-sử cách-mạng Việt-Nam, 1971), 55–56. Phan's account of the following two years is in a topical rather than chronological order. After gaining his freedom, Phan went to Peking, and the Marquis came from Japan to meet him there. After the Marquis returned to Tokyo, Phan went to Hangchow, as the autobiography of the Marquis states. See Cường-Để, *Cuộc đời cách mạng Cường-Để* (The Revolutionary Life of Cường-Để) (Saigon: Nhà in Tôn-Thất-Lễ, 1957), 98–100. Phan was evidently in Japan, no doubt organizing the erection of the monument to Dr. Asaba, early in 1918 when he heard that Mai-Lão-Bạng was still in prison. The subsequent rearrest of Mai-Lão-Bạng, Hy-Cao, and Kim-Đài is dated by GB to 28 February 1918 on the basis of French documentation; this is earlier than Phan places it in his narrative. The monument to Dr. Asaba was completed in the spring of 1918, as its inscription states. Phan was still in Japan in mid-1918,

not stay in Ch'iungchow. There was a Yunnanese called Chang T'ien-min who at the time was an officer on Lung Chi-kuang's general staff. Seeing that Lung had failed, Chang asked to join our movement; I took him to Shanghai.

I then found out what a great danger had arisen while I was in prison. The National Protection Army had been raised in Yunnan by Ts'ai Sung-po;[174]   Lung was planning a swift military maneuver, "borrowing" the Yunnan-Vietnam railway to send forward a division to strike directly at Yunnan. Lung dispatched his older brother Lung Chin-kuang to Hanoi to negotiate in person with Governor-General Sarraut. At that time Nguyễn[175] was an interpreter of the Chinese language in our country. If this plan had become a reality, I should have been handed over as a bargaining counter in exchange for the "borrowing" of the Yunnan-Vietnam railway. Little is my body, but its value at that point was not insignificant. But the French authorities were the shrewdest diplomats in the world. Knowing, with their cleverness and perspicacity, that the days of Yüan and his followers were numbered, they had no wish to incur ill will among the Chinese people. Quite apart from the fact that Lung Chi-kuang was not unlike a panther or a wolf, his proposal for "borrowing" the railway was like the State of Chin asking for passage through the State of Yü to conquer

money from Lê Dư. Trần-Hữu-Công states that Phan and he left for Yunnan on 17 July 1918, arrived there on 22 November, and returned to Hangchow at the end of the First Month of the Year of the Sheep (late February or 1 March 1919). *Năm mươi bốn năm hải ngoại*, 57–61. In the present translation, the dates given by Phan are converted into the Western calendar just as they occur in the original text, with corrections in footnotes as necessary. After Phan reaches the Year of the Sheep (1919), his narrative returns to a more or less chronological order.

174. Ts'ai Sung-po (1882–1916), also known as Ts'ai O, had been a follower of Liang Ch'i-ch'ao in Japan during 1899–1900 and had received military training there in 1900–1904, leaving, however, before Phan arrived in Japan. He was military governor of Yunnan after the Chinese Revolution and an opponent of Yüan Shih-k'ai, but died shortly after Yüan.

175. Doubtless Nguyễn-Tiêu-Đẩu, alias Nguyễn-Bá-Trác (d. 1945), formerly one of the students in Japan, in whose residence Phan lived for a time after being returned to Huế in 1926.

the State of Kuo.[176] How could the French, not being silly, allow him to do such a thing? As Lung's plan never materialized, I was once more a Vietnamese not worth a penny.

In the Fourth Month of the Year of the Snake [June/July 1917], I arrived at Canton and showed up at Madame Chou's house. She told me that in the last few months there had never been a single day when the two Vietnamese spies, So-and-so and So-and-so, had not come round to her house. Because Lung Chi-kuang had been defeated and had fled from Kwangtung, the French expected me to have got out of prison and were thus pursuing me very closely. After staying in Kwangchow for a day and a night, I set off at once for Shanghai. That was a place where both the British and French had settlements; there were hordes of people working for the French, so I dared not stay in Shanghai. On hearing that Mai-Sơn and Hồ-Hinh-Sơn were in Hang-chow, I immediately headed there.

At that very time Sở-Cuồng [Lê Dư] had just arrived in Japan from our country to follow the Marquis; he wrote me a letter inviting me to come over, saying that there were two thousand yuan that he would give me upon my arrival to use for whatever I liked. Bearing in mind that Lê Dư had just lately surrendered to the French, where could he have come by so much money? After I had thought about it for a while, the source of this money became quite obvious.

At any rate, by that time the European War had been going on for three years and showed no sign of coming to a conclusion. According to my reading of the Chinese newspapers and foreign dispatches, the German army had made the greatest gains; nine *départements* in northern France had been lost to them. When I had just left prison, I thought of taking advantage of this situation to return to our country, but the land routes through Kwangsi, Kwangtung, Hong Kong, and Siam were all beset with briars and pitfalls. The only route to Vietnam that was still feasible was the one through Yunnan—our countrymen,

---

176. A reference to the story found in *Mencius*, "Wan Chang," part I.

because of the roundabout journey and the high expenses, rarely took this route. Moreover, on the way through Yunnan there were many of my old acquaintances who might be of help to me. For these reasons I had a strong desire to make the journey this time through Yunnan; but the expenses for travel would amount to at least one thousand yuan. In view of these expenses, I felt no reluctance to take advantage of Lê's money.

Then I received a letter from Trần-Hữu-Công that read:

> Japan's stroke of policy in declaring war against Germany does not reflect her real intentions, but is only a makeshift until the opportune moment when both sides collapse; then she will certainly be in the advantageous position of Pien Chuang [Tzu], able to kill two tigers with a single blow.[177] I have now heard that a prominent person has said that Japan and Germany are secretly negotiating a special three-clause agreement, and if this should be implemented, the diplomatic chessboard would certainly change dramatically.

Because of this letter, I traveled to Japan, ostensibly to meet Lê Dư, but in reality because I wanted to get in touch with people like Inukai Tsuyoshi and Fukushima [Yasumasa] to sound out the real feelings of the Japanese toward Germany.

I stayed in Japan this time for some three months, but Lê supplied me only with monthly living expenses; the two thousand yuan were never mentioned. When I asked Lê to live up to his promise, he said that what he could give me was five hundred yuan a month and that I should have to wait four months to get all the money. By the Seventh Month of that year [August/September 1917], I had received little more than a thousand yuan, but I was so impatient to return to China that I could not wait. Eventually, in the Seventh Month, together with Trần-Hữu-Công, I went back to Hangchow.

---

177. A reference to an old story, according to which Pien Chuang Tzu, governor of the District of Pien, was advised by a friend to watch for two tigers quarreling; when one had killed the other, the surviving tiger, being exhausted, could easily be dispatched.

WE HAD JUST ARRIVED in Hangchow and were staying at Hồ-Hinh-Sơn's house when I unexpectedly received a letter addressed to me by Lê-Ấp-Tốn and Trương-Quốc-Uy in Peking. Lê-Ấp-Tốn had left our country when the Vietnam Restoration League had just been established, and had come to Kwangtung to see me about it. When the League was dispersed, he had gone up to Peking and entered a military academy there. After graduation, he had stayed on in Peking. Trương-Quốc-Uy had done the same thing. During the European War, the two busily engaged in soliciting support from the Germans, but the German minister in Peking adopted a scrupulously correct attitude, so that their efforts met with one rebuff after another. When the break between China and Germany occurred,[178] a German in Tientsin, where there was a German Concession, following a confidential directive from the minister, got in touch with members of the Vietnamese revolutionary movement and promised us assistance. This German, who had been in contact with Lê and Trương previously, advised them that an agreement should be made and signed by key persons from both sides. The letter Lê and Trương wrote to me was to invite me to come to Peking to deal with this business.

At the time when I received the letter, my joy was mixed with anxiety like that of a bird frightened by the sight of a bow. To begin with, I wrote a letter to answer Lê, asking him and Trương to negotiate with the Germans on behalf of the Vietnam Restoration League. The two parties should draft an agreement that would be satisfactory to both sides, and when it was time to sign, I would come [to Tientsin] in person.

After receiving my letter, Lê made a trip to Tientsin and held discussions with the Germans several times. They told him: "Now that Germany and China are engaged in hostilities against each other, we may have to leave China at any moment; whatever arms and money belong to us will be confiscated. If you can launch an uprising in Indochina, we will place these items at your disposal, but it would be a good idea to draw up an agreement for our later mutual benefit."

---

178. China declared war on Germany on 14 August 1917.

Thereupon Lê and Trương, together with other members of our movement in Peking such as Hoàng-Đình-Tuân, Đặng-Hồng-Phấn, and so on, considered the conditions, came up with a draft text, and went to Tientsin to see the Germans and negotiate the agreement. When Lê first entered the British Concession in order to reach the German Concession, he was suddenly seized by British soldiers. When they searched him, they found the draft agreement in his pocket, and handed him over to the French Consulate. Lê was thus under arrest. Trương, who had been walking some distance behind Lê, managed to escape. Later, Lê was transported back to Hanoi, where he was sentenced to life imprisonment on the charge of having dealings with the Germans. He died in prison. According to what we have been able to find out, this was the work of a Yunnanese who received three thousand yuan from the French *Sûreté*, and this Yunnanese was a close friend of Phan-Bá-Ngọc and had studied with Lê and Trương at the same military college.

MY PLANS TO RETURN to our country were set back by more than a month as a result of Lê and Trương's letter. Now, having heard the bad news from Tientsin, I decided to go ahead with my travel plans. To get to Yunnan there were two ways. The first way was the land route through Kwangtung and Kwangsi and across the Vietnamese border to Bắc-ninh and Hanoi, from which one could use the Yunnan-Vietnam railway to reach Yunnan. The second way was by boat from Shanghai through Nanking to Hupei, then by land through Szechwan and Kweichow to Yunnan. The first way was quick, but it would be impossible to get through; the second way was arduous and slow, but getting through did appear to be possible.

At the time of our departure from Hangchow, Trần-Hữu-Công and I kept our plan secret and did not let anyone know about it, because the goal we had in mind was very ambitious. Unexpectedly, after we arrived in Yunnan we were to find that the situation was entirely different from what we had supposed, and our futile crossing of rivers and climbing of mountains had been good for nothing but ridicule. It is impossible not to feel bitter at such interference on the part of Heaven!

IN THE FIRST DECADE of the Eighth Month[179] we left Hangchow, but did not dare to go through Shanghai. We took a boat to Soochow, then went by train to Nanking. Again we took a boat to go upstream along the Yangtze River through Hupei and Hunan as far as Ichang. There we stayed for ten days to wait for another boat. At the time, hostilities between the North and the South [factions in China] had not been brought to an end. Downriver from Ichang was the line of the Northern army, and upriver from K'ueichow[180] was the line of the Southern army. While the fighting was in progress, the [Yangtze] River was blockaded at many places. We went to see the commander-in-chief of the Northern army, Wu Kuang-hsin, to obtain a safe conduct so that we could rent a civilian boat to travel up to K'ueifu.[181] K'ueifu was a very strategic point for the Southern army. It was there that an absurd incident occurred.

When we first arrived in K'ueifu, without having had a chance to inform the commander-in-chief of the Southern army, we put up at an inn. After just sitting for a short while, we asked the proprietor where the military camp was. The proprietor said it was in front of the Potich'eng citadel. As I had heard that the Potich'eng citadel is where the temples of Liu Pei and Wu-hou [Chu-ko Liang] are located, I became excited at the prospect of visiting the ancient sites and forgot to have any second thoughts. So Trần and I set off to see the Potich'eng citadel. No sooner had we arrived at the foot of the hill than we met a patrol of soldiers of the Southern army, who asked where we had come from. Since my proficiency in the Szechwan dialect was not

179. Trần-Hữu-Công gives the date 17 July 1918. *Năm mươi bốn năm hải ngoại*, 57.
180. K'ueichow is the old name for what is now the district city of Fengchieh in Szechwan Province.
181. K'ueifu is an alternative name for K'ueichow; Phan uses the two names interchangeably.

as great as that of the local Chinese, they became suspicious of us. When they searched us, they found the safe conduct issued by Wu Kuang-hsin, thought that we must be spics of the Northern army, and took us straight to their commander-in-chief, Wang T'ien-tsung. Wang ordered them to take us to be court-martialed. The judge of the court-martial interrogated me and ordered a soldier to sharpen a sword with a flashing blade, in order to observe my reaction from my face. Luckily, in the Southern army there was a division commander, a native of Hunan called Ho Hai-ch'ing, who was an acquaintance of mine. I sent to beg for help from Commander Ho. We had been in custody for more than an hour when a note from Commander Ho arrived and we were released. Also, when we returned to the inn, our room had been searched. My curiosity about famous ancient sites had got us into a hair-raising scrape. It showed up the fact that I have plenty of nerve but not much prudence!

AT THAT TIME in Szechwan there were many bandits; on top of that, the whole place was overrun with the remnants of defeated armies. It was hard for a traveler to persuade his legs to go forward. The innkeeper said to me: "If you gentlemen do not follow in the path of a big army that will protect you, you should not go. If you went on your own, the bandits would eat you up." Fortunately, at that point T'ang Chi-yao and Hsiung K'o-wu[182] were soon to convene a military conference in Chungking and the commander-in-chief of K'ueichow was about to go there to attend this conference. I went to implore Wang T'ien-tsung to let us travel with him. By that time Wang had come to know that I was a member of the Vietnamese revolutionary movement. He deeply regretted the indignity to which we had been subjected, treated us with every courtesy, and gave orders to allow us to board

182. Hsiung K'o-wu (1881–?) had been to Japan for military training, which he completed in 1906. He supported T'ang Chi-yao and Ts'ai O in their opposition to Yüan Shih-k'ai, and took command of an army unit in Szechwan in 1916, becoming military governor of Szechwan, 1918–1920.

a boat that followed immediately behind his own. From K'ueichow it took ten days for the boats to reach Chungking, the metropolis of Szechwan. I felt just as if a squadron of brave soldiers was my personal escort.

On entering Chungking, I sought an audience with Huang Fu-sheng, commander-in-chief of the army at Chungking. Huang was one of the foremost leaders of the Chinese revolutionary party. At the age of eighteen [in 1910], along with Wang Ching-wei, he had tried to assassinate the Manchu prince regent but had been caught and imprisoned together with Wang. When the Chinese Republic was established, he had been released and appointed executive secretary to the president. I had once met and had a conversation with him at the presidential palace in Nanking. Our reunion on this day was thus a happy occasion. Nonetheless, being anxious about the prospects for the future of our country, I was eager to leave as soon as I could. Huang, unable to delay me, gave me 370 Yunnanese yuan.[183]

My departure was thus decided on. But from Chungking to Ch'ien (Kweichow), the roads were much more difficult than in northern Szechwan. When Wu-hou [Chu-ko Liang] conducted his southern expedition, this was the place that he called "the deep interior, barren of vegetation." Now, owing to the disturbed situation, bandits had arisen in swarms, and traveling across the mountains was more dangerous than ever. During the half month of my stay in Chungking, I could not rest even when sleeping or eating; a day seemed as long as a year. Fortunately, Governor T'ang, after winding up the military conference, was about to return in triumph to Yunnan. Among the commanders of the Yunnanese army, there were quite a few who were old acquaintances of mine, and thus I traveled in company with them. On this occasion, too, I felt as if I were being escorted by a great army.

After taking half a month to cross the mountains, we arrived at Pichieh, in the heart of Kweichow. As T'ang's army made camp in

---

183. TQP, followed by GB, gives the figure of 170 Yunnanese yuan, apparently a mistake.

Pichieh for several decades, I also stayed there, and when T'ang took to the road again, I went along too. After traveling for another half month, we arrived at the destination I had been dreaming of. It was the Eleventh Month [December] by that time.[184] From the Eighth Month, when I left Hangchow, until I reached Yunnan, I had crossed six provinces of China, encountering all kinds of difficulties and dangers; how was I to know that these difficulties and dangers were not to be my last? I wrote *Tây-Nam lữ-hành-ký* (Diaries of Travels in the Southwest) to record my astonishing and harrowing experiences. Regrettably, I was unable to bring it with me when I came back to our country.

THE DAY I ARRIVED in Yunnan was in the third decade of the Eleventh Month [late December].[185] Flying everywhere in the city were France's tricolor flags crossed with China's five-colored flags. Along the line of the Yunnan-Vietnam railway, the tricolor flags blotted out the heavens and overshadowed the earth. When I saw this I was dumbfounded; my jaw dropped and my legs were rooted to the ground. This was because since the Ninth Month I had been traversing remote mountains and impenetrable forests and had not been able to read a single newspaper.[186] Next morning I rushed to the *Yunnan Yüeh-pao-she* (Yunnan News Agency) to read the newspapers. I found out for the first time that the European War had been brought to an end, Germany had capitulated, and France was full of pride as a victorious nation.

For several days in succession, there was nothing but celebration of this victory. Alas! When I was in the midst of hunger and cold, suddenly I had acquired more than a thousand yuan for which I had still not had a chance to say thanks to Sở-Cuồng [Lê Dư], and I had

184. Trần-Hữu-Công gives an exact date, 22 November 1918, in *Năm mươi bốn năm hải ngoại*, 59.

185. See above, p. 227, n. 173.

186. According to what we hear, China is a civilized nation, but this is true only around the big cities in the central area; as far as the mountains and remote areas are concerned, their seclusion is much worse than that of our countryside. [Author's note.]

already thrown the money away on an aimless and confused journey. How extremely foolish I had been! When I embarked on this journey, I had thought that it would take five or six years before the European War came to an end. I had wished to take advantage of the exhausted condition of the French, just like an ant nipping an elephant's trunk, or a mosquito biting a lion's ear. To writhe in agony until I dropped dead was all that I could think of.

Not to mention one more thing: How could the Yunnanese possibly have given long-term rights over the Yunnan-Vietnam railway to the French? It had been only logical for us to go for help to Yunnan. How was I to suppose that once they arrived in Yunnanfu, the haughty spirit of the French, sweeping everything before it, would overwhelm the minds of the Yunnanese? T'ang Chi-yao had known me previously, and in addition I had also brought with me a letter from Commander-in-Chief Huang enjoining T'ang to provide me with assistance. Nevertheless, T'ang did not dare to receive me even once; he only asked the police chief, Cheng K'ai-wen (who during his years of study in Japan had been a good friend of mine), to deal circumspectly with me and politely encourage me to leave Yunnan.

I stayed in Yunnan for only twelve days. Đặng-Tử-Mẫn[187] had been in Yunnan for quite a while to raise support among the Vietnamese expatriates, but T'ang, complying with the wishes of the French, had put him in custody.[188] I therefore sent a letter to Governor T'ang requesting him to release Đặng. Without waiting for the answer, I immediately left Yunnan to return to Hangchow, setting out across the ten thousand rivers and one thousand mountains of the way by which I had come.

---

187. TQP, followed by GB, gives the name Đặng-Tử-Kính, evidently an error.

188. According to AM, on the twelfth day of Phan's stay in Yunnan, Cheng said to him: "There is a member of your movement called Đặng-Tử-Mẫn who has been here for quite a while. At the insistent request of the French, Governor T'ang has put him in close custody."

MY JOURNEY FROM Yunnan took me first to Chungking. When I arrived there, not a penny was left in my wallet. I had no choice but to go and see Huang Fu-sheng again. Huang advised me to stay in Chungking and work as a member of his staff. He gave me an official letter saying:

> Mr. Phan-Thị-Hán [i.e. Phan-Bội-Châu] is hereby specially appointed to be a staff officer in the Headquarters of the Szechwan Army with a salary of 170 yuan. *The stamp of Commander-in-Chief Huang Fu-sheng.*

This is the first time that my name was ever followed by the word *quan* (officer). Pay day was only seven days after my appointment. As soon as I received my salary, I bade farewell to Huang and left Chungking. This was because what I was after was the salary rather than officialdom.

AT THE TIME WHEN I left Chungking it was already the third decade of the Twelfth Month of the Year of the Snake [February 1918], at the turn of the New Year. I arrived in Hangchow in the third decade of the First Month of the Year of the Horse [March 1918].[189] In retrospect, the route we traveled at that time was full of hardships and difficulties of all sorts, and Trần-Hữu-Công's endurance was most admirable. From Chungking to Yunnan, then from Yunnan back to Chungking, the return trip took some seventy days. Most of the time I rented either a horse or a litter, but Trần relied on the strength of his legs. There were stretches of the road where I had to hire a coolie to carry our baggage. One coolie ran so fast, we were afraid that he might run away with the baggage, so someone had to follow right behind him. That job fell to Trần. I wrapped a blanket around myself and walked

---

189. Trần-Hữu-Công gives the date of the end of the First Month of the Year of the Sheep (late February or 1 March 1919) for his and Phan's return to Hangchow. *Năm mươi bốn năm hải ngoại*, 59–61.

slowly at some distance behind; my walking ability could not stand comparison with his.

One day we were passing through the midst of the mountains in K'weichow. The mountains were desolate; there was absolutely no one around. I was about three kilometers [nearly two miles] behind Trần. All of a sudden a great snowstorm came up, blotting out the heavens and enshrouding the earth. The roads all turned white; besides, the sun had set, so that it was impossible to find where the roads were. If I could keep going for another hour I would arrive at a village, as had been planned. However, I was so exhausted I took out a blanket to wrap around my body, and lay down and slept on a snowbank. Around me was nothing but snow. I then composed these lines on the spot, which may be found of interest:

> *One night amid the mountains steep*
> *I settled in the snow to sleep.*
>
> *The rocks were pillows for my head,*
> *The grass a cover for my bed.*
>
> *Next morn, before the moon's repose,*
> *Wrapped in my blanket, I arose.*
>
> *As I set off, for miles around*
> *No one but I was to be found.*

FROM THE YEAR OF the Horse to the Year of the Ox [1918–1925] was a period of aimlessness and loneliness; I did nothing worth mentioning in the way of revolutionary activities. Nonetheless, there were a few things that touched my heart and moved my soul that my brush cannot neglect. All these things were waves that arose and subsided by themselves, not ones that I myself stirred up and calmed down.

In the Second Month of the Year of the Horse [March/April 1918], when I was making preparations to erect the monument to our benefactor Asaba [Sakitarō], I was staying over in Nagoya, Japan.[190] In this city was our comrade Lý-Trọng-Bá, who was enrolled as a student at the Imperial High School of Technology, so I lodged nearby him for the sake of company. Unexpectedly, I received a letter from Phan-Bá-Ngọc, asking me to help release Mai-Lão-Bạng from his Kwangtung prison. The task of canvassing to obtain support was to be undertaken by Phan-Bá-Ngọc, and the expenses were to be supplied by Sở-Cuồng [Lê-Dư].

On receiving the letter, I was deeply moved by the goodheartedness of these two. Previously, when I was confined in prison in Kwangtung for four years, communication between Mai-Lão-Bạng and me had been entirely cut off. He was kept at the police headquarters, and I in the Mount Kuanyin fortress; we were as far away from each other as the eastern and western hemispheres. For this reason, afterward, when I was released in Ch'iungchow, I thought that Mai, in Kwangtung, would also have been released. It was only now, through Phan-Bá-Ngọc and Lê-Dư's report, that I found out for the first time that Mai was still in prison. The accuracy of the investigation these two had carried out was indeed astonishing. I could not say no to their request to rescue Mai from prison. The result was that when Mai was released from prison and went to Shanghai, he was arrested there. I deeply regretted that I had rescued Mai from prison only to help the informers arrest him. I cannot deny that I was extremely guilty in this matter. "Although I did not kill Chou Po-jen, it was because of me that he died."[191] How gullible I was in dealing with people and handling affairs!

---

190. While the date for the erection of the monument is correct, the affair of the release and rearrest of Mai-Lão-Bạng occurred late in February, according to the date supplied by GB (p. 177). See above, p. 227, n. 173.

191. Chou Po-jen, whose real name was Chou I, was a native of An-ch'eng who lived during the Chin Dynasty. When Wang Tun rebelled against the Chin, his brother Wang Tao was charged with being involved. Without Wang Tao's knowledge, Chou I did his best to help clear him. Later, Wang Tun asked Wang Tao what Chou I had done. Wang Tao said he had done nothing, and Chou I was therefore killed. Afterward, Wang Tao found out that Chou I had done his best to help him, and therefore made the quoted statement. The story is found in *Chin shu*, chapter LXIX.

In the Third Month of the Year of the Horse [April/May 1918], soon after I received word from Phan-Bá-Ngọc, I wrote a letter to the governor of Kwangtung, Mo Yang-hsin, to request Mai's release. In due course I received a letter from Mo, saying that the case was being handled directly by the police chief, Wei Pang-ping. I then wrote a letter to Wei. The minister of Finance of the Kwangtung government, Ts'eng Yen, was an old friend of mine, so I also sent a letter to Ts'eng to ask for his help. Toward the end of the third decade of the Third Month [early May 1918], Mai-Lão-Bạng was released. In the Fourth Month [May/June 1918], following his arrival in Shanghai, Mai sent me a letter, to which Hy-Cao [Nguyễn-Đình-Kiên] and Kim-Đài [Phạm-Cao-Đài] added personal notes. Being true men of high purpose, Hy-Cao and Kim-Đài had been deported to Poulo Condore at the same time as Cửu Cai [Trần Hoành]; together they had escaped from prison. Constructing a raft, they had committed their fate to the waves, and eventually reached Shanghai.

Years before, on the boat to Siam, passing by Poulo Condore, I had composed the following stanza of four lines:

> *This baleful island floats before my view;*
>   *My soul shrinks from its melancholy shore!*
> *The lands through which I've traveled are not few,*
>   *Yet I have not been to Poulo Condore.*

Now, on hearing the news about Hy-Cao and Kim-Đài, I was absolutely delighted; how could I possibly know that while the good news was still sinking in, ill tidings were suddenly to strike? A mere four or five days later, a letter arrived from Hồ-Hinh-Sơn with the information that all three had been arrested. As soon as I heard this, I immediately left Japan and headed for Hangchow, in the hope of finding out the true facts of the case. How strange! And how sad! Mai-Lão-Bạng's release from Kwangtung prison, Hy-Cao and Kim-Đài's escape from prison on Poulo Condore—all served only to enhance Phan-Bá-Ngọc's distinguished achievement in breaking faith with his father and betraying his country. But who was behind the scenes, there is no need to ask.[192]

AT THIS POINT I should say something about the origins of my article on Franco-Vietnamese collaboration. Although I wrote this primarily because I had been misled by Lê Dư and Phan-Bá-Ngọc, I also feel guilty because of my fault in trusting these two. In the First Month of the Year of the Horse [January/February 1918], Lê Dư had come from our country to see me in Hangchow. This was the first time that the words "Franco-Vietnamese collaboration" *(Pháp-Việt đề-huề)* ever struck my ears. Lê said that the policy of Governor-General Sarraut was different from that of the governors-general up to that time. He also told me that Sarraut was a member of the Socialist Party, and socialism was incompatible with France's colonial policy. Lê went over Sarraut's various policies one by one, such as building schools, promulgating the new reformed law code in Bắc-Kỳ, allowing our people to form associations and societies, creating the Association for Intellectual Freedom and Moral Advancement *(Hội Khai-trí Tiến-đức)*, and so on.

At first I did not entirely trust Lê's words. But then it occurred to me that if this were indeed true, we could respond to their scheme with one of our own, and it was not necessarily the case that there was no room to turn things around. I proceeded to consult Phan-Bá-Ngọc. Among those around me at the time, he was the one individual who had collaborated with me for many years and had taken risks on numerous

---

192. According to GB (p. 177), a letter from the French consul, Wilden, to Governor-General Sarraut shows that, contrary to what Phan here supposes, the arrest was the work of neither Lê Dư nor Phan-Bá-Ngọc, as Phan-Bá-Ngọc himself was arrested with the assistance of the British police in a hotel in the International Concession of Shanghai on 28 February 1918 at the same time as Mai-Lão-Bạng, Hy-Cao, and Kim-Đài. Phan-Bá-Ngọc had been denounced by a Chinese spy, who according to GB was undoubtedly the Yunnanese informer working for the French *Sûreté* mentioned by Phan-Bội-Châu earlier. (It should be noted that Phan dates the arrest of his friends some months later than the date GB indicates.)

occasions on my behalf; of those who had most distinguished themselves, no one surpassed Phan-Bá-Ngọc. At this time, when Lê Dư
had come out from our country, Lê and Phan had the closest of ties
with each other. Phan showed the utmost eagerness to support Lê's
case, and I was not aware of their ulterior motives.[193] Phan-Bá-Ngọc
said to me: "If we are to achieve something great, there is no way
to avoid using clever ruses. Now, if you were to write an article discussing the rationale of Franco-Vietnamese collaboration, both sides
would gain something from it. The French, seeing this article, would
suppose that we have become moderate, and would no longer pay any
attention to our movement. We could then send people back to our
country to associate with the French on a friendly basis, so that they
could collect information for our movement, and thus we might get a
glimpse of the actual state of the French. Secrets learned inside our
country could also be conveyed to those outside. What Lê has said
makes good sense."

I trusted this advice, since Phan-Bá-Ngọc had no reason to betray
his father and turn traitor against his country. I presently wrote a
lengthy essay entitled *Pháp-Việt đề-huề chính-kiến-thư* (A Political
Opinion Concerning Franco-Vietnamese Collaboration), "composed
by Độc-Tinh-Tử [Phan-Bội-Châu], copied by Phan-Bá-Ngọc." The
five words at the end of the essay, *Phan-Bá-Ngọc phụng-thư* (Respectfully yours, Phan-Bá-Ngọc), meant much more than appeared on the
surface.[194] Lê Dư took this letter and returned to our country. In
another four or five months, the beloved son of Phan-Đình-Phùng
became outright a loyal follower of the French.[195] Sun Tzu said: "It is
difficult to make proper use of spies." I have painfully come to realize
the truth of this saying.

---

193. The distance between us was extreme. [Author's note.]

194. It is worth noting that these five words do not occur either in the manuscript of
this letter or in the printed copies preserved in Aix-en-Provence, Archives nationales,
Fonds SPCE, Phan-Bội-Châu.

195. Phan-Bá-Ngọc must have returned to Vietnam as well as Lê Dư, because in
the subsequent dealings between Phan and the governor-general he appears as the
intermediary.

IN THE SECOND MONTH of the Year of the Sheep [March 1919], Phan-Bá-Ngọc met me in Hangchow and told me that Governor-General Sarraut was eager to talk with me about the possibility of collaboration. I said that the French authorities must send people over to negotiate and that they must first state their conditions, which must meet with my approval. Phan-Bá-Ngọc agreed and again returned to our country. In the Third Month of that year [April 1919], Phan sent me a letter from Vietnam, saying that the government had already agreed to send an envoy out to negotiate, but as for the matter of conditions, that would have to wait until the envoy arrived, so that both sides could decide on them together. In the Fifth Month of that year [June/July 1919], a Frenchman called Néron[196] arrived in Hangchow with Phan-Bá-Ngọc.

Phan had let me know about his coming in advance. I demanded that the place and date of the meeting be decided by our side and not disclosed until the last minute, and that their side send only one person, but that the number of participants from our side would be up to us. If these demands were not met, we would not negotiate. Phan-Bá-Ngọc discussed these demands with Néron, who agreed to them all.

When the day came, the meeting took place in the Hulouting (Pavilion on the Lake)[197] in the middle of the West Lake in Hangchow. I was accompanied by Trần-Hữu-Lực, Hồ-Hinh-Sơn, and three young men. After everyone had been seated and formal greetings briefly exchanged, Néron took out from his pocket a sheet of paper written in French with a translation in *quốc-ngữ*, saying that these were the ideas that Governor-General Sarraut wished to be presented to me personally. I asked one of the young men to read it aloud. I was astounded. The list of conditions was as follows.

So far as I was concerned, I must accept these two conditions:

---

196. According to the Marquis, the Frenchman whom Phan-Bá-Ngọc took to meet Phan-Bội-Châu in Hangchow was Arnaud, head of the *Sûreté* in Hanoi. *Cuộc đời cách mạng Cường-Để*, 105.

197. This seems to be a slip of Phan's memory, as the pavilion now on this site is called Huhsinting (Pavilion at the Center of the Lake).

(1) I must write a declaration to be publicized inside our country to the effect that I had renounced my revolutionary ideas and activities;

(2) I must return to our country, or alternatively, if I did not return, I must select a fixed place of residence abroad, preferably close by a French concession.

So far as the Indochinese government was concerned, it would give me these two rewards:

(1) If I returned to the country, I should be given an important position in the government of the Vietnamese court, with exceptionally favorable financial treatment;

(2) If I did not return to the country, a generous allowance would be provided to cover my long-term residence, travel, and other necessities abroad.

I had some idea of the position I should take, so I replied with a letter in *quốc-ngữ*, analyzing clearly the real meaning of collaboration and rejecting the unfair conditions. The letter was carefully written down by Lý-Trọng-Bá and was taken back by Phan-Bá-Ngọc to Governor-General Sarraut in Hanoi. This letter was the first direct communication that I had with the French. It will be put on record elsewhere; I wish my compatriots to read it, so that they can see what collaboration meant to me, and what it meant to the French—the two were as different as ice and fire.

IN THE SEVENTH MONTH of the Year of the Sheep [July/August 1919], I left Hangchow for Peking, then went on to Japan. From this time on, during the four years from the Year of the Sheep to the Year of the Dog [1919–1922], whenever I felt at loose ends, I would set out on a trip, without any particular purpose.

In the Eleventh Month of the Year of the Monkey [December 1920/ January 1921], I heard that many people from the Socialist and Communist Parties of Soviet Russia had arrived in Peking and that the headquarters of the Soviets was at Peking University. My curiosity was aroused, and I wished to learn the truth about the Communist Party. So I got out a book that was an investigation of the actual state of Russia written by a Japanese, Fuse Katsuji.[198] After going through it several times to work out its meaning, I translated it into Chinese in two volumes. This book treated in great detail the Soviet government's ideology and institutions. I rushed off to Peking taking the translation with me, wishing to use it to introduce myself to the members of the Chinese and Russian socialist parties.

When I arrived in Peking, I was able to meet Ts'ai Yüan-p'ei, the chancellor of Peking National University. Ts'ai was very pleased to see me and introduced me to two Russians, one being Mr. Somebody-or-other, the head of the Soviet delegation that was visiting China,[199] and the other being Mr. Lạp, a Chinese-language attaché on the staff of the Soviet ambassador in China, Joffe.[200] This was my first direct dealing with the Russians.

---

198. Fuse Katsuji (1886–1953) was a noted foreign correspondent for the *Ōsaka Mainichi Shimbun* who resided in Russia for some time; later he became a politician. He wrote several books on the recently established Soviet Union, including one in English, *Soviet Policy in the Orient* (East Peking: Enjinsha, 1927, reprinted Westport, CT: Hyperion Press, 1978). The book Phan translated apparently was *Rokoku kakumeiki* (An Account of the Russian Revolution) (Tokyo: Bungadō, 1918). Phan could have acquired a copy of this book in Japan when he was there to erect the monument to Asaba Sakitarō in the spring of 1918. In one of his informative studies of Phan-Bội-Châu, Shiraishi Masaya suggested that the book by Fuse was *Rōnō Rokoku yori kaerite* (Returning from Soviet Russia), but this was published only in 1921. (See Shiraishi, *Betonamu minzoku undō to Nihon, Ajia*, 657–659.) In GB's translation the author of the book is confused with Fuse Tatsuji.

199. Quite likely G. N. Voitinskii (1893–1953) of the Far Eastern Secretariat of the Comintern, who came to China in 1920 and spent some time in Peking and Canton making contacts among the intellectuals.

200. As Joffe did not come to China until 1922, Mr. Lạp—about whom no further information is available—cannot have joined his staff until that year. It is possible that Phan has dated his encounter with the Russians a year early, or that he had further contacts with him on subsequent visits to Peking. Fuse Katsuji, whose earlier book on Russia Phan had translated, gives an account of Joffe's mission in China from an East Asian point of view in *Soviet Policy in the Orient*, 197–200.

I asked Mr. Lập: " There are people in my country who would like to study in your country. Would you please indicate what prospects there are?" Mr. Lập said: " The Soviet government warmly welcomes foreigners who come to Russia to study as fellow citizens of the world. If some Vietnamese were able to go to Russia to study, their journey would be easier than most: from Peking it is possible to reach Vladivostok either overland or by sea; from Vladivostok one can go to Moscow by the Trans-Siberian Railway through Chita. Altogether, it takes only a little more than ten days. Students going to Russia must first come to Peking to obtain a letter of recommendation from our embassy. Once a letter of recommendation from the Ambassador has been obtained, the railway fare and expenses for meals from Chita to our capital will be looked after by the Soviet government. From Vietnam to Russia, the expenses should not exceed two hundred yuan, which is easy to manage. Nonetheless, the students before entering an educational institution must accept the following conditions:

(1) they must pledge their allegiance to Communism;
(2) after completing their studies and returning to their country, they must accept responsibility for propagating the ideology of the Soviet government;
(3) after completing their studies and returning to their country, they must undertake to engage in social revolution, etc.

All expenses during their period of study until their return to their country will be looked after by the Soviet government." All of the above comes from the conversation I had with Mr. Lập at that time. I am not aware of what the situation is now.

One thing I cannot forget is how dignified, courteous, and sincere the Russians appeared when they met me. Their language and their expression was at times calm, at times vigorous. I remember this being said: " Our meeting with you is the first we have had with a Vietnamese. If you could write a book in English to describe in detail the actual position of the French in Vietnam and give it to me,

I should appreciate it and not forget what you did." Regrettably, not being versed in English, I could not oblige.[201]

DURING MY TRIP on this occasion, an intriguing incident happened to me, which I shall recount here. When I left Yokohama for Talien (Dairen), I boarded a cargo vessel that also carried nine passengers, one of them being myself. There was a certain passenger who identified himself as a Japanese workman. His garb was entirely that of a workman. While on board, he and I conversed and found each other's company extremely enjoyable. As soon as the ship called at Nagasaki, he suddenly disappeared. When our ship arrived at Talien, I and the other seven passengers were all arrested by the Japanese police. I was released by the chief of police after four days in prison. He invited me to sit down and explained that I had been arrested by mistake, and that a member of the Korean revolutionary movement called Lim had just assassinated a [Korean] agent working for the Japanese in Tokyo. The agent was the president of the Chōsen Kyōshin Kai (Korean Society for Progress in Common). Lim had stabbed him and then escaped. As the Japanese police were conducting an intensive search for him, Lim had boarded the same cargo ship that I had, planning to make good his escape to Talien. On realizing that it would be impossible for him to escape, he had disappeared in Nagasaki. A member of the Vietnamese revolutionary movement mistakenly suspected as a member of the Korean revolutionary movement—this was really something quite out of the ordinary in human affairs!

DURING THE YEAR of the Monkey and the Year of the Cock [1920–1921], I traveled back and forth between Hangchow, Peking, and Canton; at times I went to the Three Eastern Provinces [i.e., Heilung-kiang or the Amur River, Kirin, and Liaoning], and a few times I

---

201. In AM Phan indicates that his conversation with Mr. Lạp was conducted in English, with Hoàng-Đình-Tuân acting as interpreter.

entered Korea by way of Antung, then crossed over to Japan to look up the Marquis. This was all merely travel for pleasure and observation, and had nothing to do with revolutionary work. Nonetheless, I never stopped writing. Whenever I ran out of money, I would sell something I had written to make a living. Chinese newspapers and magazines such as *Tung-ya hsin-wen* (East Asian News) in Peking and *Chün-shih tsa-chih* (Military Affairs Magazine) in Hangchow carried many items that I wrote. My purpose was to make a living, not to produce literature. Nevertheless, some of my writings are worth noting:

(i) *Dự chi phúc-âm* (My Good News). This book was divided into twelve long chapters, all written specifically to enlighten people and wake them up from slumber.

(ii) *Việt-Nam nghĩa-liệt-sử* (The History of the Martyrs of Vietnam). Written specifically to commemorate my compatriots who had died up to that point for our country's righteous cause. What I had heard and seen, or what had been recounted to me by other comrades, was all recorded in this book. Those who had not gone to their graves were not included, as one would have to wait until later to judge them.

(iii) *Á-châu chi phúc-âm* (Good News for Asia). The content of this book concentrated on promoting a policy of communication among Asian countries, in particular of unanimity between China and Japan. In short, it was similar to *A Modest Discourse about an Asian Alliance;* but this book was written after the rupture of Sino-Japanese amity, so that it produced no effect.

Works of the above kind were indirectly related to revolution.

ON THE FIFTEENTH DAY of the First Month of the Year of the Dog [11 February 1922], at the West Lake in Hangchow, China, there suddenly occurred an assassination incident that shocked everyone who heard about it. Because of this, in the Second Month I returned to Hangchow, and this city became the shop where I could sell my writings.

Years before, when I left Yunnan and went to Hangchow, I thought that Hangchow must be the most celebrated place in China, what with Lin Pu's historic home,[202] Yo Fei's tomb,[203] the pavilion to the memory of the hero Hsü Chi-lin, and the temple and tomb of the heroine Chiu Chin[204] all being located there. One could consider oneself fortunate to be able to pass one's time there, where there were moments when one could practically see and talk to those in the other world. Moreover, in Hangchow there were many of my old revolutionary friends. Chang Ping-lin and Ch'en Chi-mei were both natives of Hangchow; also, Mai-Sơn [Nguyễn-Thượng-Hiền] had gone into retirement from the active life there. It was a distinct advantage that there were enough people there to whom I could talk. What was regrettable was that it was next to Shanghai where there were many informers, and Phan-Bá-Ngọc, also, was a visitor who had a thorough knowledge of this area. That was why I had not dared to settle down there permanently.

It was the evening of the fifteenth day of the First Month of the Year of the Dog, the Feast of Lanterns, when lantern viewing is a custom among the residents of Hangchow. Along the banks of the West Lake the thousands of lanterns looked like a painting. Men and women had turned out in their best finery. There was a sea of people and a forest of flowers. The excitement was reaching its height. Suddenly, amidst the explosions of thousands of firecrackers, three pistol shots were heard. The crowd was startled; then came a shout: "Someone is lying on the ground! There is blood all over his body!" The military police arrived and searched his pockets. They found two thousand one hundred yuan

---

202. A man of virtue during the Sung Dynasty (980–1200) who went into hiding in a remote mountain.

203. Yo Fei was a figure well known for his unshakable loyalty and patriotism under the Sung Dynasty. When the Sung were attacked by the northern invaders, he led the resistance and won one victory after another. But Ch'in Kuai, a crafty minister, plotted to make peace with the enemy. Yo Fei was arrested and died in prison. His tomb is on the West Lake.

204. Hsü Chi-lin and Chiu Chin were the two leaders of China's Kuang-fu-hui (Restoration Association) who headed the uprising in 1907 in Chekiang Province.

in bills, and in his sleeve there was a high-quality gold watch worth about sixty yuan. The man had died. Who was he? He was Phan-Bá-Ngọc. The assassin was Lê-Tấn-Anh, a Vietnamese youth.

At the time I was staying in Peking. My friend Lin Liang-sheng, who was in charge of the *Ch'un-shih tsa-chih* (Military Affairs Magazine) in Hangchow, sent me a letter to invite me to come to Hangchow. Prior to that, there had been quite a few students from our country who had studied in Peking and graduated from the military academy. Owing to the diplomatic situation, it was difficult for them to obtain positions in the military there. On the orders of Tuan Ch'i-jui, premier of the provincial government and minister of the Army, the military commander in Hangchow, Chu Jui, started a military magazine as a means of employing our people.

Upon receiving Lin's letter, I left Peking for Hangchow to become a member of the editorial board of the *Military Affairs Magazine.* In the "Comments on Current Events," "Editorials," and "Short Story" sections of the magazine, there were many pieces written by me. This was the time when I became a writer of fiction. Though to devote my brush to catering for the tastes of this magazine's readers was not the primary aspiration of my life, with a monthly salary of seventy yuan I could provide money to buy books for two or three youths and help our comrades to travel back and forth, so I was somewhat consoled. In addition, by working for the magazine I could promote the spirit of worldwide revolution and write as vehemently as I pleased against imperialism and colonialism—to give vent to his feelings was also a source of amusement for a man of high purpose with no prospects for the future.

I carried on in this job for three years and four months. During this period I sent back to our country several items that I wrote:

— *Dư cửu niên lai sở trì chi chủ-nghĩa* (The Doctrine I Have Upheld for the Past Nine Years).
— *Y hồn đan* (A Medicine for the Spirit).
— *Thiên hồ đế hồ* (O Heaven! O Lord!).

These three items were all pamphlets, so that it would be easy for people to carry them back home. *O Heaven! O Lord!* vehemently denounced the crimes of the French. Its contents were divided into three chapters: (i) the missionaries who were stealthily exterminating our people; (ii) the law and politics that were stealthily exterminating our people; (iii) the education that was stealthily exterminating our people.

I also composed three longer writings:

— *Kính cáo ngã quốc-nội thanh-niên văn* (An Appeal to the Youth in Our Country).
— *Kính cáo kiều Tiêm ngã đồng-bào văn* (An Appeal to Our Compatriots Resident in Siam).

These were originally written in literary Chinese and translated into *quốc-ngữ*.

— *Kính cáo lân-bang Tiêm chính-phủ văn* (An Appeal to the Government of Siam, Our Neighbor).

This marked the last time that I used my brush as a spear and my tongue as a sword while I was abroad.

ON THE NINETEENTH DAY of the Fifth Month of the Year of the Rat [20 June 1924], I was in the editorial room in Hangchow opening the newspapers that had come in. I found that every Shanghai newspaper had published a telegram from Canton, "An Earth-Shaking Assassination Incident" and "Detonation of a Bomb by the Vietnamese Revolutionary Movement," all in large type. When I had finished reading, my arms and legs were shaking. At that time, every Chinese newspaper and the British and American newspapers published [in China] by the foreign communities all carried not only this news but also commentaries on it for four or five days running. People throughout the world came to know about the Vietnamese and the Vietnamese revolutionary movement; this incident was indeed most effective propaganda. The

Russian ambassador in Peking, Karakhan, pounded his desk, saying "This is what *should* happen in the cattle ranch of the capitalists!" One could see how great the impact of this incident was. Although I did not take part in it, I should not omit to put the full story on record.

One day in the Second Month of the Year of the Rat [February-March 1924], the governor-general of Indochina, Merlin, set out on his way to Tokyo, traveling through Hong Kong and Canton to Yokohama and then Tokyo.[205] The members of our movement in China had heard something of this. Those members who were in Kwangtung were champing at the bit and wanting to try to do something. However, this was easier said than done; everything is like that, let alone an attempt to create a sensation by striking a blow at the leading official of a country. How could it be easy? Moreover, Merlin's journey at this time was in order to conclude a secret deal with Japan that would have far-reaching consequences for the Indochinese situation. For this reason, the French authorities took the utmost precautions to provide security for Merlin.

Prior to Merlin's departure, the head of Indochina political affairs, Néron, had dispatched informers to Hong Kong and Shanghai, such as Trần-Đức-Quý, Nguyễn-Thượng-Huyền, and others. Wherever there were members of our movement, they would infallibly be on our trail, dogging our every footstep. Nonetheless, in spite of their utmost precautions, we still came up with countermeasures. They could not ward off the awl of Chang Tzu-fang and the pistol of An Chung-gŭn.

---

205. Merlin actually left Haiphong on 27 April, with an itinerary taking him to Hong Kong, several cities in central Japan, Korea (Pusan and Seoul), then on to Mukden, Peking, and Shanghai before returning to Hong Kong and stopping at Canton on his way back to Indochina. The purpose of his visit to Korea was apparently to show that the French recognized Japanese colonial claims on the peninsula, while the Japanese were making it clear that they fully supported the status quo in French Indochina. In consequence, both the Vietnamese and the Korean political activists had an interest in targeting Merlin. There seems to have been significant collaboration between them, and the attempt against Merlin's life was seen by both as a repetition of the deed of An Chung-gŭn. Merlin's complete itinerary is available in Tokyo, Japanese Diplomatic Archive, *Gaikoku kihin no raichō zakken—Bessatsu: Futsuryō Indoshina Meruran sōtoku raichō no ken* 6.4.4.1–12, Taishō jūsannen ichigatsu—gogatsu.

In the first decade of the Fifth Month of the Year of the Rat [2–11 June 1924], Merlin returned from Japan to Hong Kong[206] and headed for Canton to talk to the Kwangtung government about how to deal with our movement. His whereabouts were kept strictly secret, the ship on which he traveled was a French warship, and outside people could not know his itinerary. Notwithstanding, it seems that our utter sincerity had moved Heaven, so that we were able to stage a real-life drama by dealing a blow to the head of this official; it was none other than a French informer who disclosed his schedule to our movement.[207]

When Phạm-Hồng-Thái, a great martyr of our movement, left home to go to China, he was secretly nourishing a strong aspiration to become the An Chung-gŭn of Vietnam.[208] In the Third Month, when he arrived in Canton and heard of Merlin's trip, his gleaming sword was eager to leap from its scabbard. But there were hundreds of things to be arranged, and the informers were at his side day and night. With his close friend Lê-Tẩn-Anh, he worked out a painstaking plan to pull the wool over the eyes of the informers on the one hand, and surreptitiously seek his opportunity on the other. Fortunately, at the time there

---

206. Merlin's itinerary shows that he left Japan for Korea on 27 May and came back to Hong Kong from Shanghai on 16 June.

207. The Vietnamese were apparently well organized to strike at Merlin. According to a report published in the Japanese newspaper *Kokumin Shimbun* as early as 21 May 1924, seven men from Annam had left for Shanghai by boat en route to Seoul to attempt to assassinate Merlin there.

208. Phạm-Hồng-Thái (1896–1924) was a native of Nghệ-an who, through his association with the Vietnam Restoration League, was sent to Siam, then in 1918 to Canton. He belonged to the militant-action group within the League. The Korean activist Jo Hung-a ("Jo who regenerates Asia," evidently a pseudonym)—who, following Phạm's death, sent his last will and photograph to the Chinese newspaper *Hsien-hsiang pao* in which they were published on 25 June 1924—recalled forming a friendship with Phạm when they were both in Japan. Jo said that Phạm was well versed in both literary Chinese and French and had a strong interest in legal matters. Japanese and French sources indicate that Phạm was considered an "agent" of the Marquis Cường-Để. Tokyo, Japanese Diplomatic Archive, Futsukoku naisei kankei zassan— Zokuryō kankei: Indoshina kankei Annan ōzoku hompō bōmei kankei A6701-1-1-1, Taishō jūgonen jūgatsu [October 1925].

was a Russian chemist who was an instructor at the Whampoa Military Academy. Members of our movement had often asked him about the method of producing the latest model of bomb. He was prepared to help them, and manufactured two bombs fitted with electric batteries. The bombs were as small in size as a little orange, and were placed in a leather box the size of one's palm, no different from the satchels which the Westerners often carried in their hands. Phạm also went to a Chinese military academy to purchase two pistols, both the latest models designed for assassination. Having acquired these two kinds of weapons, Phạm, hero that he was, was wild with joy.[209]

According to Merlin's schedule, he was to arrive at the T'ientzu pier on the Pearl River at Canton on board a warship at 7 A.M. on the eighteenth day of the Fifth Month [19 June]. At 12 noon he was to be at the Victoria Hotel in Shamien, to have lunch with diplomats from foreign countries. At 6 P.M. he was to attend a reception given by the French Consul and the French residents in Kwangtung. Phạm-Hồng-Thái thus had a now-or-never opportunity; he was eager to unsheathe his sword and try it out, like an arrow on a bow, planning to use one of the above locations to strike at his target. Thanks to Heaven's work, the bolt was shot with an enormous detonation. It did not hurt the feelings of the Chinese people, but only fired the indignation of these members of our yellow race. Although Merlin was lucky enough to escape, the imperialists were shaken out of their illusions. This was due to the invisible guidance of the spirit of our rivers and mountains.

In the evening on the seventeenth, Phạm-Hồng-Thái rented a small boat and moored nearby the pier, hiding in the boat like a tiger, waiting for Merlin to step onto the pier to throw his bombs. Unexpectedly, before the French warship arrived, the Canton chief of police suddenly ordered all boats, large and small, in the vicinity of T'ientzu pier to

---

209. According to Jo Hung-a, Phạm could have made an attempt on Merlin's life on the latter's return to Hong Kong, but did not wish to do so because there were so many guests from other countries at the reception there. In his last testament, Phạm indicated that he was aware that his act would involve innocent people, but that he had no choice and was resigned to being condemned by the public.

disperse; they were not permitted to move inside of a security line. As soon as the ship arrived and Merlin disembarked, a limousine dispatched by the Cantonese authorities picked him up immediately, and in a moment he was whisked away. The first location at which Phạm-Hồng-Thái sought his target thus did not work out.

There was still an opportunity; with courage higher than ever, he went to the Victoria Hotel, planning to rent a room on the second floor and wait for Merlin to come, then throw the bombs. But on that day, security in both the British and the French Concessions was extraordinarily tight and only foreigners with passports were allowed to rent rooms. Thus the second location at which he sought his target also did not work out.

The decisive moment had come! He had the bombs in his hands, a pistol in his pocket, and a blaze of lightning in his heart; all was in readiness for the explosion. It was impossible to go back on his intention; he had to stake everything on a single blow. By 6 P.M., the French Consul and the French residents, men and women, were arriving one after another at the hotel, ready for the banquet and dance to welcome the governor-general of Indochina and celebrate the success of his trip. As the clock turned 6:40, the limousine carrying Merlin to the party arrived. A moment after that, through the gate of the bridge came a rather stocky man. This man had a light complexion and a short moustache. He was dressed in Western clothes, wearing Western shoes, and carrying a Western cane in his hand. From the bridge gate, he walked with an assured air straight to the door. The French military police who were guarding the door on both sides all thought that he was a French guest at the reception because his outfit and his deportment looked like those of a Frenchman, so that they suspected nothing.

It was only a short while until the time came for his righteous act. When the clock had struck "Bong, bong" seven times, and the clatter of knives and forks began to be heard at the dining tables, a spark flashed under Phạm-Hồng-Thái's fingers; then came a thunderous explosion that shook the building. The guests on both sides of the tables fell one upon another to the floor. Four persons died immediately: the French Consul and his wife, and the president of a French bank and his wife. Two other persons were seriously wounded; one was the director of a French hospital and the other was a member of his staff.

After the explosion, the British and French military police and the sailors on the warship rushed in all directions to look for the assassin. Phạm-Hồng-Thái, however, was determined not to die at the hands of the French. He therefore ran out to the bridge gate; but since the military police were blocking the way, he ran back to the riverside in front of the hotel. As the military police caught up with him, he took out his pistol and shot two bullets at them, then leaped into the Pearl River to end his life.

This explosion, according to its original intention, was aimed at Merlin, but Merlin escaped. In the other world Phạm will probably be grumbling about that. Nevertheless, it should be called a success, because the intention of our movement was to punish the evil politicians and not one individual. Since such punishment was carried out, our objective was achieved. The date was the eighteenth day of the Fifth Month in the Year of the Rat [19 June 1924]. On the nineteenth day, Phạm's body was recovered and was buried in the cemetery.

With regard to this incident, I composed a number of writings:

(i) a declaration by the Vietnamese Nationalist Party on the explosion incident in Shamien;

(ii) *Phạm-Hồng-Thái liệt-sĩ truyện* (A Biography of the Martyr Phạm-Hồng-Thái);

(iii) A composition in commemoration of Phạm-Hồng-Thái.

The Chinese and Western newspapers all praised the act of Phạm-Hồng-Thái for its courage and its perceptiveness. The explosion did not occur at the reception by Chinese officials nor at the party attended by other foreigners, but rather at the time when Governor-General Merlin was having dinner with the French residents. This was appropriate, because the place where the explosion occurred was in the French Concession, and the target was exclusively the French. This showed the revolutionary's courage and perceptiveness.

Afterward, the French minister in Peking and the Indochinese authorities both demanded that the Kwangtung government expel the Vietnamese, pay compensation for the damage, and apologize for having admitted the murderer. This the Kwangtung government resolutely refused to do. At the time, Sun Yat-sen was head of the Supreme Military Council in Canton, and Hu Han-min was the governor of Kwangtung. Sun said: "I have not heard if there are any Vietnamese here; if there are, they must all be good people; none of them is the murderer." Hu said: "During the journey of the Indochinese governor-general, when he passed through Kwangtung, everything was completely peaceful, but once he entered the French Concession, then this dangerous incident occurred. This was entirely owing to the undeniable incompetence of the British and French military police. From now on, if the French authorities wish to prevent dangerous incidents from happening, it might be a good idea for them, on a provisional basis, to ask the military police of our country to protect their country's residents in the Concession."

Two months after Phạm-Hồng-Thái sacrificed his life for the sake of our country, that is, in the Seventh Month of the Year of the Rat [August 1924], as the Sino-French negotiations had been concluded, I returned to Canton to erect a tombstone upon Phạm-Hồng-Thái's grave to commemorate him until he could be reinterred at a later date. In the Twelfth Month of that year, some members of the Chinese Nationalist Party, such as Liao Ch'ung-k'ai and Wang Ching-wei, wishing to commemorate Phạm-Hồng-Thái in order to show their sympathy toward our movement, used three thousand yuan of public funds as a grant to our members to rebury Phạm-Hồng-Thái's remains on a little hill in front of Huang-hua-kang. Huang-hua-kang is where seventy-two martyrs of the Chinese Revolution are buried. Directly facing it is the grave of Phạm-Hồng-Thái, which was constructed in imposing style. There is a huge monument inside a pavilion. The big characters on it read:

> *The grave of Phạm-Hồng-Thái of Vietnam,*
> *a man of high purpose.*

The calligraphy was by Chou Lu.

AFTER MY RETURN to Canton in the Seventh Month, I stayed until the Ninth Month [August–October 1924], as there was some work to be carried out for the movement. This was because, after my four-year imprisonment in Kwangtung, the members of the Vietnam Restoration League were scattered all over the place, and the League itself was practically defunct. In the spring of this year, young men from our country were arriving in Canton one after another; then the bomb incident occurred. Appreciation of the value of our revolutionary movement suddenly increased; there was hope, at long last, that it could be revived.

Chiang Kai-shek was then principal of the Whampoa Military Academy, and Li Chi-shen was its director. With Nguyễn-Hải-Thần, I went to see these two men. We took a tour of the Academy and proposed to have our students enrolled in it. Chiang and Li were both strongly in favor. Three Russian instructors at the Academy came to meet me; we talked for a while, and then had our photograph taken together.

Knowing that the current trend was gradually turning toward a worldwide revolution, I presently discussed with the other comrades winding up the Restoration League and turning it into the Việt-Nam Quốc-Dân-Đảng (Vietnamese Nationalist Party). I quickly drafted a program of activities, as well as a constitution, for the Vietnamese Nationalist Party, and printed them for circulation. The Party was organized into five big departments:

(i) the Political Department;

(ii) the Economic Department;

(iii) the Executive Department;

(iv) the Supervisory Department;

(v) the External Relations Department.

This scheme of organization was by and large modeled on that of the Chinese Kuomintang, with some modifications, in order to adapt the means of revolution to the times.

Less than three months after the program of activities and the Party's constitution had been made public, Nguyễn-Ái-Quốc[210] came back to Canton from the Russian capital Moscow. He communicated with me about their revision on several occasions. In the Ninth Month of that year [October 1924][211] I had left Kwangtung for Hangchow. In the Fifth Month of the Year of the Ox [June 1925], I planned to return to Kwangtung to meet the comrades there to discuss the question; unfortunately, I was arrested and taken back to our country. I do not know how the program of activities and the constitution of the Vietnamese Nationalist Party have been revised since.

IN THE FIFTH MONTH of the Year of the Ox, I was planning to go back to Kwangtung for two reasons. One was the above-mentioned question of reforming the Vietnamese Nationalist Party. The other was the commemoration ceremony in honor of Phạm-Hồng-Thái on the first

---

210. It is worth noting that in the original text Phan gives Nguyễn-Ái-Quốc the respectful title of *tiên-sinh*, meaning "teacher, master," in spite of the fact that the latter was some twenty-three years his junior.

211. From Nguyễn-Ái-Quốc's correspondence with the Comintern, it appears that he arrived in Canton on 11 December 1924, and a week later, on 18 December, he reported his contacts with Phan and others. Hồ-Chí-Minh, *Toàn tập*, I, 314. (It may be noted that according to *Hồ Chí Minh biên niên tiểu sử* [A Chronological Biography of Hồ-Chí-Minh], Nguyễn-Ái-Quốc arrived in Canton on 11 November.) GB, on the basis of the date Phan gives here for his departure for Hangchow, rightly deduced that Phan could not have met Nguyễn-Ái-Quốc in person in China; the documentary evidence supports this. See the Introduction, pp. 19–20.

anniversary of his death, which was to be carried out on the eighteenth day of the Fifth Month, the day of his martyrdom.

During the years when I was staying in Hangchow, I used to send money through a German bank to Trần-Trọng-Khắc [Trần-Hữu-Công] in Berlin for his school fees in Germany. Each year without fail I secretly made two trips to Shanghai, usually in the Sixth Month and the Twelfth Month. This time, on account of the ceremony in memory of Phạm-Hồng-Thái, I made the trip a month in advance. On the eleventh day of the Fifth Month [2 July 1925], I arrived in Shanghai, thinking that after sending the money at the bank I should immediately board a ship heading for Canton, as from Shanghai to Canton it would take five days by ship. I left Hangchow carrying with me four hundred yuan, the amount to be sent to Trần-Trọng-Khắc for his tuition.[212] I did not realize that every minute of my activities was being reported to the French by Nguyễn-Thượng-Huyền, a man who lived with me and was supported by me. When this Nguyễn-Thượng-Huyền first arrived in Hangchow, he was with Trần-Đức-Quý; I was quite dubious about him. But later I heard that he was a great-nephew of Mai-Sơn [Nguyễn-Thượng-Hiền], well versed in literary Chinese, the holder of a *cử-nhân* degree, and familiar with French and *quốc-ngữ*. Owing to his capabilities, I kept him on as my secretary without suspecting that he was an informer for the French.

At 12 noon on the eleventh day of the Fifth Month, my train from Hangchow arrived at the North Station [Shanghai]. In order to go quickly to the bank to send the money, I left my luggage at the depository and carried only a small bag with me. As soon as I came out of the train station, I saw a rather luxurious automobile and four Westerners standing by it. I did not realize that they were French, because in Shanghai there was a great mixture of Westerners and there were swarms of foreign visitors. It was quite common for cars to be used to pick up hotel guests. Little did I know that this car was there

---

212. This money was still with me when I went into prison. Trần-Trọng-Khắc had to study on an empty stomach; I really let him down. [Author's note.]

to kidnap someone! When I had gone a few steps from the station, one of the Westerners came up to me and said in Mandarin: "This car is very nice; please get in." I politely refused, saying "I do not need a car." Suddenly, one of the Westerners behind the car with a great heave pushed me inside it, the engine accelerated, and we were off like a shot. In no time we had already entered the French Concession. The car drew up to the waterfront, where a French warship was docked. I now became a prisoner on this warship.

While on the warship, I wrote a long poem in the traditional style for my bosom friend Lin Liang-sheng, an extract of which follows:

> *From twenty years of running to and fro*
> *Death is the only gain I'll have to show.*
>
> *Ah! Woe betide the man whose land of birth*
> *Has lost its freedom; he is nothing worth.*
>
> *Alas that, luckless, I must bear the cost,*
> *Child of a land of independence lost!*
>
> *Among a servile people I was bred,*
> *So filled with shame as not to lift my head.*
>
> *I could not but resent my feeble powers,*
> *Yet would some venture try for what was ours.*
>
> *Though Chi's state I had yet to overthrow,*
> *I hoped at mighty Ch'in to strike a blow.*[213]
>
> *The call of years was answered; came the day*
> *My countrymen rose up in armed array.*
>
> *Anew our nation's soul to life returned;*
> *The brute-force Power's fury hotly burned.*

---

213. These lines reflect the ancient historical position of Vietnam, with the State of Chi the nearer and weaker, the State of Ch'in the more distant and more powerful enemy; the analogies are to the collaborationist mandarin administration and the French colonial government in Vietnam.

With wires are all our streams and mountains bound,
While thorns our heaven and our earth surround.

On what branch for support should we rely?
On what but China's mighty power hard by!

A wide place is this earth on which I dwell;
Why must I be confined in one small cell?

When at Shanghai's North Station I arrived
I knew not what my enemies contrived.

A car drew up; four men stood in the way
With ill intent; I was their destined prey.

One push—and I am helpless in the car!
It starts! The French Concession is not far.

My body's caged within an iron fence
Like pigs and chickens—there's no difference!

Had I a country to stand firm for me,
Then such humiliation would not be.

Our nations must together stand or fall.
My death is naught; the bond between us, all.

Great China! And magnificent to view!
Yet you protect not them that look to you.

A rabbit dies—the fox is then fair game;
An empty bottle puts the jar to shame.

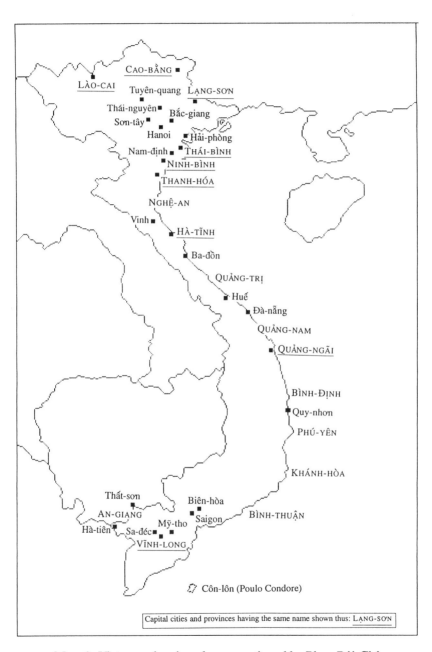

CAO-BẰNG ■
LÀO-CAI ■
Tuyên-quang ■   LẠNG-SƠN
Thái-nguyên ■   Bắc-giang
Sơn-tây ■
Hanoi   ■ Hải-phòng
Nam-định ■ ■ THÁI-BÌNH
■ NINH-BÌNH
THANH-HÓA

NGHỆ-AN
Vinh ■
■ HÀ-TĨNH

■ Ba-đồn

QUẢNG-TRỊ

■ Huế
■ Đà-nẵng
QUẢNG-NAM
■ QUẢNG-NGÃI

BÌNH-ĐỊNH
■ Quy-nhơn
PHÚ-YÊN

KHÁNH-HÒA

Thất-sơn   Biên-hòa
AN-GIANG   ■ ■ Saigon   BÌNH-THUẬN
Hà-tiên ■ Sa-đéc ■ Mỹ-tho ■
VĨNH-LONG

Côn-lôn (Poulo Condore)

Capital cities and provinces having the same name shown thus: LẠNG-SƠN

MAP 1. Vietnam, showing places mentioned by Phan-Bội-Châu

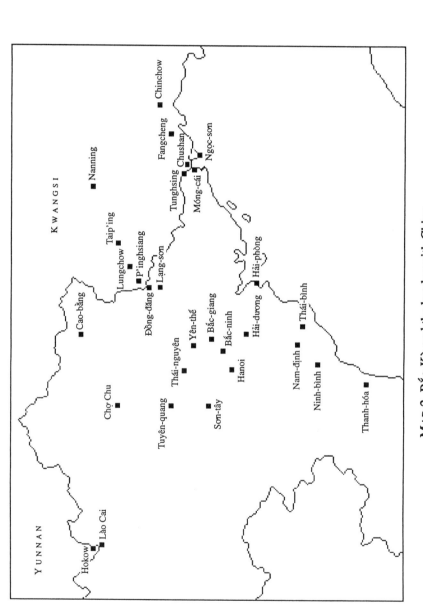

MAP 2. Bắc-Kỳ and the border with China

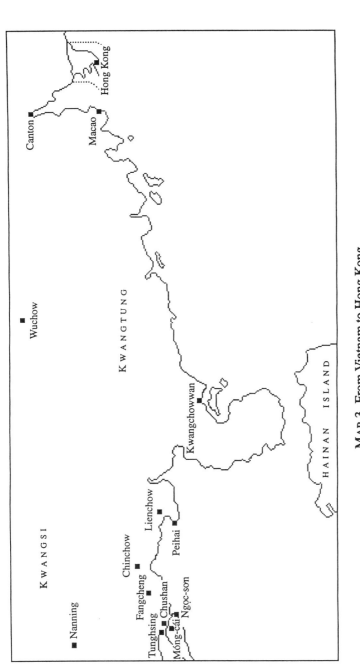

MAP 3. From Vietnam to Hong Kong

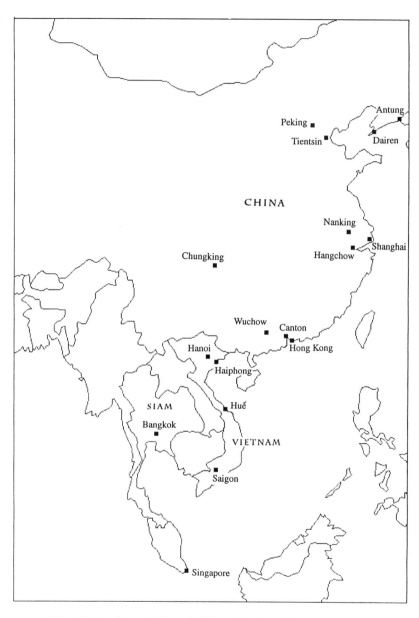

MAP 4. Southeast Asia and China, showing places mentioned
by Phan-Bội-Châu

MAP 5. East Asia, showing places mentioned by Phan-Bội-Châu

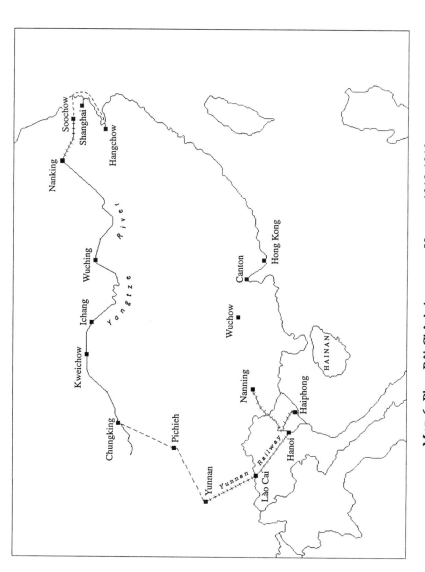

MAP 6. Phan-Bội-Châu's journey to Yunnan, 1918-1919

Select Bibliography

The following is a short list of materials in Western languages for readers who would like to learn more about Phan-Bội-Châu and the Vietnam of his times.

BOUDAREL, Georges. "L'extrême-gauche asiatique et le mouvement national vietnamien." In *Histoire de l'Asie du Sud-est: Révoltes, réformes, révolutions*, Pierre Brocheux, ed. Lille: Presses Universitaires de Lille, 1981.

————. "Phan-Bội-Châu et la société vietnamienne de son temps." *France-Asie/Asia* 199, 23, no. 4 (1969): 1–82.

————. "Phan-Bội-Châu: Mémoires." *France-Asie/Asia* 194–195, 22, no. 3/4 (1968): 4–210.

BUTTINGER, Joseph. *Vietnam: A Dragon Embattled.* 2 vols. New York: Praeger, 1967.

CADY, John. *The Roots of French Imperialism in Eastern Asia.* Ithaca, NY: Cornell University Press, 1967.

DUIKER, William J. "Hanoi Scrutinizes the Past: The Marxist Evaluation of Phan Boi Chau and Phan Chu Trinh." *Southeast Asian Studies* no. 4 (September 1973).

————. *The Rise of Vietnamese Nationalism, 1900–1941.* Ithaca, NY: Cornell University Press, 1976.

FURUTA Motoo. "Vietnamese Political Movements in Thailand: Legacy of the Đông-Du Movement." In *Phan-Bội-Châu and the Đông-Du Movement*, Vĩnh Sính, ed. New Haven, CT: Yale Center for International and Area Studies, 1988: 150–181.

MARR, David G. *Vietnamese Anti-Colonialism, 1885–1925.* Berkeley: University of California Press, 1971.

————. *Vietnamese Tradition on Trial, 1920–1945.* Berkeley: University of California Press, 1981.

MCALISTER, John, Jr. *Vietnam: The Origins of Revolution*. New York: Harper and Row, 1970.

MCALISTER, John, Jr., and Paul MUS. *The Vietnamese and Their Revolution*. New York: Harper and Row, 1970.

NGUYỄN Khắc Kham. "Discrepancies between *Ngục Trung Thư* and *Phan Bội Châu Niên Biểu*." In *Phan-Bội-Châu and the Đông-Du Movement*, Vĩnh Sính, ed. New Haven, CT: Yale Center for International and Area Studies, 1988: 22–51.

NGUYỄN Thế Anh. "Phan Bội Châu et les débuts du mouvement Đông-Du." In *Phan-Bội-Châu and the Đông-Du Movement*, Vĩnh Sính, ed. New Haven, CT: Yale Center for International and Area Studies, 1988: 3–21.

SHIRAISHI Masaya. "Phan-Bội-Châu and Japan." *Tōnan Ajia Kenkyū* (Southeast Asian Studies) 13, no. 3 (1975): 427–440.

———. "Phan-Bội-Châu in Japan." In *Phan-Bội-Châu and the Đông-Du Movement*, Vĩnh Sính, ed. New Haven, CT: Yale Center for International and Area Studies, 1988: 52–100.

TRƯƠNG Bửu Lâm. *Patterns of Vietnamese Response to Foreign Intervention, 1858–1900*. New Haven, CT: Yale University Press, 1967.

UNSELT, Jorgen. *Vietnam: Die nationalistische und marxistische Ideologie im Spätwerk von Phan-Bội-Châu (1867–1940)*. Wiesbaden: Franz Verlag, 1980.

VĨNH Sính. "Phan-Bội-Châu and Fukuzawa Yukichi." In *Phan-Bội-Châu and the Đông-Du Movement*, Vĩnh Sính, ed. New Haven, CT: Yale Center for International and Area Studies, 1988: 101–149.

VŨ Đức Bằng. "The Dong Kinh Free School Movement, 1907–1908." In *Aspects of Vietnamese History*, Walter Vella, ed. Honolulu, HI: University of Hawai'i Press, 1973.

WOODSIDE, Alexander B. *Community and Revolution in Modern Vietnam*. Boston, MA: Houghton Mifflin, 1976.

———. *Vietnam and the Chinese Model*. Cambridge, MA: Harvard University Press, 1971.

Index

About the Translators

Vinh Sinh, professor of History at the University of Alberta, was born in Huế, Vietnam, and educated at the Tokyo International Christian University, the University of Tokyo, and the University of Toronto, where he received his Ph.D. He has published extensively on modern Japanese intellectual history and Japan's international relations with the West and East Asia.

Nicholas Wickenden, associate professor of History at the University of Alberta, was educated at the University of Alberta and King's College, Cambridge, receiving his Ph.D. from the University of Cambridge. Among his interests is the interrelationship among cultures in world history.